HANDFULS ON PURPOSE

SERIES IV

BY

Pastor JAMES SMITH

Author of "A Survey of the Wondrous Cross,"
"Spiritual Patterns," etc

WM. B. EERDMANS PUBLISHING COMPANY

Grand Rapids   1964   Michigan

American Edition

———

Published in 1947, by

WM. B. EERDMANS PUBLISHING CO.
by
Special Arrangement with

PICKERING & INGLIS, LTD.
14 Paternoster Row, London, E.C.4
229 Bothwell St., Glasgow, C.2
Manchester—Newcastle—Liverpool—Edinburgh

PHOTOLITHOPRINTED BY CUSHING - MALLOY, INC.
ANN ARBOR, MICHIGAN, UNITED STATES OF AMERICA
1964

Guide to Series 1 to 12

OLD TESTAMENT

NEW TESTAMENT

SERIES 1 to 10 .. By Pastor JAMES SMITH
SERIES 11 and 12, .. By ROBERT LEE
SERIES 13, COMPLETE INDEX TO SERIES

Preface

"Behold, how great a matter a little fire kindleth" (James 3. 5).

L ITTLE did we think when, with fear and trembling, we launched the first small monthly part, that it would so soon grow into so many volumes. For this special token of the Master's favour we are sincerely thankful. It is an unspeakable delight for us to know that very many weary gleaners have found therein "Handfuls on Purpose." All who choose to glean here, are as much at liberty to take home for their own use what they find as Ruth was, when she gleaned among the sheaves in the fields of Boaz.

We esteem it a great privilege to have the opportunity of ministering in any small degree, to the encouragement and usefulness of the lowliest of Christ's servants, believing that "inasmuch as ye did it unto one of the least of these My brethren, ye have done it unto Me" (Matt. 25. 40). In this volume, which we trust will also be found helpful in "the quiet hour," we have once more humbly attempted to fulfil the Apostle's injunction, "Let him that is taught in the word *communicate* unto him that teacheth in all good things" (Gal. 6. 8). What we have prayerfully received, we herewith prayerfully give.

JAMES SMITH

GENERAL INDEX OF SUBJECTS

Including Expository and Gospel Outlines, Bible Readings, and Seed Thoughts

INDEX OF TEXTS

Handfuls on Purpose

Expository Outlines   Old·Testament

FORWARD.

"Ye have compassed this mountain long enough"
(Deuteronomy 2. 1-7).

> "I will trust, and not be afraid,
> Be it in light, or be it in shade;
> The enemy visible and strong,
> Or creeping stealthily along;
> O! by Thy grace I shall be bold,
> If that Thy grace doth me enfold."

AS pilgrims and strangers on the earth there are two dangers to which we are ever exposed, that of sitting at ease in our present comfortable condition, or of rushing impatiently into new spheres and circumstances. Commit thy way unto the Lord, and He shall direct thy paths. Consider—

I. **The Arrest.** "Ye have compassed this mountain long enough." The mountain they had been compassing was not for them, "no, not a foot breadth" (v. 5). There were other possessions waiting on them.

It is a blessed thing to be saved from the wrath to come, but it is a miserable thing never to get beyond that. Are there not many of the Lord's people to whom it might be said with regard to their spiritual experience, "Ye have compassed this mountain long enough?" Press on toward the mark of your high calling in Christ Jesus.

II. **The Command.** "Turn you northward." The

good land of promise lay stretched away northward. They were to set their faces toward all that had been freely given them by God. Christian pilgrim, remember the man with the muck rake in Bunyan's allegory. See that your neck is not allowed to stiffen looking only at the things of earth and sense. "Turn you northward." Look up and expect the fulfilment of His exceeding great and precious promises in your daily experience. Instead of the muck of earth look for the crown of glory.

III. **The Warning.** "Ye are to pass through the coast of your brethren, the children of Esau; meddle not with them" (vv. 4, 5). Mount Seir had been given to Esau to possess it (Josh. 24. 4). When God blesses His people He does it *righteously*, even in the presence of the ungodly. We have a *just* God and a Saviour. In the face of an assembled universe this will be manifestly so. It was not the Lord, but one of Job's miserable comforters who declared that "The *heavens* are not clean in His sight."

IV. **The Reminder.** Just as we are the Lord's remembrancers so He is ours. In verse seven they are reminded of His—

1. FAVOUR. "The Lord thy God hath blessed thee in all the works of thy hand." His favour always means blessing. The *grace* of God that bringeth salvation to all men hath appeared. His favour is better than the best of a mere earthly life.

2. WISDOM. "He knoweth thy walking through this great wilderness." He is mindful of us. He knoweth the way that we take. Our Lord Jesus Christ was tempted in all points like as we are, and is touched with the feeling of our infirmities. Yes, He knows thy walking, whither it is through great shadows of trial and suffering, or along the sunny path of painless prosperity. So that you may fearlessly say—

"Where He may lead I'll follow,
  My trust in Him repose,
And every hour in perfect peace,
  I'll sing, He knows, He knows."

3. PRESENCE. "The Lord thy God hath been with thee." Have we no evidence in the past that the Lord our God hath been with us? Will His faithfulness fail toward us in the future? Be encouraged, O soul, if thy heart seeks His honour and His Name's glory. He cannot deny Himself. He would be denying Himself and robbing His Word of its power and glory if His presence failed the humble, childlike, believing spirit. He *hath been* with thee; He will bless thee still.

4. SUFFICIENCY. "Thou hast lacked nothing." "When I sent you, lacked ye anything?" And they answered, "Nothing" (Luke 22. 35). Out of Heaven and from the flinty rock the God of all grace satisfied their needs. There may be many things we *want*, but we shall lack no good thing when He is with us. My God shall supply all your need. Many a time they murmured in the wilderness, but the Lord their God declares that they *lacked nothing*. We are rich indeed when we have what He wishes us to have, *whatever* that may be. "Be content with such things as ye have, for He hath said, I will never leave thee nor forsake thee" (Heb. 13. 5).

A SOLEMN CHARGE.
Deuteronomy 4. 1-9.

"Thy words rule men a statute ne'er have ruled,
  Not penalty but conscience gives them power;
Men find out soon or late themselves befooled,
  And bruised and broken seek Thy Spirit's dower.
How have Thy words up-flamed as into swords,
  How have they gone straight to the world's great heart,
How freedom thence has fetched her battle words,
  How Thy word-pictures glorified all art."

"O ISRAEL, thou shalt keep the commandments of the Lord your God which I command you" (vv. 1, 2). This is

a very clear evidence of inspiration. The statutes and
judgments taught by Moses were the authoritative *words
of God*. As Newberry points out, the I's of Moses here are
emphatic in the Hebrew. He speaks in God's stead. This
Paul declares in writing to the Hebrews (chap. 1. 1).
This solemn charge to keep the *words of God* comes loudly
and urgently upon us to-day. Several reasons are given
for this.

I. Because they are Powerful. They—

1. BRING LIFE. "Do them, that ye may live" (v. 1).
Man shall not live by bread alone, but by every word of
God, The words that I speak unto you they are spirit and
they are *life, begotten* by the incorruptible Word of God.

2. SECURE AN INHERITANCE. "That ye may go in and
possess." It is by laying hold of His promise that the
soul enters into the possession of the inheritance provided
and offered. "Thy Word was found, and I did eat it, and
it became the joy and rejoicing of my heart." The hungry
one must eat to be satisfied.

II. Because they are Perfect (v. 2). Nothing is to be—

1. ADDED. "Ye shall not add unto the Word." The
Law (Word) of the Lord is perfect. It is finished. We
can no more add to the revelation of God than we can
add to the *finished* work of Christ or the work of Creation,
although man in his pride makes many attempts. We
presume to *add* to the grace of God when we go about
seeking to establish our own righteousness. "Add thou
not unto *His words*, lest He reprove thee, and thou be found
a liar, for every word of God is pure" (Prov. 30. 5, 6).

2. DIMINISHED. "Neither shall ye diminish aught
from it." "If any man shall take away from the words
of the book of this prophecy, God shall take away his
part out of the book of life" (Rev. 22. 19). The Scriptures

of truth *cannot be broken*, so that no repair is ever needed. To add or to diminish is only to mar the perfect *Man* of our counsel.

III. **Because they are Precious** (vv. 4-9). Precious because they are—

1. UNFAILING. "Ye that *did cleave* unto the Lord your God *are alive* every one of you this day." Joshua and Caleb did trust the Word of the Lord, and they were *living* witnesses to His unfailing faithfulness (Num. 26. 65). The living Christ is the eternal Word. He will not fail thee; be not faithless.

2. ENLIGHTENING. "Keep them, for this is your wisdom and your understanding in the sight of the nations." "The Word of the Lord makes wise the simple" (Psa. 19. 7). Apart from it, Israel would sink down to the level of the heathen nations around them. If His Word does not abide in us we, too, will fall back into a savourless state, good for nothing, or like a fruitless branch.

3. COMFORTING. "What nation is there so great who hath God so nigh unto them?" etc. (v. 7). Israel as a redeemed people were distinguished for the *nearness* to which God came to them. This nearness was only enjoyed when they walked in obedience to His Word (2 Sam. 7. 23). "The Lord is *nigh* unto all that call upon Him in *truth*" (Psa. 145.. 18). All who have *believed* are made nigh through the blood of Christ. *His nearness* is the distinguishing mark of all who live in the power of the Spirit of truth. The more we are *like* Christ, the more near will He be.

4. ENNOBLING. "What nation is there so great that hath statutes and judgments so righteous as all this law?" (v. 8). What soul is there so great that hath the words of the living God dwelling richly within? His words are more to be desired than gold Moreover, in keeping of

them there is great *reward* (Psa. 19. 9-11). They do no iniquity that walk in His ways (Psa. 119. 3). The incorruptible Word in the heart will beautify the whole character as the seed in the earth when it springs up beautifies the whole field with a comeliness not its own, yet not separate from it.

5. ENDURING. "Take to thyself and teach them to thy sons, and thy sons' sons" (v. 9). The words of God are enduring for us, and will be as effectual to our believing children and our children's children. Timothy knew the Scripture from his *youth*, and we need not wonder at it, when love for the Word of God dwelt in Eunice his mother and in Lois his grandmother (2 Tim. 1. 5). The Word of the Lord endureth for ever. It has an enduring purity, suitability, influence, and faithfulness. "He that heareth My Word, and believeth on Him that sent Me, hath everlasting life" (John 5. 24). Believest thou this?

> " A charge to keep I have,
> A God to glorify,
> A never failing Word to trust
> That lifts me to the sky."

BACKSLIDING: ITS CAUSE AND CURE.
Deuteronomy 4. 23-31.

> "My Lord, I covet not the breath
> Of grand renown,
> But rather that which lies beneath
> A blood-bought crown.
> Fain would I hold, if but small cup,
> To thirsty lips,
> Fain would I shine but to light up
> Some soul's eclipse."

WHATEVER occupies the chief place in our hearts and lives takes the place of God and becomes our god. We are constantly in danger, as Israel was, of allowing *visible* things to usurp the place of the Eternal One, whom we see not.

When the Lord spake out of the midst of the fire in Horeb
no manner of *similitude* was seen (v. 15). One of the
reasons given is, "For the Lord thy God is a jealous God"
(v. 24). Jealous of our *faith*, and the adoration of our
hearts. Backsliding is always manifested by *preferring*
some earthly thing to the Lord.

I. The Cause. To be forewarned is to be forearmed.
They are here warned beforehand of how they may
retrograde from a God-pleasing life. Circumstances may
change, but in principle the causes are still the same.

1. FORGETFULNESS. "Take heed unto yourselves, lest
ye *forget* the covenant of the Lord your God" (v. 23).
Forgetting God's Word and forsaking the secret place of
prayer. It is so easy to forget our own spiritual need
amidst the rush of everyday life. Take heed to yourselves. To forget His promise is to lean on a paralysed
arm of flesh.

2. FALSE WORSHIP. "Take heed lest ye *make* you a
likeness of anything which the Lord thy God hath forbidden" (v. 23). Forbidden *images* are sure to appear
in the minds and thoughts of those who forget God, and
the horror of it lies in this, that they are self-made; the
deliberate work of a Christ-doubting soul.

3. SELF-CORRUPTION. "Ye shall *corrupt* yourselves"
(v. 25). When we turn away from the light we turn into
darkness. When we cease to *live* by faith on the Son of
God we begin to corrupt like a member severed from the
body.

II. The Effect. Backsliding in heart will soon show
itself in the life. There will be—

1. DISPOSSESSION. "Ye shall soon utterly perish *from
off* the land" (v. 26). Their days in the land and their
enjoyment of it would not be prolonged if they turned
from following the Lord. It is altogether impossible for

any soul to enjoy the inheritance in Christ and to prolong
their fellowship with Him who has departed from the
Lord in their heart. As a matter of *experience* they shall
soon be utterly cut off.

2. DIVISION. "The Lord shall *scatter* you," etc. (v. 27).
They were to be scattered among the nations and left few
in number. Individual backsliding is always accompanied
with division and separation. When they are not of us
they will go out from us. When the Lord is dethroned
from His true place in the midst of His people schism takes
place in the Body of Christ—His Church.

3. WEAKNESS. "Ye shall be *few* among the heathen"
(v. 27). Few in the midst of the heathen means terrible
weakness and helplessness. Robbed of their aggressive
power and distinguishing glory as the people of God,
instead of a conquering army they become the slaves of
their own lust and pride. What a picture of a backsliding
Church, crying out about its fewness in number in the
midst of an overwhelming and ever growing heathenism.
This melancholy situation is doubtless the result of
unfaithfulness to God.

III. The Cure. Thank God, that although we may
have turned away from Him He has still left the door of
restoration open.

1. CONFESS. "For the Lord thy God is a *merciful* God,
He will not forget the covenant which He sware" (v. 31).
This declaration of His mercifulness and faithfulness in not
forgetting His covenant is a powerful plea for those who
have forgotten His covenant to confess their sins that they
might be forgiven. If we confess, He is faithful and just
to forgive and to cleanse.

2. SEEK. "If from thence thou shalt *seek* the Lord thy
God, thou shalt find Him" (v. 29). But note that it is
Himself that must be sought. It is Himself that we need.

After our Lord rose from the dead He showed them Himself. What else could satisfy their troubled souls and meet all their need. Seek Him, and seek Him from thence, from just where you are, in all your false worship, divisions, and helpless weakness, and bondage. O backsliding Church, thou hast destroyed thyself, but in *Me* is thy help. Return, O wanderer.

3. Obey. "Thou shalt turn unto the Lord thy God, and be *obedient* unto His voice" (v. 30). This is our security, to hold fast the Word of God. Giving heed to other voices can only lead into shame and hopeless failure. The mighty power of Jesus Christ lay in His obedience to the Father's voice and will, and shall it be otherwise with His disciples? To obey is better than sacrifice. This is My beloved Son. *Hear ye Him.*

DELIVERANCE AND TESTIMONY.
Deuteronomy 6. 21-25.

"How long, O Lord, how long,
Until shall burst the song?
The throne of evil shattered,
The hosts of hell all scattered;
Heaven here on earth begun,
Thy will by all men done,
How long, O Lord, how long?"

THIS great groaning earth still needs deliverance as much as ever Israel did out of the furnace of affliction and the house of bondage (Rom. 8. 22, 23). Every Israelite was enjoined to bear testimony to his inquiring son of all that the Lord had done for them. From the statements here put into his mouth we learn much of what this great salvation was. We learn from it—

I. The Need of Deliverance. While in Egypt they were—

1. Exiles. They were at that time "afar off" from

the holy city of divine fellowship. Ye who sometimes were *afar off* are now made nigh by the blood of Jesus. Exiled from the enjoyment of the grace of God implies bondage to the world and sin.

2. SLAVES. "We were Pharaoh's bondmen in Egypt" (v. 21). Burdened and oppressed under a thankless and loveless master, ever striving in vain to please an irreconcilable enemy. Such were some of us, led captive by the devil at his will.

II. The Manner of Deliverance. It was—

1. OF THE LORD. "The Lord brought us out of Egypt" (v. 21). It was not their own devising, neither was it after their own thoughts. It was a *new thing*, like the redemption that is in Christ Jesus. Every saved one has to confess, like Jonah, that "salvation is of the Lord."

2. THROUGH A MAN. Moses was called and ordained for this great work, away in the back part of the desert of Midian, while he stood by the burning bush. The Man, Christ Jesus, was also called of God, away in the back part of eternity, as He stood by the burning glory of the presence of the Holy One, when He laid help upon One that was mighty.

3. BY ALMIGHTY POWER "He brought us out with a mighty hand" (v. 21). When the Lord makes bare His holy arm to smite His enemies and set His people free, who shall be able to resist? The arm of His redeeming power has been made bare in Jesus Christ, who is mighty to save.

4. WONDERFUL. "The Lord showed signs and wonders" (v. 22). There were many wonders associated with the emancipation of Israel from Egypt. There were not only the *signs in Egypt*, but the great "Red Sea" wonder that separated them from the house of bondage. Every conversion from sin to God is a wonder. A supernatural deliverance.

5. COMPLETE. "The Lord brought us *out*" (v. 21). They were not partly out of Egypt and partly in the wilderness. "Not a hoof was left behind." The salvation of God implies the salvation of the *whole man*, spirit, soul, and body. When our head and heart have been taken out of the horrible pit our *feet* also will be lifted out of the miry clay (Psa. 40. 2).

6. WITH JUDGMENTS. "Signs and wonders, great and sore, upon Egypt and upon Pharaoh" (v. 22). In the salvation of Israel both Egypt and Pharaoh, its king, come under the judgments of God. In the crucifixion and death of Christ (which means the salvation of God) both the world and the prince of this world have been judged. All who obey not the call of God's sovereign grace will assuredly come under the terrible plagues of the righteous judgments of the Almighty.

7. TWOFOLD. "He brought us out, that He might bring us in," etc. (v. 23). He brought them out of Egypt that He might bring them into Canaan. He brings us out of the kingdom of darkness that He might bring us into the kingdom of His dear Son. Out of bondage and poverty into the liberty and wealth of sonship. Out of the weakness of self-effort into the power of the Holy Ghost. To get *in* we must get *out*. But we may be out and yet not in.

III. The Responsibilities of the Delivered. To seek—

1. THE GOOD THAT COMES THROUGH HOLY FEAR. "Fear the Lord our God, for our good always" (v. 24). It is still true that spiritual riches and honour belong to those who humbly fear the Lord (Prov. 22. 4). Fearing to grieve the Spirit of God will secure the unceasing good of His comforting presence, and maintain a conscience void of offence.

2. THE RIGHTEOUSNESS THAT COMES THROUGH IMPLICIT OBEDIENCE. "It shall be our righteousness if we do all

these commandments'' (v. 24). "If ye love Me, keep My commandments.'' Our *rightness* with God in our daily life depends on our walking day by day in the light of His Word. As ye have therefore received Christ Jesus the Lord, so walk ye in Him.

COMMANDMENTS FOR CANAAN.
Deuteronomy 6.

THE first three verses of this chapter give us the secret of a happy, fruitful, satisfied life. "He that *doeth* these sayings of Mine shall be likened unto a *wise* man" (Matt. 7. 24). We have here then—

I. A Solemn Declaration. "The Lord our God is one Lord" (v. 4). This is His glorious and fearful Name (chap. 28. 58). "I and My Father are one" (John 14. 9).

II. An Absorbing Attitude. "Thou shalt love the Lord with *all* thine heart, soul, and might" (v. 5). If the Lord absorbs the affections there will be no more room for self or the world. No provision for the flesh (Phil. 1. 21).

III. A Gracious Responsibility (vv. 6-9). When the Lord is loved His words will be treasured, thought of, talked, written, lived (Psa. 1. 2; Job 23. 12).

IV. An Unmerited Possession (vv. 10, 11). The inheritance of the saints, present or future, is not the fruit of their own labour, but the outcome of infinite grace (Eph. 3. 16-19).

V. A Needful Reminder. "Beware lest thou forget the Lord which brought thee out of bondage" (v. 12). It will preserve our sympathies for the unsaved to remember that "such were some of us" (1 Cor. 6. 11).

VI. A Conditional Promise. "Do that which is right in the sight of the Lord that it may be well with thee"

(v. 18). "Walk *before* God" (Gen. 17. 1). Behave as in the presence of God (Matt. 23. 8).

VII. **An Expected Testimony** (vv. 21-25). "Thou shalt say," etc. Their testimony, like ours, consisted of—

1. A CONFESSION of their past condition. "Bondmen in Egypt" (v. 21).

2. AN ACKNOWLEDGMENT of the Lord's righteous judgments against sin (v. 22).

3. A DECLARATION of His power to save "from thence" (v. 23).

4. AN ASSURANCE of His faithfulness to His Word "that He might bring us in" (v. 23).

5. A WARNING against the sin of unbelief (v. 24).

6. AN ENCOURAGEMENT to implicit obedience (v. 25).

PRIVILEGES AND RESPONSIBILITIES.
Deuteronomy 7.

IN this chapter we have, as it were, the pomegranates of promise and the bells of warning hanging from the robe of our great High-Priest. Let us note—

I. **The Privileges of the Lord's People.** They are—

1. CHOSEN. "The Lord thy God hath chosen thee" (v. 6). Chosen in Christ (Eph. 1. 4). According to God's purpose (Rom. 8. 28; 1 Peter 1. 2-9).

2. REDEEMED. "The Lord redeemed you out of Egypt" (v. 8). Redeemed by blood (1 Peter 1. 18, 19). From the curse of the law (Gal. 3. 13). To God (Rev. 5. 9).

3. ASSURED. "Know that thy God is the faithful God" (v. 9). He is faithful that has promised. "These things have I *written* that ye *may know*" (John 5. 13).

4. FAVOURED. "Blessed above all people" (v. 14).

They have light in their dwelling (Exod. 10. 23). All
the wheels of providence *work together* for their good
(Rom. 8. 28).

5. PRESERVED. "The Lord will put none of the diseases
of Egypt upon thee" (v. 15). The diseases of Egypt were
the fruits of unbelief (Exod. 9. 14; Heb. 12. 6, 7).

6. HONOURED. "The Lord thy God *is* among you"
(v. 21). "I will *dwell* in them, and walk in them" (2 Cor.
6. 16). And Christ dwells *in* our hearts *by faith* (Eph. 3 17).

7. POWERFUL. "No man shall be able to stand before
thee" (v. 24).   Stephen, being full of the Holy Ghost,
"they were not able to resist *the Spirit* by which he spake"
(Acts 6. 10; Micah 3. 8; Acts 1. 8).

II. The Responsibilities of the Lord's People.
There must be—

1. No COMPROMISING WITH THE ENEMY. "Make no covenant with them," etc. (vv. 2, 3). "Be not unequally
yoked" (2 Cor. 6. 14). Beware of the modern Gibeonites
(Josh. 9. 6; see Exod. 10. 24-26).

2. No CONNIVANCE AT FALSE WORSHIP. "Ye shall
destroy their altars," etc. (v. 5). The Christian *faith* is
iconoclastic. Earnestly contend for it. It was when the
Ark was *set by* Dagon that Dagon fell (1 Sam. 5. 2, 3;
John 12. 32).

3. No SWERVING FROM THE DIVINE COMMAND. "Thou
shalt keep the commandments which I command thee"
(vv. 11, 12). Notice the connection between Christ's
"commandments," "sayings," or "words," and *love*
in John 14. 21, 24, 31; 15. 9-17.

4. No FEARING THE FACE OF MAN. "Thou shalt not
be afraid of them" (v. 18). The fear of man ensnares
our liberty (Gen. 12. 12) and grieves the Spirit. Have
the boldness of Peter and John (Acts 4. 19, 20).

5. No Coveting the Riches of the World. "Thou shalt not *desire* their silver or gold" (vv. 25, 26). Paul coveted no man's silver (Acts 20. 33). How many have erred from the faith through this? (1 Tim. 6. 10). Covet earnestly the best gifts (1 Cor. 12. 31).

THE DIVINE PURPOSE IN TRIAL.
Deuteronomy 8. 2-6.

"When my sense of safety pales,
Show Thy nail-marked hand in mine;
When my sense of comfort fails,
Place my trembling hand in Thine.
I held of Thee, Thee holding,
Thy strong love me enfolding."

Although "trials make the promise sweet," yet to the people of God suffering has its mystery as well as sin. Abraham suffered, being sorely tried not because of his disobedience or unbelief, but because of his faith (Gen. 22). So the "afterwards" yielded peaceful fruits. If we cannot *see* the wisdom of His hand in affliction we can *trust* the love of His heart. While the Israelites were in the wilderness it was to them verily a time of trial.

I. The Nature of it. It was—

1. Long. "These forty years" (v. 2). Our Lord fasted forty days, and was tempted of the devil. "These forty years" remind us of the patience of God. He can afford to wait. The great wheels of the divine purpose move slowly but surely.

2. Severe. "Suffered thee to hunger" (v. 3). God could easily have prevented this, but He *suffered* it. It is good for us at times to feel the pinch of need (2 Cor. 12. 8, 9).

3. The Result of Unbelief. "They could not enter in because of unbelief" (Heb. 3. 19). Unbelief always disinherits from the enjoyment of the promise. The name of those who profess to be the followers of Christ and who, like these wanderers, live an aimless life is legion. Doubting the Word of God, they cease to be warriors for God.

4. UNDER HIS LEADING. "The Lord thy God led thee" (v. 2). Blessed be His holy Name for this. Although we may fail to lay hold of all that He in His mercy has provided for us, yet will He not forsake those whom He hath redeemed. He abideth faithful.

II. The Blessings enjoyed while in it.

1. BREAD FROM HEAVEN. "He fed thee with manna" (v. 3). During the covenanting struggle, in what were called "the killing times," one woman declared that "she got more good out of one verse of the Bible now than she used to get out of a chapter before."

2. THEIR CLOTHING PRESERVED. "Thy raiment waxed not old upon thee" (v. 4). It is wonderful how far a very little will go when the blessing of God is on it (Matt. 16. 9). The robe of God's righteousness which adorns every blood-bought pilgrim never gets the worse for the wear. The clothes suggest the *outward* appearance of our daily life.

3. THEIR FEET KEPT. "Neither did thy foot swell these forty years" (v. 4). He is able also to preserve the feet of His saints in their going out and in their coming in (Psa. 121. 8). This implies preserved ability to *walk* in His ways and to witness for Him. It is when we turn aside from the Lord's way that the feet of faith fail and we begin to limp.

4. HIS PRESENCE WITH THEM. "The Lord thy God led thee" (v. 2). It was while in the furnace of affliction that the three Hebrews proved the preserving presence of their God. If they were chastised, they are reminded that the

rod was in the hand of their redeeming God (v. 5). "Why can ye not trust God?" said a wife to her alarmed husband the other night when a terrific storm was shaking the house and making the tiles fly off the roof. "Lo, I am with you alway" (Heb: 12. 5, 6).

III. **The Purpose of it.** God has a *purpose* (Rom. 8. 28), and that purpose is as big as the universe, and as definite as the light of truth. To Israel it was threefold—

1. To HUMBLE THEE (v. 2). Those who walk humbly with their God will love mercy and do justly. The haughty head of pride is ever ready to lift itself up to the grieving of the gentle Spirit of God, who delights to dwell with the contrite and humble in heart. To be humbled is a great mercy, as it puts the soul in a better position for the enjoyment of hidden heavenly things.

2. To PROVE THEE. "To know what is in thine heart" (v. 2). The furnace of trial is intended to make *manifest* the real inner character. Did not the Lord say to Abraham, after he had been severely tested, *"Now I know that thou fearest God?"* (Gen. 22. 12). We would never have heard of the "patience of Job" but for the fiery trials. Faint not, then, at the rebuke of the Lord. Whom He loveth He "chasteneth" (v. 5).

3. To TEACH THEE. "To make thee know that man doth not live by bread alone, but by every word that proceedeth out of the mouth of the Lord" (v. 3). What the manna was to the Israelites the Word of God should be to us—"bread from Heaven," "angels' food," "the living bread." Evermore give us this bread. The Word was made flesh, and dwelt among us. In closing His testimony regarding Himself as the "Bread" our Lord connects the *bread* with the *words* of truth, saying, "The *words* that I speak unto you are spirit and *life*" (John 6. 63). If affliction and adversity make us realise our vital need of

C Vol. IV.

His Word it will be as the opening of a living fountain of water to a parched soul. This is the cup of the New Testament, drink ye all of it.

WILDERNESS EXPERIENCES.
Deuteronomy 8.

"There are those who walk in gloom,
    But there are those who walk in light;
There are tempted, overcome,
    But victors as well in the fight.
Shine or shade, vanquished or winning,
By Thy grace shield us from sinning."

IF we were half as anxious to be saved from *sin* as we are to be kept from sorrow it would be a wholesome fear. This chapter is very rich in suggestive thought. The great cardinal blessings that should characterise every Christian life are here indicated.

There are four blessings mentioned in the first verse as the result of obedience. (1) Life: "Ye may live." (2) Fruitfulness: "Multiply." (3) Progress: "Go in." (4) Possession: "Possess the land."

The Christian life is—

I. **A Life Under the Guidance of God.** "The Lord thy God *led* thee" (v. 2). He led them in the pillar of cloud and fire. The fiery cloud was to them what the *Word* of God is to us—*spirit and power*. The Holy Ghost shall guide you into all truth (John 16. 13). As many as are led by the Spirit of God are the sons of God.

II. **A Life of Humility before God.** "Thy God led thee to *humble* thee" (v. 2). We would never of ourselves choose the self-humbling path. To be *humbled* is just to be put into that position in which God Himself can find more room in our lives. The process of *proving* is always painful, but profitable. It is to bring out what is in our hearts that we may be in God's sight either approved or condemned (Gen. 22. 12; 2 Chron. 31. 32).

III. **A Life Sustained from God.** "He fed thee with manna" (v. 3). "He brought thee forth water out of the rock of flint" (v. 15). The *sustenance* of their life was as miraculous as their salvation. "The Bread of God is He which cometh down from Heaven and giveth life unto the world" (John 6). Christ not only saves but satisfies (Phil. 4. 19). If any man eat this bread he shall live for ever. The Word was God, and the Word was made flesh, and dwelt among us.

IV. **A Life of Dependence on God.** "By *every word* that proceedeth out of the mouth of God *doth man live*" (v. 3). Words are for the hearing of *faith*. We live by faith on the Son of God. "Thy words were found, and I did eat them" (Jer. 15. 16). There is in the Word of God that which exactly suits every spiritual constitution. "They did all eat the same spiritual meat." Lord, to whom can we go? Thou only hast the words of eternal life.

V. **A Life of Hope in God.** In verses 7-9 there is given a description of the good land that lay before them, so that they were to forget the things that were behind, and press on to the better things before. "Press on that ye may obtain" (Phil. 3. 12-14) and receive *the end* of your faith, even the *salvation of souls* (1 Peter 1. 9) (Alford). We hope in God through our Lord Jesus Christ. It is the hope of His coming that not only leads to the salvation of others, but also to the purification of ourselves (1 John 3. 3).

VI. **A Life of Praise to God.** "When thou art full, then shalt thou bless the Lord thy God" (v. 10). The Lord would have us to praise Him with a *full* heart. The *lean* are sure to cry out about their leanness (Isa. 24. 16). They cannot glory in their infirmities. It is the *satisfied*

that bless the Lord (Psa. 103. 1-5). He that eateth to the
Lord will be sure to give thanks (Rom. 14. 6). The hungry
soul cries: Lord bless *me*. The satisfied soul says: Lord, I
bless *Thee*. Thanks be unto God for His unspeakable gift.

VII. A Life Empowered by God. "The Lord thy God
giveth thee power to get wealth" (v. 18). In *saving* His
people out of the poverty of Egypt; in *sustaining* them in a
waste, howling wilderness; in *leading* them into the land
of promise and of plenty He was giving them power to get
wealth. The *power*, then, was that which enabled them to
lay hold on, and take possession of, the fuller gifts of His
grace. This power we have in the Holy Spirit, who by His
sustaining and guiding presence enables us to lay hold on
and enter into the possession of the *fulness of the blessing* in
Christ Jesus our Lord. In the gift of the Spirit God has
given us power to get wealth—the wealth of Christ's
unsearchable riches now, and the wealth of His unspeakable
glory hereafter. This blessing of the Lord it maketh
rich. Why cry out about your leanness and poverty when
God hath given thee power to get wealth? Buy of Me, that
thou mayest be rich (Rev. 3. 18). Receive ye the Holy
Ghost.

THE LAND OF PROMISE.
Deuteronomy 9-11.

"What He wills, I say I must;
     What I must, I say I will;
He commanding, it is just
     What Ho would I should fulfil.
     Whilst He biddeth I believe
     What He calls for He will give;
     To obey Him is to live."

CANAAN may fitly represent the *present* inheritance of the
believer, although many seem content to abide in the
wilderness with the promise of "bread and water," instead of passing over into full deliverance and joyful

abundance (Heb. 3. 17). From the above chapters we might learn the—

I. Character of this Possession. "It is a land watered and watched by the Lord from the beginning of the year to the end" (chap. 11. 10-12). And may typify the grace and fulness given us of God in Jesus Christ (John 1. 16, 17).

II. Difficulties to be Expected. "Nations greater and mightier than thyself" (chap. 9. 1, 2). Paul tells us about these mightier ones in Romans 7, and also how to conquer in verse 25.

III. Condition to be Remembered. "Speak not in thine heart, saying, For *my* righteousness the Lord hath brought me in," etc. (chap. 9. 5, 6). The condition of receiving the greater blessing is not our righteousness but *emptiness* (Isa. 40. 29).

IV. Attitudes to be Maintained. In chapter 10. 12 they are exhorted: (1).To fear; (2) to walk; (3) to love; (4) to serve; (5) to keep; and in chapter 11. 22 (6) to cleave (see 2 Peter 1. 8).

V. Faith to be Exercised. "Every place whereon the soles of your feet shall tread shall be yours" (chap. 11. 24). The moment the feet of faith rests on the promise the blessing is secure (Mark 11. 24).

VI. Promise to be Trusted. "The Lord thy God is He which goeth before thee" (chap. 9. 3). I will dwell in them (2 Cor. 6. 16). It is God *in us* that doeth the works (John 14. 10).

VII. Victory to be Gained. "None shall be able to *stand* before thee," and the *fear of thee* shall be upon the land (chap. 11. 25). How does the present-day Church answer to this? (Acts 6. 10; Luke 21. 15).

THE LORD'S REQUIREMENTS.

Deuteronomy 10. 12-22.

"Broken from all other trusting,
Enfranchised from all 'former lusting;'
Thy freedman, Lord, on Thee calling,
Guard me in my dolorous falling.
Anoint my eyes with Thy own seeing,
Interpenetrate my being
That by Thee all 'apprehended,'
This weary conflict may be ended."

THE secret of rest and victory lies in ceasing to struggle against the requirements of God. It was not till Jacob had yielded to the man from Heaven, at the brook Jabbok, that he became a prevailing prince. Here is a question that should come with searching power to the heart of every child of God: "What doth the Lord thy God require of *thee*?" (v. 12). Surely such a question ought to constrain us honestly to make this inquiry: "Lord, what wilt Thou have me to do?"

I. The Lord has Requirements.

1. As OUR CREATOR. "The Heaven of heavens is the Lord's, the earth also, and *all that therein is*" (v. 14). As the creatures of His creative hand we live and move on and in the things which are God's (Psa. 24. 1). What have we that we have not received? As our Maker He requires the thankful homage of our lives.

2. As OUR REDEEMER. "He is thy God, that hath done for thee these great and terrible things, which thine eyes have seen" (v. 21). In redeeming them out of the house of Egyptian bondage it was by *great* things in mercy for them, and *terrible* things in judgment against their enemies. Christ hath redeemed us from the curse of the law. Ye are bought with a price, *therefore* glorify God in your body and your spirit, which are His. "Him only shalt thou serve" (Matt. 4. 10).

II. What these Requirements are. "What doth the Lord *thy* God require of *thee*?" The claim is based on the fact of His saving grace. *Thy* God who hath done such great things for thee. He requires—

1. A FILIAL FEAR. "Fear the Lord thy God" (v. 12). Not as a *slave* who fears his master because of the lash, but as a loving, dutiful *son* fears to grieve or dishonour his father. God is our Father, but He is also Judge, and hath power to cast both soul and body into hell. "Yea, I say unto you, fear ye Him."

2. AN OBEDIENT WALK. "To walk in all His ways" (v. 12). If we would walk in *His ways* we must be willing to set the Lord continually before us, then our walk will be "worthy of the Lord in all well-pleasing" (Col. 1. 10). What doth the Lord require of thee but to walk humbly with thy God? (Micah 6. 8).

3. AN AFFECTIONATE HEART. "To love Him" (v. 12). He who looketh upon the heart· requires truth in the *inward* parts. What is more sickening and repulsive than feigned love? It is the most loathsome stage of the leprosy of sin. Mere *words* uttered in the ear of God will not meet the requirements of His *heart* concerning us. Thou shalt *love* the Lord thy God with all thy heart. If any man love not the Lord Jesus Christ, let him be accursed.

4. A WHOLE-HEARTED SERVICE. "To serve the Lord thy God with all thy heart" (v. 12). This is a divine requirement that needs to be specially urged in His Name. We are not saved merely to rejoice in salvation, but to glorify God by a life of consecrated service to Him. This service implies selling, giving, following (Mark 10. 21). To the lame man Peter said, "Such as I have, I give." Present your bodies a living sacrifice unto God. This is *your* reasonable service (Rom. 12. 1).

5. A SUBMISSIVE WILL. "Be no more stiff necked"

(v. 16). Having presented ourselves to God, as Isaac did to his father, let us be as silently submissive as he was (Gen. 22). "Behold, here am I, let him do to me as seemeth good unto him" (2 Sam. 15. 26). The clay that remains *stiff* in the hands of the potter will not be fashioned into a vessel of great honour. "Not My will, but Thine be done."

6. A CHARITABLE SPIRIT. "Love ye therefore the stranger, for ye were strangers in the land of Egypt" (v.19). This is another most salutary requirement of the Lord. It was while we were strangers and enemies that God loved us, and that His Son died for us, therefore if the *love of God* is in us we will have compassion on those who are out of the way. Such were some of you, but ye are washed. Having been once a stranger yourself ye should "know the heart of a stranger" (Exod. 23. 9). Remember the words of the Lord Jesus as recorded in Luke 10. 29-37.

7. A TENACIOUS FAITH "The Lord thy God,... to Him shalt thou cleave" (v. 20) This is our life, *cleaving* to the Living One. Let our cleaving be as tenacious as the limpit on the rock, which clings the closer the more it is buffeted. "I will not let Thee go." My heart is fixed (Psa. 57. 7). Cleaving to the Lord is the secret of strength, and such will always be brightened with His brightness. Lord to whom can we go?   ———

THE BLESSED POSSESSION.
Deuteronomy 11. 10-17.

"Wilt thou, O Lord, me holier make?
  Wilt Thou, O Lord, me holier keep?
The power of sin within me break,
  Behold me as I troubled weep.

Lord, I go dimly, give me light,
  That I may not unworthy prove;
Shield me, O shield with gentle might,
  In the long patience of Thy love.

Purge and repurge me all within,
  In thought and word, desire and deed;
Fain would I final conquest win,
  Help me, as Thou for me didst bleed."

IF the Lord cared for the land given to His people for a
possession so much that His eyes were always upon it,
"from the beginning of the year, even unto the end of the
year," surely His caretaking eye will always be upon
His own inheritance and "peculiar treasure," purchased by
the blood of His own Son. Oh, how much this possession
needs to "drink the rain from Heaven," and to be cleansed
and purged by the power of His own presence. How often
this *holy land* gets defiled. Observe here—

I. A Wonderful Assurance. Concerning the inheritance reserved for them in Canaan they are assured that—

1. IT IS NOT LIKE THE OLD. "The land is not like the
land of Egypt, from whence ye came out" (v. 10). A
state of liberty and plenty is never like a state of bondage
and poverty. "For ye were once darkness, but are now
light in the Lord" (Eph. 5. 8, R.V.). Once afar off, but
now made nigh by the blood of Christ.

2. IT IS NOT WATERED BY WORKS. "In the land of Egypt
thou wateredst it with thy foot. But the land, whither ye
go to possess it, drinketh water of the rain of Heaven"
(vv. 10, 11). "Watering with the foot" of course has
reference to the *laborious* process of irrigation by which the
waters of the Nile were led from place to place, or perhaps
the working of a *tread mill* wheel for lifting up the water
from the river into a cistern for watering purposes. It is a
terrible task to get our inheritance *refreshed* while in the
house of bondage; but *in* Christ our possession is continually
refreshed by the rain of His Holy Spirit from Heaven. No
self-effort is needed to make the "things freely given us of
God" spring up in living beauty and reviving power before
us and in us. *He* shall come down like rain upon the
mown grass.

3. IT IS WATCHED OVER BY THE LORD. "The eyes of the Lord are always upon it, from the beginn ng of the year even unto the end of the year" (v. 12). Even in midwinter, when no sign of life is visible, and when every living thing seems to have gone back to the stillness of death, and when king frost has imprisoned the earth as in iron bands. So also in the spiritual life He hath not forsaken His own, although there be no *outward* tokens of abundance of fresh life within. "From the beginning of the year unto the end" surely teaches us that in every *season* of the Christian life His carefulness over us is the same. I am the Lord, I change not (Psa. 33. 18).

II. A Simple Condition. God's terms are always easy. "My yoke is easy, and My burden is light." The condition of abiding in His possession and enjoying continual blessing is threefold—

1. HEAR HIM. "Ye shall hearken diligently" (v. 13). Hear, and your soul shall live. "Hearken diligently unto Him, and ye shall eat that which is good, and your soul shall delight itself in fatness" (Isa. 55. 2).

2. LOVE HIM. "Ye shall love the Lord thy God" (v. 13). He not only seeks an opened *ear*, but also an opened *heart*. As His love for us gives us an entrance into His heart, so our love to Him gives Him an entrance into our hearts.

3. SERVE HIM. "To serve Him with all your heart and with all your soul" (v. 13). All the affections of the heart and all the life and energies of the soul must go into our service if it is not to be perfunctory, fruitless, and hypocritical.

III. A Solemn Warning.

1. AGAINST SELF-DECEPTION. "Take heed to yourselves, that your heart be not deceived" (v. 16). The heart is easily deceived, just because it is naturally deceitful. One of the chief devices of the devil is to make men believe that there is no devil. "Watch ye therefore, lest ye be secretly enticed" (Job 31. 27).

2. AGAINST FALSE WORSHIP. "Take heed lest ye turn aside and serve other gods" (v. 16). No image was to be set up in the land (Lev. 26. 1). The hearts that become deceived and turn away from God will soon have other gods set up in their own imaginations whom they will *secr tly* worship. When Jesus Christ is dethroned in the heart some self-made god will take His place.

3. AGAINST LOOSING THE INHERITANCE. "Take heed lest ye perish quickly from off the good land which the Lord thy God giveth thee" (v. 17). This is a solemn truth. By allowing the heart to deceive us, by setting its affections on other than God Himself, we thereby perish from out of the practical enjoyment of the gifts of God's grace. The Lord thy God is a jealous God. Thy sin will shut up the dew of Heaven from thee (1 Kings 8. 35). The *rain* referred to in Amos 4. 7 is most suggestive of the moving of the Holy Spirit. The attitude of the heart toward God determines where the refreshing power of His presence shall come. Where His reviving Spirit does not come everything is sure to *wither*, so there is *experimentally* a perishing from off the good land. ———

THE SECRET OF VICTORY.
Deuteronomy 11. 22-25.

"Victor, yet Victim manifest,
Love to its mighty task addressed;
Victim, yet Victor—righteousness,
Suffering our fallen race to bless.

Victim, yet Victor—on the Cross,
Redeeming our stupendous loss;
Victim, yet Victor—sacrifice,
By which eternally death dies."

THE Lord Jesus Christ has left us an example, how a Victim to the *will of God* can become the Victor in the *work of God*.

Learn here, O soul, that there is no other way into a life of triumph in His sight. We must be vanquished by the power of the Holy Ghost before we can be overcomers in this present evil world. The battle is the Lord's, and He conquers *in* us. In these Scriptures indicated above, we have again before us some old words that breathe the vital breath of life for us.

I. The Conditions.

1. A CONSECRATED LIFE. The yielded up life is here detailed in the following pointed and all-comprehensive terms (v. 22). (1) "Ye shall diligently *keep all* these commandments." (2) "Ye shall *love* the Lord your God." (3) "Ye shall *walk in all* His ways." (4) "Ye shall *cleave* unto Him." The consecrated—filled up—life is one that is daily being consumed, or eaten up, of zeal for the Lord, yet a life that is also daily replenished by the indwelling Spirit of burning. This holy fire, burning on the altar of the heart, is never to go out. Yield *yourselves* unto God, that your members may be instruments of righteousness.

2. AN ADVENTUROUS FAITH. "Every place where the soles of your feet shall tread upon shall be yours" (v. 24). "Faith laughs at impossibilities, and says it shall be done." Abraham's faith was adventurous when he went out, not knowing whither he went. Every promise *claimed* is a promise *possessed*. Believe, and thou shalt see. Those who are afraid of the deep will not catch many fishes. Have the courage to "launch out." We need *pioneers* in the realms of faith as well as in the dark places of the earth, and no other field of exploration can ever yield such reward, for " every place where the sole of your feet shall tread upon shall be *yours*."

II. The Promises.
Every promise of God rings like a dinner bell to the hungry, believing heart. They are open doors into the superabundant fulness of God, covenant

bows that stretch across the dark brow of every cloud of difficulty, crowning it with glory. They are—

1. As GREAT AS OUR NEED. "Then the Lord will drive out all these nations from before thee" (v. 23). "Then shall no man be able to stand before thee," etc. (v. 25). Emphasis should be put on the first word, "*then*." When they are in heart right with God, *then* He will magnify His Name in them by working miracles for them. This is a law in the kingdom of grace that is unalterable. Sanctify yourselves, and the Lord will do wonders. It is God's *little children* that are said to be overcomers (1 John 4. 4). It does not matter how strong the man is who would rob us of our goods the Lord is stronger than he. Let your trust be in Him (Luke 11. 21).

2. As SURE AS HIS WORD. "The Lord your God shall lay the fear of you upon all the land, as *He hath said unto you*" (v. 25). "Prove Me, and see if I will not do it for you." "God is not a *man* that He should lie" (Num. 23. 19), as if no man is worthy of our trust. What are adverse circumstances in the face of His Word? (Gen. 17. 15). Faith will always find it even as He hath said (Mark 14. 16). Hath God not also pledged that He will *not alter* the thing that has gone out of His lips? (Psa. 89. 34). All His promises are seasoned with the salt of eternal faithfulness. Yes, we have a *sure word* wherein we do well to take heed. The words that I speak unto you they are spirit and life. Believest thou this?

THE PLACE WHICH THE LORD SHALL CHOOSE.
Deuteronomy 16. 7, 15, 16.

"There is a sacred, hallowed spot,
Oft present to my eye,
By saints it ne'er can be forgot,
'Tis much-loved Calvary."

> "There is a place where Jesus sheds
> The oil of gladness on our heads;
> A place than all beside more sweet,
> It is the blood-stained mercy-seat."

"THE place which the Lord thy God shall choose." These
words occur three times in this chapter and twelve times
in this book. The *place* called Calvary was as much the
appointment of God as the occasion. Abraham and Isaac
came to *the place* of which God had told Abraham (Gen. 22.9).
God as the offended one surely has the right to choose the
place where He will meet with man. Did He not say to
Moses, "Thou shalt put the mercy-seat above the ark, and
there I will meet with thee?" (Exod. 25. 21, 22). We shall
look at the connections in which these words, "The place
which the Lord thy God shall choose" are used as so many
fingerposts pointing to the Cross of Christ. Each time the
God-chosen place is referred to there seems to be associated
with it some fresh truth that reminds us of "the place
called Calvary." Holy Spirit lead us into all truth. That
place is connected with—

I. His Name. "The place which the Lord your God
shall choose to cause His Name to dwell there" (chap. 12.
11). Oh, how closely and how vitally the *Name of God* is
associated with the Cross of Christ! God in Christ recon-
ciling the world unto Himself. It is the glory of *the place*
called Calvary that the blood shed there was the blood of
God (Acts 20. 28). His saving Name dwells there.

II. Burnt Offering. "In the place which the Lord
shall choose, there thou shalt offer thy burnt offerings"
(chap. 12. 14). Christ the great burnt offering was offered
in the place chosen by God outside Jerusalem. He gave
Himself an *offering* and a sacrifice to God. The burnt
offering aspect of our Lord's death declares His *perfectly
accepted* life and character by God in our stead.

III. Eating. "Thou must eat them before the Lord

thy God in the place which the Lord thy God shall choose''
(chap. 12. 18). After the sacrifice comes the feasting.
In this God-fixed place the offerer was also to be fed and
strengthened. The shadow of the Cross falls on this
place. ''Except ye eat the flesh and drink the blood of
the Son of Man ye have no life in you.'' ''My flesh is meat
indeed.'' From the crucified One we may still hear these
words: ''Hearken diligently unto Me, and eat ye that
which is good.''

IV. Vowing. ''Thy vows thou shalt take, and go unto
the place which the Lord shall choose'' (chap. 12. 26).
If at the Cross we have found a sacrifice for our sins and
food for our souls, surely the next thing is a yielding of
ourselves in covenant promise unto God. Let the vows
made in secret be paid openly in the presence of the people,
paid in the coin of true-hearted adoration and active,
self-denying service.

V. A Price. ''If the way be too long for thee, then thou
shalt turn it (sacrifice) info money, and shalt go into the
place which the Lord thy God shall choose'' (chap. 14. 25).
This worshipper brought the price of his offering in his
hand to the place where God was pleased to put His name.
But God's own Son hath appeared before Him for us with
the price in His hand. ''Ye are bought with a price''
(1 Cor. 6. 22). '' Ye are not redeemed with corruptible
things, as silver and gold, but with the precious blood
of Christ.''

VI. The Passover. ''At the place which the Lord thy
God shall choose, there thou shalt sacrifice the Passover''
(chap. 16. 6, 7). This is another fingerpost pointing to
Him who was ''Christ our Passover sacrificed for us.''
''When I see the blood I will *pass over* you.'' God finds
enough in the blood of His Son to enable Him righteously
to pass over all who take shelter beneath it.

VII. **Rejoicing**. "Thou shalt rejoice in thy feast unto the Lord thy God in the place which the Lord shall choose" (chap. 16. 14, 15). This holy rejoicing is intimately associated with the awful Cross. We joy in God through our Lord Jesus Christ by whom we have now received the reconciliation (Rom. 5. 11). Bunyan's pilgrim leaped for joy in the presence of the Cross. It is through Christ's sufferings that His own joy is imparted. "My joy I give unto you."

VIII. **Personal Appearing Before God**. "Three times a year shall all thy males appear before the Lord thy God in the place which He shall choose" (chap. 16. 16). Those who would be made participants of His saving grace must present themselves *personally* before Him, and those who would keep themselves in the enjoyment of His favour must come often. The thought of *personal consecration* to God may also be here. Those saved by His grace are called upon to present *themselves* unto God a living sacrifice. They shall not appear before the Lord empty (see Rom. 6. 13).

IX. **Teaching**. "If there arise a matter too hard for thee, then shalt thou arise and get thee up into the place which the Lord thy God shall choose" (chap. 17. 8). Difficulties will arise, but light was to be found in the chosen place where His holy Name was recorded—the mercy-seat. This is a precious lesson for us. If you would be taught of God, arise, get thee up to Him, who is the great Teacher come from God. Lord, to whom can we go? Thou only hast the words of eternal life. He is made of God unto us wisdom. "Learn of Me, for I am meek and lowly in heart, and ye shall find rest."

X. **Service**. "If a Levite shall come . . . with all the desire of his soul unto the place which the Lord shall choose, then he shall *minister* in the Name of the Lord his

God'' (chap. 18. 6, 7, R.V.). This reference is beautifully applicable to our Lord and Master. Coming to Him *with all the desire of the soul* as a Levite (separated one) will always lead into active and acceptable service. This is the door into the holy ministry. If Christ is desired with all the soul, then the ministry will be *in the Name of the Lord*.

XI. **The Gathering of all before the Lord.** ''When *all* Israel is come to appear before the Lord thy God in the place which He shall choose'' (chap. 31. 11). This is a general appearing of men, women, and children, of all *within thy gates*, and forcibly reminds us of the judgment seat of Christ before which we must all appear. He will judge the world by that Man whom He hath *appointed*. At this great and solemn assembly the book of the law was opened (v. 10). Now for instruction, but then for judgment (Rev. 20. 12-15). ''Be not deceived; God is not mocked'' (Gal. 6. 7).

CHARACTERISTICS OF A GOD-RAISED PROPHET.
Deuteronomy 18. 15-22.

''On faith wings lifted up, I heard the stainless praise
  Of the redeemed hosts above,
Even as it was heard on Patmos Isle by the disciple
  Whom the Lord did love.

I saw, too, in the streets of shining gold that led
  Up to the Lord Christ enthroned there
The glorious company of the redeemed from first
  Of time, who the 'new Name' did bear.

Oh, it was such a beatific glimpse that thus to me
  In my deep thought was given,
That now I walk this scarred, sin-shattered earth
  As tho' already I were there in Heaven.''

EVERY true prophet of God is a *seer*. One whose *eyes* have been opened to see sin and redemption, God and Eternity in Eternity's own light. Such a faith vision is sure to revolutionise the life by bringing the grace of God and the glory of Heaven into it. From references in the New Testament it is very clear that the prophet spoken of here was—

The Lord Jesus Christ.

1. He was raised up by God (Matt. 17. 5; John 1. 45; John 6. 14).

2. He was taken from among His brethren (Heb. 2. 14-17).

3. He was made like unto Moses (compare Num. 12. 3; Matt. 11. 29).

4. He spake the word of God (Heb. 1. 1, 2; John 8. 24; 17. 14).

5. His words will be required of by those who hear them (Heb. 2. 1-4; John 12. 48).

6. His words come to pass (John 4. 19).

Balaam was a man whose "eyes were opened," but whose heart was unchanged, for he "loved the wages of unrighteousness." Every God-raised servant, every Spirit-ordained worker (Acts 13. 2), will bear the marks of this true Prophet. He will—

I. **Belong to the Brethren.** "Raised up from among their brethren" (v. 18). All God's prophets were taken out from among His own people. It is so still. We must be brought into the family of God, into the holy brotherhood, before we are in a position to serve. First sons, then servants.

II. **Resemble the Great Prototype.** "Like unto Thee" (v. 18). As a prophet Jesus Christ was made like unto Moses in His lowly birth, in His princely character, and in His work as a Deliverer. So are the servants of Christ raised up like unto their Master, born of God, partakers of the divine nature, and co-workers together. He hath left us an example, that we should follow His steps (John 17. 18).

III. **Be Possessed by the Word of God.** "I will put My words in his mouth" (v. 18). His words are put in as treasure in.an earthen vessel. They are *put in* because there is on the part of the servant a real hunger for the truth of.God, and an open mouth to receive it. The words of God are living words, and burn as a fire in the bones. To receive His words is to receive His thoughts, and *to know* what the will of the Lord is (Isa. 55. 8-11).

IV. **Fearlessly Speak the Truth.** "He shall speak unto them all that I command him" (v. 18). He declares the whole counsel of God, keeping back nothing. The received word has such a breaking forth power that "we cannot but speak the things which we have seen and heard" (Acts 4. 20). Nothing can be more straight than rays of light. Nothing so dogmatic as truth. It is little faith that wavers; the strong in faith glorify God.

V. **Speak in the Name of God.** "He shall speak in My Name" (v. 19). God's words and thoughts must be uttered in the Name of God. No servant is responsible for the words of his master. "It is not ye that speak, but the Spirit of the Father which is in you." When the thoughts of Christ are declared in His Name He takes the responsibility of making them effectual to the purpose whereunto they were sent; He is sufficiently jealous of *His own Name* to relieve the servant of any anxiety. "It shall not return unto Me void."

VI. **Be Known by his Fruits.** The question is put: "How shall we know the word which the Lord hath *not* spoken?" (v. 21) so that they may distinguish between self-ordained and God-sent prophets. The answer is: "It the thing spoken in the Name of the Lord follow not, nor *come to pass*, that is the thing which the Lord hath not spoken" (v. 22). There is a heart-piercing principle underneath this. We may speak in the Name of the Lord, but if the Lord hath not spoken that thing *to us* it will come to naught. If the message falls *fruitlessly* on the ears of the hearers it is an evidence that the Lord hath not spoken it. The proof of a prophet speaking in his own name was that there were no results from his testimony; the thing came not to pass. How does this apply to our work in the Name of the Lord? A prophet must needs *hear* before he could speak in power. The Lord give us the open ear (see John 15. 15, 16). ———

UNFIT FOR THE BATTLE.

Deuteronomy 20. 1-8.

"O Lord,
Forbid that I in Thy Church be
Barren as that roadside fig tree
For ever useless. What a doom!
Lord, let it not upon me come,
But graff'd in Thee, the living Vine,
To bear 'much fruit' each day be mine."

"THE thought of being unfit for work is like to break his heart." So said a woman lately when speaking of her aged father. What a blessing it would be if *unfitness* for the Lord's work created such distress of soul! Why should it not? If a man has a withered hand and not able to work we pity and help, but if he has a withered *soul*, and incapable of serving Christ, how few are in any way concerned. Let us learn from this portion that—

I. **There is a Battle to be Fought.** "We wrestle not against flesh and blood, but against principalities, against powers, against spiritual wickedness in heavenly places" (Eph. 6. 12). Consider the—

1. POWER OF THE ENEMY. "Horses and chariots, a people more than thou" (v. 1). The forces of evil are both numerous and formidable, they are marshalled in three great companies: the world, the flesh, and the devil. In times past we fought under the banner of the prince of darkness (Eph. 2. 2).

2. SECRET OF STRENGTH. "The Lord thy God is with thee" (vv. 1, 4). In this battle without the presence of the living Christ we can do nothing. The battle is not yours, but the Lord's *in you*. Greater is He that is in you than he that is in the world (1 John 4. 4). Some trust in the chariots and horses of their own strength and energy; but we will remember the Name of the Lord (Psa. 20. 7; see Isa. 31. 1).

3. WORD OF ENCOURAGEMENT. "Let not your hearts faint, fear not, and do not tremble" (vv. 3, 4). "Fear not, I am with you, be not dismayed, for I am thy God." "We shall be more than conquerors through Him" (Rom. 8. 37). "Now is the prince of this world to be cast out" (John 12. 31). "Be of good cheer, for I have overcome the world."

II. There are Some who are Unfit for the Battle. Who are they?

1. THOSE WHOSE WORK OF DEDICATION HAS NOT BEEN COMPLETE. "What man is there that hath built a new house, and hath not dedicated it? let him go and return to his house" (v. 5). The Lord knew that although such were coerced into the army their *hearts* would be in their houses. Every undedicated thing on which the heart is set will unfit for the whole-hearted service He requires. Consecrating all our possessions to God is the way to be delivered from all anxiety about them, so that they may not in any way hinder from doing the work of the Lord

2. THOSE WHO HAVE NOT TASTED THE FRUIT OF THEIR LABOUR. "What man is he that hath planted a vineyard, and hath not yet eaten of it? let him go and return unto his house" (v. 6). The man who had not yet reaped any fruit from his work was also disqualified. This to us is a severe test. Christians whose lives have not been fruitful at home are not likely to be fruitful abroad. The missionaries

who have been most blessed in the foreign field are those who have been most successful in the home field. If as preachers we have not reaped from the planting in our own vineyards we need not expect to reap when we sow in the vineyards of others. The way to be made fit for the great *aggressive* work of God is to begin at home. Let him return to his house and eat the fruit of his labour there, then let him fight the battles of the Lord abroad.

3. THOSE WHO HAVE OBLIGATIONS TO OTHERS UN- FULFILLED. "What man is there that hath betrothed a wife, and hath not taken her? let him go and return unto his house" (v. 7.) The man whose whole affections are set on another, while he may be outwardly in the service of Christ, is just as guilty as the man who said "I have married a wife, and therefore I cannot come," his *heart* is absent. Any unfulfilled promise to a fellow-creature, or any uncharitable feeling to such, is enough in the sight of God to disqualify for service. Some debt, however small, may act as a fly in the ointment. First be reconciled to thy brother, and then come and offer thy gift of service (Matt. 5. 23, 24).

4. THOSE WHO ARE FEARFUL AND FAINT-HEARTED. "What man is there that is fearful and faint-hearted? let him go and return unto his house" (v. 8). The language in each case is very decided, "*let him go.*" It will be better for him and for the cause that he should go. The fearful and the faint-hearted in the great work of God are very numerous. As it was in the days of Gideon, so is it still (Judges 7. 3). But the cause of Christ does not suffer through their *going*. The purging of the ranks is the strengthening of the force. Three hundred consecrated souls are of more value in this battle than twenty-nine thousand seven hundred self-important doubters. The battle is the Lord's, only those who *are His* and *for* Him can fight it.

THE BLESSEDNESS OF THE OBEDIENT.
Deuteronomy 28. 1-14.

THE words of Robert Blair on "Friendship" are beautifully applicable to Him who is the Friend of sinners:

> "Thou hast deserved of me
> Far, far beyond whatever I can pay;
> Oft have I proved the labours of thy love,
> And the warm efforts of thy gentle heart."

We are blessed with all spiritual blessing in Christ Jesus.
The blessings recorded in this chapter are but figures of
the true—shadows of better things to come for all those
who are obedient to the will of God. Obedience is always
connected with blessing, as disobedience is with the
curse (chap. 27. 26). Luther said that "he had rather
obey than work miracles." But the obedient will work
miracles—miracles of grace by the power of Him who
worketh within. To obey is better than sacrifice. The
obedient life will be blessed with—

I. **Material Comforts.** "Blessed shall be thy basket
and thy store" (vv. 2-5). A blessed basket, like the
widow's cruse, is one that is never entirely empty. Your
bread and water shall be sure. "The little that a righteous
man hath is better than the riches of many wicked"
(Rom. 8. 28).

II. **Unfailing Protection.** "The Lord shall cause thine
enemies to be smitten before thy face," etc. (v. 7). The
Lord your God, He it is that fighteth for you, as He hath
promised (Josh. 23. 10). It is a true father's delight to
exercise his wisdom and power in behalf of his child. How
much more will your heavenly Father? The enemies of the
Church, like those of the soul, are many, subtile, and
mighty, but greater is He that is *for us*. When He works
who shall hinder?

III. **Prosperous Work.** "The Lord shall command

the blessing upon all that thou settest thine hand unto"
(v. 8). "*Godliness* is profitable unto all things, having
the promise of the life that *now is*," etc. (1 Tim. 4. 8).
The Christian's life is like a tree planted by rivers of
water, the roots of his being lie buried in God Himself
as the source of his all sufficiency, so there is unwithering
prosperity (Psa. 1. 3).

IV. Abiding Fellowship. "The Lord shall *establish*
thee an holy people *unto Himself*" (v. 9). *Called* by
His sovereign grace, *separated* by His cleansing blood,
established in His risen Son, *reconciled* unto Himself, and
transformed into His own image. Truly our fellowship is
with the Father and with His Son Jesus Christ. "Built up
in Him and established in the faith" (Col. 2. 7). He who
hath established us *in Christ* is God (2 Cor. 1. 21). Every
soul so established belongs to the established Church of
God. Abide in Him. The gates (authorities) of hell
shall not prevail against such.

V. Powerful Testimony. "All the people *shall see*
that thou art called by the Name of the Lord" (v. 10).
Those called by His Name are to be ruled over by Him
(Isa. 63. 19). If the Lord rules over us and *in us*, then the
savour of His Name, as ointment, will be poured forth.
The *Name* of the Lord upon us implies His life and character
begotten in us. This is the *life* which is the *light* that
lightens the path of sorrowing sinners in their search of
salvation. Let your light so shine before men.

VI. Abundant Supply. "The Lord shall open unto
thee His good treasure" (v. 12). What a privilege to
have the treasures of His infinite grace opened to us!
This He hath done in the gift of His Son, and by the
ministry of the Holy Spirit. The things which are freely
given us of God, in Christ, are abundantly plentiful,
and unspeakably precious. Who shall ever be able to

exhaust the *unsearchable* riches of Christ? When the Lord opened for us this treasure He opened our supply for time and eternity.

> "When all created streams are dried,
> His fulness is the same;
> I will with this be satisfied,
> And glory in His Name."

VII. Special Honour. "The Lord shall make thee the head, and not the tail; and thou shalt be above only, and thou shalt not be beneath" **(v. 13).** This will of course be fulfilled in the latter days, when Israel, as God's ancient people, shall be restored (Isa. 9. 15; Rom. 11. 26), and when the peoples of the earth shall be blessed through them. But surely these words have a message to present-day believers. "Thou shalt be *above only.*" Your life is hid with Christ in God—"above only"—therefore set your affections on things above, and not on things which are on the earth. They are from beneath, but ye are from above. Born from above, and one with Him who is now set in the heavenlies "far above all" (Eph. 1. 20, 21). This honour have all the saints.

PRECIOUS PROMISES.
Deuteronomy 30. 1-10.

> "None God loseth but who leaveth,
> None who leaveth but God grieveth;
> God grieveth by his forsaking,
> Froward heart its own doom making."

To forsake God is to forsake the FOUNTAIN OF LIVING WATER, and to choose the broken cisterns of unfailing disappointment. We have no choice between the ocean fulness of God's infinite grace and the dry and barren wastes of man's vain imaginations. In these verses there are seven promises given to those who *return* unto the Lord and *obey* His voice (vv. 1, 2). This of course implies

the *conversion* of the soul and the *consecration* of the life.
Two unalterable conditions by which the promises of God
are received and enjoyed.　They will be—

I. Delivered. "Then the Lord thy God will turn
thy captivity" (v. 3).　He will loose thy bands of
iniquity and recover thy soul out of the snare of the
devil (2 Tim. 2. 26).　He delivers from the power of
darkness those who were sold under sin (Rom. 7. 14;
2 Cor. 1. 10; Isa. 55. 7).

II. Restored. "From thence will the Lord thy God
gather thee" (v. 4).　He not only delivers from the
dominion of Satan, and the fascinations of sin and the
world, but brings home to the bosom of His own great
heart of love that we might have fellowship with
Himself.　The prodigal in Luke 15 was *delivered* when
he *left* the far country, but he was not *restored* until he
fell into the arms of his gracious father.　The love of
Christ *constrains* us.

III. Supplied. "The Lord thy God will bring thee
into the land, and He will do thee good" (v. 5).　These
promises were of course given primarily to the children
of Israel; but *all Scripture*, Spirit breathed, is profitable for the *man of God* (2 Tim. 3. 16, 17).　All who
have been reconciled to God through the death of His
Son are made *heirs* of God, and joint-heirs with Christ
(Rom. 8. 17).　What may be only a barren rock to
the carnal eye will yield honey and oil to the believing
heart.

IV. Chastised. "The Lord thy God will circumcise
thine heart," etc. (v. 6).　A circumcised heart is one
chastened and subdued, so that the whole affection of
the soul is weaned from the world and self, and centred
on the Lord.　Chastisement is the sorrowful sign of
sonship (Heb. 12. 8).　It is also a positive necessity to

fruit-bearing (compare Heb. 12. 10, 11 with John 15. 2).
The *stony* heart must be taken away to make room for
the heart of flesh that can *feel* the gentle touch of God
(Ezek. 36. 26).

V. Defended. "The Lord thy God will put curses
upon thine enemies" (v. 7). What a difference there is
between chastisement and *condemnation* (Exod. 11. 7).
We are not to curse our enemies, but pray for them.
Vengeance is Mine, saith the Lord. Hand all your
enemies over to Him. Take no thought for your life.
This was how the early apostles acted. "Grant unto
Thy servants that with all boldness they may speak Thy
Word" (Acts 4. 29). Ye are as the apple of His eye.

VI. Fruitful. "The Lord thy God will make thee
plenteous in every work of thine hand" (v. 9). The trees
of the Lord's planting and watering are never fruitless.
They flourish like the palm tree (Psa. 92. 12). They take
root *downward* and bear fruit *upward*, "and the remnant
that is escaped of the house of Judah shall yet again take
root downward, and bear fruit upward" (2 Kings 19. 30).
"Except a corn of wheat fall into the ground and die, it
abideth alone " (John 12. 24). The downward (dying)
process of the self-life is the strengthening of the new
Christ-life upward. The best fruits are those ripened in
the sunshine.

VII. Rejoiced Over. "The Lord will rejoice over thee
for good" (v. 9). A wise son maketh a glad father. "He
will rejoice over thee with singing" (Zeph. 3. 17). Surely
happy are the people who are in such a case. See how the
father rejoiced over his long lost son when he *returned*
(Luke 15. 24). Oh, what a joy to know that we are a joy to
Him, whose soul was exceedingly sorrowful for us. Thus
His joy may remain in us, and so our joy may be full
(John 15. 11).

LIFE AND DEATH.
Deuteronomy 30. 15-20.

> "Sweet peace, where dost thou dwell? I humbly crave
>   Let me once know;
> I sought thee in a secret cave,
>   And asked if peace were there;
>   A hollow wind did seem to answer, 'No!
>   Go seek elsewhere.' "

IT was Douglas Jerrold who said: "I am convinced the world will get tired, at least I hope so, of this eternal guffaw about all things." There is no apparent sign of this *tiredness* yet. The most sacred and solemn things are so frequently turned off with an empty giggle. But there are awful realities in life, and only madmen can afford to treat them lightly. One of the most stern facts that can assail an immortal soul is that our *present choice* determines our future and irrevocable weal or woe. Observe here—

I. A Solemn Alternative.

1. WHAT IS IT? "Life and good, death and evil" (v. 15). Life or death, and their accompaniments good and evil. This *good* and *evil* must be eternally associated with life and death. This spiritual life is the everlasting favour of God, as spiritual death is the everlasting absence of such.

2. HOW DOES IT COME? "See I have set before thee this day," etc. (v. 15). God in His infinite mercy has been pleased to set this privilege of life *before us*. It is set before us in the Gospel. It is brought very near: "The Word is very nigh unto thee, in thy mouth, and in thy heart" (v. 14). "Thy Word hath quickened me" (Psa. 119. 50). "This is the Word of faith which we preach" (Rom. 10. 17, 18).

II. A Merciful Counsel. "I call Heaven and earth
to reckon this day against you, that I have set before you life and death, THEREFORE *choose life*" (v. 19). This

is the entreaty of Moses, the man of God, who had personally proved the value and blessedness of such a choice (Heb. 11. 24-26).

1. WHERE IS THIS LIFE? "The Lord thy God, *He is thy life*" (v. 20). "I am come that ye might have life." This life is in His Son. "He that hath the Son hath life" (1 John 5. 12). "When Christ *who is our life* shall appear," etc. (Col. 3. 3, 4). This life which yields eternal good is not in us by nature, it is the gift of God (Rom. 6. 23).

2. HOW IS THIS LIFE TO BE HAD? "*Choose* life" (v. 19). It is not by the works of the law, but by a deliberate whole-hearted consent of the will. Mary chose the better part, a part that would not be taken from her. It is not enough to hope and desire this life, the *choice* must be made, and *life* must be chosen as the *one thing* needful. "Choose ye this day whom ye will serve."

III. **The Blessed Results.** There will be—

1. LOVE. "That thou mayest love the Lord," etc. (v. 20). It is vain to expect that you will be able to *love* the Lord until you have made Him the choice of your heart. The more He is trusted the better will He be loved.

2. OBEDIENCE. "That thou mayest obey His voice." Here again loyal-hearted obedience is the outcome of making the Lord Himself the sole object of our choice. We cannot lash ourselves into acceptable obedience. The love of Christ constraineth us.

3. ADHERENCE. "That thou mayest cleave unto Him." Our clinging to Him or our abiding in Him will be determined largely by the measure in which our hearts have really chosen Him as the source and strength of our lives.

4. RESTFULNESS. "That thou mayest *dwell* in the land." In *Him* we live, and move, and have our being

(Acts 17. 28). Our sufficiency is of God. The gifts and calling of God are without repentance (Rom. 11. 29). Make Christ your all, and you will find your all in Him.

> "My heart is fixed, Eternal God,
>   Fixed on Thee;
> And my eternal choice is made,
>   Christ for me."

THE SONG OF THE ROCK;
OR, WHAT CHRIST IS TO HIS PEOPLE.
Deuteronomy 32.

THERE are two rocks mentioned here. One represents the gods of the heathen, or the false foundations on which sin-blinded men build their vain hopes (v. 37). The other speaks of Christ as our strong, unchanging Saviour. So "that their rock is not as our Rock" (v. 31). "Their rock *sold* them" (v. 30). "Our Rock *saves* us" (v. 15). Christ, our Rock, is here represented as the—

I. **Giver of Life.** "The Rock *begat* thee" (v. 18). With other religions it is only a being converted to a *system*. With the Christian it is a being *born of God* (1 John 5. 1). Nothing less will suffice (John 3. 3). HE must quicken (Eph. 2. 1)

II. **Saviour of Men.** "The Rock of his salvation" (v. 15). Christ's Name, works, death, resurrection, all proclaim Him a Saviour, and that to the exclusion of every one and everything else (Acts 4. 12). Those who build without this Rock will be confounded (Luke 6. 48, 49). Their rock is only the treacherous sands of their own imaginations.

III. **Source of Supply.** "He made him suck honey and oil from the Rock" (v. 13). The honey and the oil may speak of sweetness and refreshing, of strength and anointing, or of the grace of Christ and the power of the

Holy Ghost. See the connection between Christ's death and the gift of the Spirit in Galatians 3. 13, 14; 4. 4-6.

IV. Perfect Worker. "He is the Rock, His work is perfect" (v. 4). What He begins He finishes (Phil. 1. 6). The believer's wisdom, righteousness, sanctification, and redemption begun in Christ are perfected in Him (Col. 2. 10; Eccles. 3. 4). The work He had perfected *for* us, He wishes to perfect *in* us (Phil. 2. 13).

V. Incomparable Master. "Their rock is not as our Rock" (v. 31). The rocks of the ungodly fail them in the day of trial (v. 30; 1 Kings 18. 26). Ye serve the Lord Christ, the chiefest among ten thousand. He will never forsake you (Heb. 13. 5, 6). Our Rock is immutable, all the storms of earth and time cannot move it, nor will all the ages of a coming eternity change it. A young woman lay a-dying whose father was an infidel, but whose mother was a Christian. "Now that I am dying," said the girl to her father, "shall I believe you or mother?" He answered, "Believe your mother." Truly their rock is not as our Rock, even our enemies themselves being judges.

THE BLESSED PEOPLE.
Deuteronomy 33.

"Lord we would not always bring Thee
Plaints, and wails, and sobs, and sighs;
We would eager sing before Thee
Of our Cross-drawn ecstasies."

To "count your many blessings" is an excellent thing for driving away the clouds of dull care. This chapter begins with "This is the blessing wherewith Moses the man of God blessed the children of Israel." But what is the blessing wherewith Jesus the Son of God blesses the children of faith? The *blessing* then divided among the tribes may now, in a spiritual sense, be inherited by each individual believer in Christ. Surely there is enough here to make thy "cup run over." All His saints are *loved* by Him, they are *in His hand*, they *sit* at His feet and *receive* His words (v. 3). Loved, secured, rested, taught. Viewing these blessings as patterns of spiritual things, as figures of the true, and shadows of things to come, we would point out that the people of God are blessed because they are—

I. A Living People,   "Let Reuben live and not die" (v. 6). What Abraham prayed for Ishmael is true of every heaven-born soul, they "live before God." They have been "quickened by the Spirit," and "raised from among the dead," and made "alive unto God." "Because I live ye shall live also."

II. A Praying People. "Hear, Lord, the *voice* of Judah, and be Thou an help to him" (v. 7). So we read that Judah prevailed above his brethren (1 Chron. 5. 2). They always prevail who have God for their help. Hath He not said, "Call upon Me, and I will deliver you?"

III. An Enlightened People. "Let thy Thummim and thy Urim be with thy holy one (Levi), and they shall teach," etc. (vv. 8-10). It was with Levi as it is with the *saints* of God now. They teach the difference between the holy and the profane (Ezek. 44. 33). Those possessed with the *lights* and *perfections* (Urim and Thummim) that come through the gift of the Holy Spirit will be witnesses unto Him (Acts 1. 8). We may have here in type what is taught in 1 John 2. 17.

IV. A Protected People. "The beloved of the Lord shall dwell in safety *by Him*, and the Lord shall *cover him* all the day long, and he shall dwell *between His shoulders*" (v. 12). The beloved of the Lord are: (1) *By Him* for fellowship. (2) *Under Him* for safety. (3) *On Him* for rest. He hath loved us with an everlasting love. Beloved for the Saviour's sake (Matt. 3. 17).

V. A Fruitful People (vv. 13-17). The blessing of Joseph is full of the precious things of Heaven—the dew, the sun, and the moon—but the crowning blessing of all is "the *good will of Him* that dwelt in the bush." No wonder that Joseph was a *fruitful* bough, and that his branches ran over the wall. If we have the "good will of Him" who dwelt in Christ, then the "precious things of Heaven" will also be ours (1 Cor. 3. 22, 23).

VI. A Sacrificing People. "They shall offer sacrifices of righteousness" (v. 19). To offer to God the sacrifices that are *right* is to crucify the flesh with its lusts. The unrenewed heart is incapable of such offerings. The first sacrifice of righteousness we are called upon to offer is *ourselves* (Rom. 12. 1). Let the next be thanksgiving (Psa. 116. 17). The constraining motive is the love of Christ (2 Cor. 5. 14, 15). In yielding *ourselves* unto God we yield our members as instruments of righteousness unto Him (Rom. 6. 13).

VII. A Courageous People. "Dan is a lion's whelp" (v. 22). The lion's whelp has begotten in it the lion's nature, and will grow up into the lion's image. We have been created after the image of Him who is called the "Lion of the tribe of Judah." May we go in the fearlessness of His strength.

VIII. A Satisfied People. "O Naphtali, satisfied with favour, and full with the blessing of the Lord" (v. 23). What an inheritance! To be filled with the blessing of the Lord is indeed to be *satisfied with* FAVOUR. This favour, which is the *grace* of God, is abundantly able to do this (Phil. 4. 19). We will never be *satisfied* until we are full with His blessing. This grace that fills and satisfies and makes to abound to every good work is within the reach of all (see 2 Cor. 9. 8).

IX. A Happy People. "Happy art thou, O Israel"

(v. 29). They ought to be a happy people whom God *went forth* to *redeem* that they might be a *people to Himself*, and to make Him a Name that He might *do for them great things* and terrible (2 Sam. 7. 23). Sought, redeemed, separated, used. Happy is that people that is in such a case, yea, happy is that people whose God is the Lord (Psa. 144. 15) ———

THE DEATH OF MOSES.
Deuteronomy 34.

"A change from woe to joy, from earth to Heaven,
  Death gives me this; it leads me calmly where
The souls that long ago from mine were riven
  May meet again; death answers many a prayer.
Bright day shine on! be glad; days brighter far
Are stretched before my eyes than those of *mortals* are."
                                            —NICOLL.

WHEN Moses stood on the top of Pisgah it was not as "a trembling candidate for God's compassion," but as a *servant* who had found great favour with Him, as one whose work was finished before his strength and vigour were exhausted Like the law which he represented, he was set aside before his natural force was abated. There are some things about this unique departure of Moses that suggest characteristics which belong to the death of every saint. It was—

I. **A Going Up.** "And Moses went up to the top of Pisgah" (v. 1). Going up to die. What a thought! Mounting up in spirit to the gate of Heaven that we might depart and be with Christ. "Like Enoch, he was not, for God took him." In dying the body departs to the earth, but the spirit to God, who made it and saved it. Those who live on the hill top of communion with the Father have not far to go when the home-call comes.

II. **Lonely.** Moses was alone with God on the mount (v. 6). With regard to the friendships of earth, every man is *alone* when he meets God. Over this Jordan no human hand can guide. But the dying servant of God does not feel any loss at the absence of the kinsman according to the flesh; they are so filled with the glory of His presence that they forget the things which are behind. Alone, but without any feeling of loneliness. At home with God.

III. **Full of a Satisfying Vision.** "The Lord showed him all the land" (v. 1). This vision of the land of promise had been before him for many years, but now the Lord *caused him* to see it (v. 4). If he did not enter into it, he did in spirit enter into the *rest* that comes through trusting in a faithful God. Moses is not alone in his seeming failure here. Are there not many spiritual privileges into which we have failed to enter because of our unbelief? Yet, blessed be the God of all grace, the vision of His mercy and faithfulness in Christ will satisfy the soul while in its last pantings on earth. "I shall be satisfied when I awake in His likeness."

IV. **In the Presence of the Lord.** "The Lord said unto him," etc. (chap. 10. 4). To die in His presence is to die *into* His presence, and to be for ever with the Lord. "Blessed are the dead that die *in the Lord*. Yea, saith the Spirit" (Rev. 14. 13).

"It is not death to die when He is near."

No, it is only entering into a fuller possession of the life of God. "Yea, though I walk through the valley of the shadow of death I will fear no evil, for Thou art with me" (Psa. 23).

V. **According to His Word.** "So Moses the servant of the Lord died, according to the word of the Lord" (v. 5). It is still so with the saints of God, His Word is, "He that believeth in Me shall never die." Be it unto me according to Thy Word. "O death, where is thy sting; O grave, where is thy victory? Thanks be unto God who giveth us the victory through our Lord Jesus Christ." In *His* victory death is swallowed up (1 Cor. 15. 54-57).

VI. While His Faculties were Unimpared. "When he died his eye was not dim, nor his natural force abated" (v. 7). We have no reason to expect that *physically* it shall be so with us when the hour of our departure comes (Psa. 90. 10). But the new man created after Christ Jesus, his eye shall not be dim, nor his force abated. "Even the *youths* shall faint and be weary, and the young men shall utterly fall; but they that wait upon the Lord shall exchange strength, and mount up with wings as eagles" (Isa. 40. 30, 31). Those who die *in* the Lord die in His strength. In Him the eye of our hope need never grow dim, nor the natural force of our faith ever abate.

VII. Followed by a Unique Funeral. "He buried him, but no man knoweth of his sepulchre unto this day" (v. 6). It is no real loss although no man may know where a servant of God lies buried, God knows. He superintends the funeral of every servant of His. In the resurrection not a member will be left behind. The devil contended with Michael about the *body* of Moses (Jude 9). Did he wish to claim it because Moses had killed an Egyptian, or because he had failed to sanctify the Lord in the wilderness of Zion? (Num. 20. 10-13). The *body* is the Lord's as well as the spirit (1 Cor. 6. 19). Is the Lord not contending for our bodies even now? (Rom. 12. 1), and is not the devil still disputing this?

WHAT GOD HATH WROUGHT FOR US.
2 Corinthians 1. 21, 22.

1. He hath *stablished* us.
2. He hath *anointed* us.
3. He hath *sealed* us.
4. He hath *assured* us. "Giving the earnest of the Spirit *in our hearts.*"

CONDITIONS OF SUCCESS.
Joshua 1. 1-9.

"Workman after workman dies,
And unfinished their work lies;
But their work is Thine, O Christ,
Thou wilt keep Thy pledged tryst.

Still Thy promise words observe,
To send workers Thee to serve;
Our God will fresh ardour give,
Workmen die, but Thou dost live."

"AFTER the death of Moses the Lord spake unto Joshua." Although God buries His workmen He does not bury His work. Before Elijah is called away his mantle was cast over Elisha. The great purposes of God, begotten and nurtured in a past eternity, will not fail of their accomplishment in time. To be successful in God's work is just to fall in with His will, and to do it in His way. All that is pleasing to Him is a success. In these verses there is given us an infallible prescription for *good success*, or how to "do wisely" (margin).

I. An Understanding of the Purpose of God. "The Lord spake, saying, Arise, go over this Jordan" (vv. 1, 2). Joshua did not need to say, "Lord, what wilt Thou have me to do?" This *call* he could never doubt. The way for him was perfectly plain, and in the doing of it he was fully conscious that he was doing the will of God. Unless we have made our *calling* sure all else will be uncertain (Gal. 1. 1). The next thing is, *"Understand* what the will of the Lord is."

II. Faith in the Promise of God. "Every place that the sole of your foot shall *tread upon* have I given you" (v. 3). All things are possible to them that believe. The land had to be claimed by their feet. Every promise *claimed* is an inheritance given. Believe that ye receive, and ye *shall have*. Are there not much land in the "heavenly places" yet unpossessed? (Isa. 36. 3; 2 Cor. 2. 14).

III. Assurance of the Presence of God. "I will be
with thee; I will not fail thee, nor forsake thee" (v. 5).
This threefold promise is to faith an inexhaustible legacy.
His presence with us means all that He is in Himself for us.
"Lo, I am with you, and in My Name ye shall cast out
devils." This assurance leads to boldness and victory
(Dan. 3. 17). Know ye not that God dwelleth in you?

IV. Courage in the Name of God. "Be strong and
very courageous" (v. 7). If we believe that He is with
us, then we may be bold as a lion to face the giant foe
(1 Sam. 17. 45). What nerved Elijah to confront the 450
deceivers? Greater works than these shall ye do if ye
believe on Him (John 14. 12-14). "Be strong *in the Lord*,
and in the power of His might" (Eph. 6. 10). "I can do
all things through Christ which strengtheneth me."

V. Faithfulness to the Leadings of God. "Turn not
from it to the right hand or to the left." God's Word
must be to us our only and infallible guide. In keeping to
it there is great reward. The example of our Lord Jesus
Christ should be ours. How devoted He was to the words
of His Father. "The words that I speak unto you I speak
not of Myself." To reject His Word is to be rejected
(1 Sam. 15. 26). Sons of God are led by the Spirit of God.

VI. Delight in the Word of God. "Thou shalt medi-
tate therein day and night" (v. 8). Those who really find
delight in the Scriptures of truth will be like trees planted
by rivers of water (Psa. 1. 2), always fresh and fruitful.
Those who hide His Word in their hearts will, as good men,
be able to bring out good treasure (Matt. 12. 35). Is it not
in these hearts of ours where the Lord layeth up sound
wisdom for the righteous by the working of His Holy
Spirit through the Word? (Prov. 2. 6). Christ Himself
is called the Word of God (Rev. 19. 13).

VII. Obedience to the Will of God. It was not

enough that Joshua heard the call and knew the will of God, if whole-hearted obedience and submission did not follow. The surrender of our *will* to God is as indispensable to spiritual life and prosperity as breathing is to the natural life. The answer the people gave to Joshua is certainly the answer we should give to our Lord and Leader: "All that thou commandest us we will do, and whithersoever thou sendest us we will go" (v. 16) "Then thou shalt make thy way prosperous, and then thou shalt have good success" (v. 8). He who is our great Example became obedient unto death. Whatsoever He saith unto you, do it. Then shalt thou do wisely.

RAHAB.
Joshua 2. 8-24.

"Bone-weary on my wretched quest,
An aching heart still longs for rest;
Dark memories my soul appal,
And old sins like to fire-sleet fall;
I lay me, Lord, at Thy Cross down,
Guilty, hell-worthy, all I own."

JOSHUA sent spies to view the land, but this did in no way help the *promise* of God. His Word is true whether we_see it or not. We walk by *faith*, not by sight. No one can justify Rahab's doubtful dealings with the King of Jericho (vv. 3-6); but no one is an angel because they are seeking after salvation. The God of all grace knows that it is only out of the depths of darkness and guilt that *any one* can come into the light of life. Let him that is without the sin of pretending to be what he is not cast the first stone. Let us follow her step by step into the higher life. She—

I. **Heard.** "We have heard how the Lord dried up the waters of the Red Sea for you," etc. (v. 10). The tidings of God's great salvation had reached her ears. How shall they believe on Him of whom they have not heard?

Tell out His wondrous doings among the people. The opening up of the Red Sea, and the opening up of the new and living way through the atoning blood of Christ, these things were not done in a corner.

II. Confessed. "As soon as we heard our hearts did melt because of you" (v. 11). The tidings of what the Lord had done for His own people broke the backbone of their pride and caused their self-confident hearts to melt like wax within them. Oh, that it were so now! She makes honest confession of her utter helplessness and hopelessness. There is no attempt at self-justification. Without strength.

III. Believed. "I *know* that the Lord hath given you the land" (v. 9). The terror of the Lord had fallen upon all the inhabitants of the land, but Rahab only *believed*. Hers was a faith produced by *fear*, but such faith will save as well as the faith that works through love. The fear of the Lord is the beginning of wisdom. Knowing, therefore, the terror of the Lord we persuade men.

IV. Prayed "Now therefore, I pray you, swear unto me by the Lord," etc. (v. 12). Having believed she now pleads for a place in this great deliverance that Jehovah was accomplishing for His people. It was a great request for a condemned harlot to make, but her faith made her bold. "By *faith*," the apostle says, "the harlot Rahab perished not" (Heb. 11. 31). Her request was not only for herself, but also for her "father's house," and even that was not all. She pleaded for an assuring evidence that her request would be granted, for she added, "and give me a *true token*." There is a delightful simplicity about this sinful but anxious inquirer. An assuring token every believer may have (Heb. 6. 18). The Spirit also beareth witness with our spirit. He is the TRUE TOKEN.

V. Received. "The men answered her, Our life for yours, we will deal kindly and *truly* with thee" (v. 14).

She has now received the *promise*. If she rested on the promise of men, surely the promise of God is greater. Faith lays hold on the Word of God. If they believe not Moses and the prophets, neither will they be persuaded though one rose from the dead. "He that believeth not God hath made Him a liar."

VI. Worked. "She let them down by a cord through the window" (v. 15). The apostle James fastens on this deed to prove that she was justified by her *works* (James 2. 15). Her works justified her faith in the sight of the men she was dealing with, and justified her most nobly and perfectly too. *Show* me your faith without works (impossible), and I will show thee my faith by my works. Faith without the works that manifest life is dead. We are justified before God without works by faith only; but faith in God will be justified before *men* by works of love and kindness. Faith which *worketh* by love.

VII. Obeyed. The men said, "Thou shalt bind this line of scarlet thread in the window, and bring thy father and thy mother," etc. And she said, "According to your words so be it. And she bound the scarlet line in the window" (vv. 18-21). The sailor believes in the wind, so he spreads his sails to the breeze. Rahab honoured her father and mother by earnestly seeking their salvation as well as her own. The life of faith is a life of simple obedience. Put all right in the home of your heart, and take refuge under the scarlet line of Christ's precious blood that ever speaketh for us. It is a fearful thing to count the *blood of the covenant* an unholy thing (Heb. 10. 39). The scarlet line was to Rahab the sign of the covenant, so she bound it in the window *immediately*.

VIII. Triumphed. "Joshua saved Rahab, and all that she had, and she dwelt in Israel" (Josh. 6. 25). She received exceeding abundantly above all that she did ask or think, for she afterwards became the wife of a prince in Israel, and the mother of Boaz, who took to wife the graceful Ruth. Thus she was brought into the honourable and glorious line of our Lord's genealogy (Matt. 1. 5). All who believe are made the sons and daughters of God, brought into His family, and made partakers of the divine nature. Rahab, through her faith, was both saved and sanctified.

CROSSING THE JORDAN.

Joshua 3.

> "With every wild ring mist dispersed,
> In great deeps of Thy love immersed;
> Holding Thee as my heart's treasure,
> In love's measure without measure.
> O God, keep me a child of light,
> Yea, ev'n with Thine own brightness bright."

THE soul that has ceased to long for a fuller experience of the riches of God has ceased to grow in grace. Every Christian will have his or her Jordan to cross before entering into the fulness of the blessing of the Gospel of Christ. In the minds of men Jordan has been always associated with death, although it is not easy to see here any connection between them. After death we enter into rest, and our *works follow*, but when the children of Israel crossed the Jordan their work was *before* them. By their own works were they to drive out the enemy and take possession of their inheritance by the power of the sword. Their salvation from Egypt was all of *grace*, but they entered into possession of the land of plenty through the stern *works* of *faith*. See how it came about. There was—

I. **A Word of Warning.** "When ye shall see the ark of the covenant of the Lord your God, . . . then ye shall go after it. Come not near unto it, that ye may know the way by which ye must go" (vv. 3, 4). This warning is twofold. 1. *They must follow when the ark moved.* The ark was the symbol of Jehovah's presence and the sign of the covenant. This is an unalterable condition of spiritual progress; we must be prepared to follow the Lord anywhere and at any time. 2. *They must have a space between them and it.* "About two thousand cubits by measure" (v. 4). The reason given for placing such a distance between them and the ark is, "For ye have not passed this way heretofore." Surely this is intended to remind us that there is always a distance between the ETERNAL I AM and the creatures of but yesterday (Psa. 89. 7). And also that every *new path* should be entered upon in entire dependence upon Him. Ye have not passed this way heretofore, therefore make sure that the ark of His guiding presence is before you.

II. **A Call to Preparation.** "Sanctify yourselves, for to-morrow the Lord will do wonders among you" (v. 5). It is a law in the spiritual kingdom that if God is to be glorified *through* us He must first be sanctified *in* us (Lev. 10. 3). The Holy God must have holy instruments for the accomplishing of His wonders among men. *Sanctify yourselves.* Put off the old man with his deeds if you would in your inmost soul pass over into the more "abundant life" and the "greater works" of your wonder-working God.

III. **A Word of Encouragement.** The Lord said unto Joshua, "This day will I begin to magnify thee in the sight of all Israel" (v. 7). On the day that Joshua called for a sanctified people did God begin to honour Joshua. Seek the honour that cometh from God only; it maketh rich and addeth no sorrow. All human honours are like cut flowers, they soon wither in the wearing, but the honour of God crowns with everlasting reward. This diadem of divine favour is never put upon the head of those who seek it for their own glory. Begin to sanctify the Lord in your life, and God will begin to magnify you in the sight of the people. Become a prince with God, and you will have power with men.

IV. A Strange Halt. "The priests that bear the ark shall stand still in Jordan" (v. 8). Crossing the Jordan does not seem to represent the passing of a soul from time into eternity so much as the passing of a soul from a lower into a higher experience of the things of God. The ark of the covenant halted right in the river as the Lord's guarantee to His people that the mighty floods of difficulties that would hinder them from taking possession of His inheritance will be rolled back before the feet of faith (v. 13). It is surely significant that near this very spot, *Bethabara* (the house of passage), the feet of the Son of God rested, who is the true Ark, in whom the law was hid. And that while He stood there the clouds rolled back, and *Heaven opened*, and the Spirit like a dove descended upon Him. That baptism has opened up a passage for us from the wilderness experience into the milk and honey land. In this Jordan, that separates between the self-life and the Christ-life, our "Ark of the Covenant" still stands by His intercession, keeping the way open for all who by faith will enter in. Oh, that it were true of God's people now, as it was then, that "all people passed clean over" (v. 17). Receive ye the Holy Ghost. Without this mighty baptism how wilt thou do in the swelling of Jordan?

V. An Assuring Promise. "As soon as the soles of the feet of the priests that *bear the ark* of the Lord rest in the waters of Jordan, they shall stand upon an heap" (vv. 13-16). "He that hath ears to hear let him hear." Ye who have been made priests unto God, and who bear the Christ, the Ark of the Lord (Acts 9. 15), be comforted and encouraged. No river of opposition whose destiny, like Jordan, is the dead Sea will ever hinder you from the enjoyment of the promises of God if in your heart you bear the Son of God. "What ailed thee, . . . thou Jordan, that thou wast driven back?" (Psa. 114. 5). "Greater is He that is in you."

VI. A Proof of His Presence. "Hereby ye shall know that the living God is among you. He will without fail drive out from before you" (v. 10). The proof of His presence is *overcoming power*. The overcomer is always an inheritor (see Rev. chaps. 2 and 3). If we are not living a victorious life we may well question whether the Lord is with us. Hear the apostle's testimony, "I can do all things through Christ who strengtheneth me." "If God be for us, who shall prevail against us?"

THE MEMORIALS.
Joshua 4.

"As in the stillness of the night
  I lie awake;
The hours, like birds wing weary, flight
    Towards Heaven take;
And from the beating of my heart,
    Untaught of art,
Fancy, from every pulse and pause,
    Quaint symbols draws."

EVERY God-ordained memorial is a great mercy. We all are so ready to *forget* the great things He hath done for us. His memorials do not always appear in cairns of stones, in temples made with hands, or philanthropic institutions. Every living stone built upon Christ, the living foundation, is a memorial of His redeeming power.

I. How these Memorials were Raised.

1. BY PREPARED MEN. "Joshua called the twelve men whom he had prepared" (v. 4). Not every one can build a memorial for the glory of God's grace. A work of *personal preparation* is needed by our heavenly Joshua. We must be called of God and believing.

2. By Representative Men. "Out of every tribe a man" (v. 2). It is a blessed privilege to be chosen of God to represent Him before the people, and to raise a monument to His Name. These twelve men acted for the whole nation, each one having a "stone laid upon his shoulder." Privileged men will be burdened ones, but the *burden of the Lord* is not bondage (Matt. 11. 29, 30).

II. Where these Memorials Rested.

1. In the Midst of Jordan. "Joshua set up twelve stones in the midst of Jordan, where the feet of the priests stood" (v. 9). On that very spot where the ark of the covenant rested were these memorial boulders piled. Jesus Christ, the Ark of our Covenant, went down into the Jordan of death and separation for us, and rose again. So they *came up* out of Jordan on the tenth day of the first month (the day on which the lamb was taken for sacrifice, Exod. 12. 2, 3). Now the memorials of the Last Supper still remind us of Him who stood in the midst of Jordan that we might pass clean over.

2. In the Lodging Place of Gilgal. "Those twelve stones which they took out of Jordan did Joshua pitch at Gilgal" (vv. 3-20). Gilgal means the place of *rolling*. All their past sins and failures are now rolled away. They stand, as it were, on resurrection ground. This *second* testimonial has a different voice. It speaks of rest and possession as the first spoke of deliverance. These stones, taken out of the place of death, now become memorials of life and blessing, having been *saved* from the flood, and appointed as *signs* to others.

III. What these Memorials Mean. These two heaps of stones, one in Jordan and the other in Gilgal, may have been intended to teach the children of Israel what Calvary and Pentecost are intended to teach us, the *salvation* and *sufficiency* of God. These stones declared the—

1. MERCY OF GOD. "The Lord your God dried up the waters" (v. 23). Nothing impossible with Him; He hath opened up for us a new and living way. "That ye may know the exceeding greatness of His power to us-ward who believe."

2. FAITHFULNESS OF GOD. "Until everything was *finished*" (v. 10). He that hath begun the good work will carry it on. The angel of the Lord *stood by* till Joshua the high priest got everything that he needed (Zech. 3. 1-5). The Holy Spirit is able and willing to do the same for every trusting one.

3. GRACE OF GOD. As long as the priests stood in Jordan the way stood open, but when the priests came out the waters returned and overflowed (v. 18). Then the day of grace was passed, and the door shut. The grace of God that brought salvation still appears. "Behold, *now* is the accepted time."

4. LOVE OF GOD. "Let your children know" (v. 22). This is the language of Him who will have all men to be saved, and to come to a *knowledge of the truth*. "Suffer the little children to come to Me, and forbid them not."

5. POWER OF GOD. "That all the people of the earth might know the hand of the Lord, that it is mighty" (v. 24). These stones are a witness to the saving power of God. They are as brands plucked out of the fire. Let all the people know it. Tell it out. "He is able to save to the uttermost." ───────

"WHAT IS THIS THAT THOU HAST DONE?"
Genesis 3. 13.

I. What is the cause of it? (v. 6).

II. What is the nature of it? Disobedience.

III. What is the effect of it? 1, Guilt. 2, Nakedness (v. 7). 3, Tears (vv. 8, 9). 4, Sorrow (v. 17). 5, Sacrifice (v. 21). 6, Covering.

WHAT MEAN THESE STONES?
Joshua 4. 21-24.

"Upon a bench before the door
   He sits with weak and staring eyes;
He sits, and looks, for straight before
   The grave that holds his daughter lies.

Dark palsied mass of sever'd rock,
   Deaf, blind, and sear to sun and rain;
A shattered grave-stone's time-worn block
   That only shows the name of—JANE."

THERE are "sermons in stones," in mill-stones, mile-stones, and grave-stones. "What mean these stones?" might be written over the gateway of every cemetery, although God alone knows what they all do mean. According to the Lord's declaration, these *twelve* stones piled up at Gilgal were to teach the rising generation of Israelites what He had done for their fathers (vv. 22, 23). The history of these stones may be regarded as figuratively setting forth their deliverance by the power of God. Just as we might say now, What mean these Jews? or, What mean these Christians? In either case we are face to face with witnesses, with memorials of the past. What mean these stones?

I. **They Speak of Bondage.** Once they lay buried in the dark rolling Jordan, the floods overflowing and imprisoning them within its deep and dismal bosom. Such was Israel in Egypt, when the deep, dark waves of oppression rolled over them, and floods of persecution swept about them. Such also is the condition of every unsaved soul. They lie buried in the darkness of death, imprisoned by iniquity, and the stream of worldliness flowing over them.

II. **They Speak of Helplessness.** The Israelites in Egypt could no more save themselves out of the stream of Pharaoh's tyranny and bondage than these stones could lift themselves out of the river of Jordan. They were utterly helpless. No more can ye who are accustomed to do evil. Who can bring a clean thing out of an unclean, or life out of a thing that is dead? There is only one who can (Eph. 2. 1). That one is not you, but God.

III. **They Speak of Discovery.** "God *dried up* the waters" (v. 23). This was God's way of bringing the stones to light. These stones would never have been found out by man had not God the Lord wrought this great and merciful work of rolling back the drowning flood. This is what He did for His people in the house of bondage. He dried up the pride and power of Pharaoh, and unbosomed from the flood of affliction those who for long lay helpless beneath the ever flowing stream of oppression and death. Yes, our God can *dry up* the waters that bury and conceal from His sight and favour. If these stones had feelings, what would these feelings be when the waters were turned back, and they brought suddenly into the sunlight of Heaven? Those who know the power of God in *conversion* know what this means; the rolling back of the dark waters of judgment, and the soul brought into the light of God's favour through the atoning blood of Jesus Christ His Son. Resurrected from the dead into a new kingdom, and now *nothing* between, Hallelujah! But there is here a solemn thought for those who would *cover* themselves from God in the waters of formalism and hypocrisy. He will suddenly *dry up* these water coverings. What then?

IV. **They Speak of Deliverance.** These twelve stones were taken out of the midst of Jordan and *carried* on the *shoulders* of *prepared* men (vv. 4, 5), and laid down in a *lodging* place (v. 8). What a picture of Israel's salvation and of ours! Carried out of bondage into rest and liberty on the shoulders of the Shepherd, who has come to seek and to save that which was lost (Luke 15. 5). His presence is a *carrying* presence (Exod. 33. 15). He who hath delivered

us from so great a death will yet deliver (2 Cor. 1. 10) out
of the horrible pit on to the songful Rock (Psa. 40. 2).

V. They Speak of Testimony. They are memorial
stones. Signs of what the Lord hath done. Once they
were buried and useless in Jordan, now they are exalted
and witnesses for God. Israel was to be a witness for Him,
but, alas! through iniquity her testimony soon withered.
All God's *called out* ones are to be witnesses (Acts 1. 8).
Witnesses of a rolled back flood of wrath, and of the
mighty *uplifting* and *transplanting* power of the grace of
God. "Ye are My witnesses." What mean these stones?
"Let your children know" (v. 22).

GILGAL.
Joshua 5. 1-12.

"Rest in Christ, and be at rest,
Vain elsewhere will be your quest;
The heart is made for God alone,
And restless is, as wave-washed stone,
Till it welcomes Him for guest,
Then it enters His own rest."

By welcoming the will of God Israel entered into the rest
of God. Many could not enter in because of unbelief (Heb.
3. 18, 19). Gilgal was the first lodging place after they
crossed the Jordan. As we may expect, the first day spent
in the land of promise would be very memorable. Who
can forget the day of conversion when the soul for the first
time tasted the fruits of salvation? Gilgal was to them—

I. A Place of Memorials. Here the twelve stones were
pitched that were taken out of the midst of Jordan as
witnesses to the fact that God had dried up the river.
Every soul that has passed over into the kingdom of God's
dear Son has many memorial stones of the goodness and
power of God their Saviour.

II. A Place of Sacrifice. "They kept the passover on

the fourteenth day of the month." They passed over Jordan on the *tenth* day, and on the *fourteenth* they kept the passover.

Days have a meaning in the purpose of God. The lamb was taken on the *tenth* day and killed on the *fourteenth* (Exod. 12. 3-6). These two days suggest *chosen* out by grace and *passed over* in mercy. This is what the grace of God, that bringeth salvation, hath done for all that believe.

III. A Place of Rest. Here they found a "lodging place" (chap. 4. 8). The promise had been left them, and they entered into His rest (Heb. 4. 1). Let us therefore fear lest any of you should seem to come short of it. The evil heart of unbelief goes another way (Heb. 3. 12). "Come unto Me, and I will give you rest."

IV. A Place of Humiliation. "Them Joshua circumcised" (vv. 5-7). The spiritual significance of this act seems to be the putting away of all confidence in the flesh (Phil. 3. 5). The circumcised in heart can say, "In me, that is, in my flesh, dwelleth no good thing." It is needful after entering into rest through faith in Jesus Christ that we should learn *experimentally* that the flesh profiteth nothing in the service of God, and that we are crucified with Christ.

V. A Place of Freedom. "This day have I rolled away the reproach of Egypt from you" (v. 9). Whom the Son makes free are free indeed. The "reproach of Egypt" points back to poverty, bondage, and unbelief; but, blessed be God, He can roll the past all away. Your sins and your iniquities will I remember no more—rolled away. All that believe are justified from *all things*. There is freedom from guilt, from condemnation, and from the fear of man, *irreproachable* by the rolling away mercy of God.

VI. A Place of New Food. "They did eat the old corn

of the land on the morrow'' (v. 11). The *old* corn was
something new for them, as all but Joshua and Caleb had
been born in the wilderness, and had in all likelihood
never tasted it before. ''The old corn of God's precious
promises,'' old, yet ever new, can only be enjoyed by
those who by faith have taken possession. Here the
wilderness fare (manna) ceased, thereby declaring that
what is sufficient merely to *preserve* life is not enough
for those who have the battles of the Lord to fight.
Those who would witness and win souls for Christ need
more than the *milk* of the Word, they must have the
old corn, strong meat, if they would be strong to do
exploits and be more than conquerors.

STOOPING TO CONQUER.
Joshua 5. 13-15.

'' 'My way, not Thine,' O Lord,
It pierced me like a sword;
'Thy way, not mine,' uplifts,
And each temptation sifts.

'My way, not Thine,' misleads,
And brings forth all ill deeds;
'Thy way, not mine,' brings peace
And all its sweet release.''

As seen from the former part of this chapter, Gilgal has a
deeply significant meaning (v. 9). When God *rolls away*
one thing it always makes room for another. The place
of blessing is often followed by the place of *testing*.
This is what happened to Joshua as he came and stood by
Jericho. It seems to us that these three verses are heavy
laden with spiritual instruction to all whose ears are open.
We might look at his—

I. **Determination.** ''It came to pass *when* Joshua
was by Jericho'' (v. 13). After the trying and refreshing
experiences at Gilgal he is now face to face with his great

life's work as he stood "by Jericho." What are his thoughts now as he is within sight of those terrible walls? Like Nehemiah, he goes calmly to view the difficulties. "What wilt Thou have me to do?"

II. Interruption. "Behold, there stood a man over against him with a drawn sword in his hand" (v. 13). This was another crisis in the life of Joshua, such as Jacob had (Gen. 32. 24), and also Balaam, but he (Balaam) failed to take advantage of it (Num. 22. 41). Such seasons as these in one form or another come in every Christian's life. Sudden interruptions, privileges, switches that may turn the force of our lives into brighter lines of blessing or shunt us into inactivity or uselessness. No man is ever the same after he has been brought face to face with the Divine One (Rev. 3. 20).

III. Interrogation. "Art thou for us, or for our adversaries?" (v. 13). Joshua, as a man wholly devoted to the cause of God, sees but two great classes and causes. "*Us* and our adversaries." There is a prince who works for and in the adversaries (Eph. 2. 2), but "greater is *He that is in you*, than he that is in the world" (1 John 4. 4). This question might be put with profit concerning *every* new difficulty that may arise in our way, aye, and to every questionable thought and feeling and act, for all will either help us or our adversaries.

IV. Revelation. "Nay, but as captain of the host of the Lord am I come" (v. 14). The Prince of Heaven does not come to take the place of a *private* in the army of Jehovah. If He is not leader, then He is not there. The Lord Jesus Christ is not the servant of the Church, but the Head. Perhaps as Joshua stood by Jericho he was tremblingly thinking of himself as captain of this great host, but here he learns that *another* must get all the responsibility, and that he is only a *follower*. Have we learned this most important lesson? Have we given our Lord His true place in all our work for Him? Not I, but Christ.

V. Adoration. "Joshua fell on his face to the earth, and did worship" (v. 14). When any one has had their eyes opened to see the grace and power of Jesus Christ, as Joshua did, they will not *try* to be humble, they will fall on their faces; they will not pray for the spirit of worship, but they will worship. This lowly attitude betokens entire surrender, a perfect willingness to take the place appointed him by the Captain of Salvation, who in all things and circumstances claims the pre-eminence.

VI. Petition. "What saith my Lord unto His servant" (v. 14). Those who have a *humble* heart will also have an *open* ear. It was when Abram fell on his face that God talked with him (Gen. 17. 3). Daniel had his face towards the ground when he heard the voice of His words (chap. 10. 9). When we have been humbled before the Lord, let us then *hear* what God the Lord will speak. "Learn of Me, for I am lowly in heart."

VII. Submission. "The Captain of the Lord's host said, Loose thy shoe from off thy foot, for the place whereon thou standest is holy, *and Joshua did so*" (v. 15). Every place is holy where the Holy One is. Taking off the shoe had much the same meaning as taking off the hat has now. It was an act that indicated reverence (Exod. 3. 5). The high priest ministered before the Lord with naked feet. If in olden times they cast off their shoes who stood before the *messenger* of God, what shall they do now *in* whom God by His Holy Spirit dwells? Surely this, that the whole inner man be laid naked and bare before His Holy presence. Such an attitude of soul will always honour God and gain victories for Him (see chap. 6. 27). He stooped and conquered. "He that humbleth himself shall be exalted."

THE FALL OF JERICHO.
Joshua 6.

"Faith is a courier swift and sure, who will carry us to the absent."
—MADAM DE JASPARIN.

THE terror of the Lord had fallen upon the Canaanites on hearing what the Lord had done. Joshua believed God, and He overcame. All really holy men are a terror to the ungodly. Those who live only for God will have a power for Him that the wisdom and strength of the world cannot resist (v. 1). All human defences melt in the powerful presence of the Holy Ghost. Power for testimony is oneness with God, witness the life of Jesus Christ. It was easy for Joshua to overcome, just because he trusted in God, who goeth before in the spirit of conviction, showing to the enemy their utter weakness in the presence of the Almighty. We shall notice three leading thoughts in this chapter—

I. **A Doomed City**, OR THE SINNER'S STATE. It was—

1. UNDER THE CURSE OF GOD. "The city shall be accursed" (v. 17). The sentence of death had been passed upon it forty years ago (Exod. 23. 27, 28), although then they were glorying in their strength, ignorant of their condition in the sight of God, just as many still are insensible of their state. Their doom was as surely fixed when they were rejoicing as when they were trembling. The Scriptures hath concluded all *under sin*, and so under the curse of a broken law. The sentence of death has already passed upon all men, for that all have sinned (Rom. 5. 12).

2. STRAITLY SHUT UP (v. 1). If it had been straitly shut up by God as Noah was shut up in the ark, then they might have laughed the Israelites to scorn. When He shutteth no man can open, but *they shut themselves up* against God. He that *covereth his* sins shall not

prosper. This is characteristic of the vain effort of proud, defiant sinners, shutting themselves within the walls of their *own righteousness*. Every *mouth* must be shut up.

3. QUICKLY BROUGHT DOWN. "The wall fell flat" (v. 20). Their only refuge failed, and great was the fall of it. What is the value of a refuge that will not stand the day of trial? It is like a rotten ship in a storm. These great walls, the *work of their own hands*, were all their confidence (Isa. 28. 17). Such hopes will only make ashamed.

II. A Strange Assault, OR THE VICTORY OF FAITH (Heb. 11. 30). The means appointed by God are often foolishness with man. But the believing heart delights to obey. The means appointed were the—

1. COMPASSING OF THE CITY (v. 3). Here we see the *measure* of faith. Paul says: "By *faith* the walls of Jericho fell." They must have had great faith; their faith as well as their feet must *compass* the city. Our faith also must compass the object of desire if we would possess it. "According to your faith," etc. It is in the compassing that the faith is tried, for nothing is seen but huge walls of difficulty. Nothing is felt but human inability. But these only make the trusting heart more confident in God.

2. BLOWING OF THE TRUMPETS (v. 4). Here we see the *means* of faith. The means faith uses are far different from the inventions of the carnal mind. They are the simple, seemingly weak, things of God; but they are the weapons, not of doubt or experiment, but of faith. The sling and the stone would be no use to Saul, but they are mighty in the hand of David. The trumpet of the Gospel must be blown in faith if the victory is to be won. The holy lips of the priests alone were to blow. Holy men must still speak, being moved by the Holy Ghost.

3. CARRYING OF THE ARK (v. 6). Here we see the *object*

of faith. The ark, the symbol of Jehovah's presence. All was arranged according to the ark. What confidence! The Ark that divided Jordan is coming. Their faith would not be in their blowing or marching, and yet if they do not march the ark does not follow. So our faith must look up to Him who has said, "Lo, I am with you alway," and press on with the compassing and the blowing.

4. SHOUTING OF THE PEOPLE (v. 20). Here we see the *expectation* of faith. This is not the work of the priests alone, but of all the people (v. 5). Through what has been done faith has been increased in the hearts of all Israel. Now all are trusting and expecting, and all shout the downfall and the victory. Why so few great victories for God? Because so *few expect*. So few join in the shout. Oh, how much blowing there is in these days of much preaching, but how little shouting among the people.

III. **A Family Spared**, OR THE GREAT SALVATION (v. 25). "By faith the harlot Rahab perished not" (Heb. 11. 31). Notice that she—

1. BELIEVED. "I know that the Lord hath given you the land; . . . for the Lord your God, He is God" (chap. 2. 9, 11). She hid the message as well as the messengers. Her old beliefs and prejudices were cast aside. She *heard* and believed (vv. 2, 11). "Who hath believed our report, to whom is the arm (power) of the Lord revealed." He that believeth shall be saved.

2. OBEYED. "She bound the scarlet line in the window" (chap. 2. 21). Her faith was justified in the sight of men by her works. She hid the messengers and exposed the line (James 2. 25). "Faith without works is dead." By the scarlet cord she is to be justified or condemned. Is the crimson blood between you and the approaching vengeance, which must come upon all who obey not the Gospel? When I see the line (blood) I will pass over you.

3. TESTIFIED. She not only saved herself, but "all that she had" (v. 23). How she would persuade them we know not, but drowning ones will catch at a straw; the hope might seem vain, but the honour of Joshua was at stake. The *name of the Lord* is a strong tower. "Believe on the Lord Jesus Christ, and thou shalt be saved, *and thy house.*" "Behold, now is the accepted time;" not when the walls are fallen flat. "Come thou and all thy house into the ark."

———

THE FAILURE AT AI;
OR, THE POWER OF SECRET SIN.
Joshua 7.

"Shine on, thou bright beacon, unclouded and free,
  From thy high place of calmness o'er life's troubled sea.
  But, barque of eternity, where art thou now?
  The wild waters shriek o'er each plunge of thy prow,
  On the world's dreary ocean, thus shattered and tossed—
  Thou, lone One, shine on, 'If I lose Thee, I'm lost.' "

THE fall of Jericho was followed by the temporary fall of Israel. We have much need to beware of the dangers of success. When Uzziah was strong his heart was lifted up to his destruction (2 Chron. 26. 16). The seed of pride and self-confidence is often sown in the joyful but unguarded hour of victory, or amidst the dangerous applause of men. There are still Achan desires lurking in the heart, just waiting a chance to enrich *themselves* with the things that are to be wholly devoted to God (chap. 6. 17, margin). Sin always brings failure. To lose fellowship with Christ is to lose all power for testimony for Him. There are two intensely solemn thoughts here—

I. **The Shameful Defeat of Israel**, OR THE BELIEVER'S FAILURE. It was—

1. UNEXPECTED. They said: "Let not all the people go up" (chap. 3). They were very confident of success, but very ignorant of their own condition in the sight of

God. Confidence and *earnestness* in a Christian worker will never stand in the stead of *holiness*. Our power lies not even in our past experiences. Is thy *heart* right with God? Even *unexpected* failure has its tap-root of evil somewhere.

2. COMPLETE. "They fled before the men of Ai" (v. 4). Why did they flee? Because the Lord was not with them. There is none so helpless as the Samsons when their strength is gone. The man whose strength God alone is must ever be a helpless object without Him (John 15. 5). But ask them: Do you believe God is with you? They say: Yes. Look how He helped at Jericho. But the past is not the present. All our efforts will be as completely abortive unless the presence and power of God is in it. We don't win the victory simply because we are Christians any more than the children of Israel did because they were Israelites. We must be Christians after the holy mind and will of God if we would be overcomers.

3. HUMBLING. "O Lord, what shall I say?" etc. (v. 8). Israel's failure brings dishonour upon Israel's God. How keenly our failures should cut us to the heart when we know that by them our Master is dishonoured. How we should bow our heads to the dust, confounded and ashamed, saying, like Joshua, "O Lord, what shall I say?" etc. If past failure does not bring humbling and self-searching before God we will never find out the true source of power. Those who expect failure are never humbled because of it, and by them the Lord is not magnified in the sight of the people. He that humbleth himself shall be exalted.

4. NEEDFUL. "Wherefore liest thou upon thy face? Israel hath sinned. Neither will I be with you except ye take away the accursed thing" (vv. 10-13). Many are mourning over their *failure* who have more need to mourn over their *sin*. The Lord cannot use us at times because of secret sin. Although we may be ignorant of

it, God is not. He cannot treat sin lightly because *we* don't realise it. If they had not failed here they would just have gone on in their sin. God can have no fellowship with unrighteousness. The accursed thing must be taken away or His presence will be taken away. Our failures should set us also a searching of the tent of our heart. "Search me, O God!"

II. The Sin of Achan, OR THE SINNER'S DOOM. His history is very short and very sad. Four thoughts include all. His—

1. DESIRE. "I saw, then I coveted them" (v. 21). Sin often begins with a *look*. Eve saw the fruit. Lot saw the well watered plains. Ahaz saw an altar and copied it (2 Kings 16. 10). But Achan's sin lay not in *seeing* the gold, etc., perhaps he could not help that, but he "*coveted them*." He loved the forbidden gain, until desire moved his hand. The pleasures of sin will always attract the more when one looks on them with a *desire*. Christians have much need to watch their hearts. Certain circumstances might bring ruinous results if every *thought* is not led *captive* to Christ.

2. DISOBEDIENCE. "He took of the accursed thing" (v. 1). God had warned them in any wise to keep themselves *free* from the accursed (devoted) thing (chap. 6. 18). He sinned willingly, not ignorantly. The fact that he *hid* the goods proves that he was *conscious* of his wrongdoing. Just as many still willingly disobey God by preferring the world to Christ, and ofttimes keeping up the *appearance* of godliness to deceive men. Achan's hypocrisy is not uncommon in these days, even among professedly workers for Christ. Although the Lord has clearly said, "*Love not the world*," alas, how much of it is hid in the heart!

3. DETECTION. "And Achan was taken" (v. 18). Be sure your sin will find you out, whether you be saint or

sinner, Christian or not. Amongst all the thousands of Israel he was found out, because nothing is hid from the eye of God, with whom every sinner has to do. How solemn the discovery, exposed to the eyes of all the people, and every hidden thing brought to light. What a forecast of the Great Judgment! He that covereth his sins shall not prosper.

4. DESTRUCTION. "And all Israel stoned him with stones" (v. 25). There was no way of escape. How shall ye escape? What a contrast between Rahab's house and Achan's. The one saved, the other lost (chap. 6. 25). The faith of the one and the disobedience of the other made all the difference. As parents, are you acting the part of Rahab or Achan? What will the end be, salvation or destruction? There is sin in the camp. "Is it in me, Lord?" What the law could not do God can now accomplish through the sending forth of His Son.

THE ALTAR ON MOUNT EBAL.
Joshua 8. 30-35.

"Strength divine, He will not wield,
　High and deep His woe's tide swelled;
No one near His Lord to shield?
　Only one—and him 'compelled.'

How human, O Christ, Thou wast,
　Fainting, falling in the street;
Yet the 'work' on Thee was cast,
　Came from Thee flawless, complete."

THE altar on Mount Ebal is the fulfilment of God's command (Deut. 27. 2-8) and a foreshadowing of the Cross of Christ. The great coming event, the death of the Son of God, casts its shadow before. The whole scene before us is most impressive and suggestive. "Open Thou mine eyes to behold wondrous things out of Thy law."

I. **The Mount of Ebal**, OR THE PLACE OF CURSE. Ebal

was right in the centre of the land, and here they were commanded to put the curse (Deut. 11. 29). *Ebal* means "stony," or "heap of barrenness." It may be a figure of what Jerusalem was to become in after years, or of a stony heart and a barren life. In both cases the curse has come because of unbelief (Gal. 3. 10).

II. **The Altar of Sacrifice**, OR THE CROSS OF CHRIST. "Then Joshua built an altar unto the Lord God of Israel, in Mount Ebal" (v. 30). It is sublimely suggestive that the altar was built in the place where the curse was put; this is the thought that we have in Galatians 3. 13, "Christ being made a curse for us." This altar was made of "whole stones, over which no man hath lift up any iron" (v. 31). The warning given was, "If thou lift up thy tool upon it, *thou hast polluted it*" (Exod. 20. 25). In the making of *atonement* there is absolutely no allowance for the *work* of man. All man's cutting and carving only pollutes the *saving grace* of God. *Unhewn* stones were stones prepared and *finished* by God. As Ruskin said, "God *alone* can finish." The altar of Christ's Cross raised in the place of the curse, and the offering of Himself unto God for us is a divinely finished work, and finished with materials of His own forming. Modern hewers attempting to improve this only mar and pollute, while they betray their ignorance and unbelief. The altar was for God, and never was intended for an *ornament*; it was an awful necessity.

III. **The Law of Moses**, OR THE WORD OF GOD. "And he wrote there upon the stones a copy of the law of Moses" (v. 32). These plastered stones, on which the law was written, were different from the altar stones (Deut. 17. 2-8). Where the altar was built there the law was declared. With the Cross of Christ comes the revelation of the Word and will of God. The pillar of truth stands by the altar of the Cross. Surely the *law* of the Lord has a new meaning in the presence of the *altar* of the Lord. The altar declares atonement for the sin of a broken law. "Christ hath redeemed us from the curse of the law, being made a curse for us." "The *words* that I speak unto you are spirit and life."

IV. The Ark of the Covenant, OR JESUS IN THE MIDST. "And all Israel stood on this side, and on that side the ark; half of them over against Mount Gerizim, and half of them over against Mount Ebal" (v. 33). The ark of the covenant, as the symbol of God's presence standing *between* the cursing and the blessing, seems like a foreshadowing of that solemn scene recorded in Matthew 25. 31-46. "Before Him shall be gathered all nations. He shall *separate* them one from another, as a shepherd *divideth* his sheep from the goats." As surely as the unfailing covenant of Jehovah was in the ark, so surely shall His Word *in Christ* be fulfilled. Jesus Christ is the divinely appointed Man, by whom He will judge the world in righteousness (Acts 17. 31).

V. The Twofold Purpose, OR BLESSING AND CURSING. "He read all the words of the law, the blessings and cursings" (v. 34). *All the words* of the law were read, all the blessings and all the cursings were pronounced and justified. There was no neutral condition possible. In the presence of God we are either blessed or cursed. To be unblessed is to be accursed. The only alternative to *life* is *death* (Deut. 30. 19). Salvation or condemnation. All the threatenings as well as the promises of God will be read out in literal fulfilment on that day when the judgment is set. _____

THE ANXIOUS GIBEONITES.
Joshua 9.

Two sins were committed in connection with the Gibeonites. 1. Joshua judged according to his own wisdom instead of asking of God (v. 14, margin), and so made a

league with them, contrary to the command of God. Let
us beware of being flattered into disobedience. 2. The
Gibeonites came with a false pretext. They did evil that
good may come. Had they been humble and honest like
Rahab they might have been saved all the same. Rahab
was greatly exalted (Matt. 1. 5). They were greatly
humbled (v. 23). But laying aside the faults let us look
at some of the facts in their life as illustrating the way of
grace and salvation. We see them—

I. Greatly Alarmed (vv. 9, 10). And no wonder,
when they believed that they were all under the condemnation of God, and that the sentence of death was passed
upon them (Rom. 3. 23). They were sore afraid (v. 24),
just because they *believed*. The devil believes and trembles.
The false peace of the sinner is founded on the sands of ''I
don't believe it.'' It is impossible for a man to believe
God's Word and remain unaffected thereby. Oh, that
many had this deep sense of their own state before
God! What concern, anxiety, sleeplessness, and sorrow
it would create! Visit Gibeon, converse with the citizens,
price their articles. What a change has come over the
whole city, just such a change as comes into the heart
when the conscience is truly convicted of sin.

II. Pleading for Salvation. ''Make ye a league with
us'' (v. 6). We have not to do just now with the way
they came, but with the *object* of their coming. They
wanted saving *grace*. They were convinced that on this
lay their only hope. Resistance was useless. When
sinners are awakened they deeply feel that mercy is their
chiefest need. Self-justification is out of the question.
Their only refuge is in the grace of God (Eph. 2. 8). They
said, ''Make a league with us.'' They wanted the *promise
of Joshua* as a guarantee of safety. This is what our Joshua
gives to all that come to Him, so that they are assured of
salvation, and can rest, like the Gibeonites, on the *word* of

Him who will not lie. Go not away without the promise. What the Gibeonites feigned we can say in truth. "We be come from a far country" (v. 6), like the prodigal in Luke's Gospel.

III. Graciously Reconciled. "Joshua made peace, and made a league with them to *let them* live" (v. 15). He might in justice have condemned them. He had the power and authority for it, but he let them live. It was purely a permission of grace; moreover, there was added to the peace the *oath of confirmation*, which is the end of strife (Heb. 6. 16). Three things stand out in connection with this reconciliation: (1) The *Acceptance*, (2) The *Covenant*, (3) The *Oath*. The sinner in coming to Jesus is accepted through mercy. Then he enters into the covenant (or league) of grace, and then the seal of the *promise* of God makes the engagement eternally secure (Eph. 1. 13).

IV. Wholly Consecrated. They said, "We are in thy hand, as it seemeth good and right unto thee to do unto us, do" (v. 25). The effect of grace is not to make them proud and defiant. How beautiful when the soul, melted down by the mercy and love of God, yields so sweetly to its great Deliverer! This is the language of consecration: Thou hast saved us, we are Thine, just do Thy will in us and with us. We owe our life to Thee, it is Thine own, Thy will be done. This is the pure effect of the grace of God when truly enjoyed. If His love has not constrained you to yield all to Him it must be little of the love that you enjoy.

V. Actively Engaged. "Joshua made them hewers of wood and drawers of water" (v. 27). We must not only be humble and submissive, but willing and active. It is very humbling work they get to do. Some are willing, like Naaman, to do some great thing, but it is in doing the

little things that our true character is seen. If we profess
to be very humble God is sure to try us with some lowly
service. But the true heart finds nothing too mean that is
His will. An angel would sweep a street as heartily as
proclaim "Time to be no more," if sent. We have
been saved to serve (Luke 1. 74). Hewers of wood for
the *altar* and drawers of water for the laver are still in
great demand.

VI. **Bitterly Despised.** "Come and help me to
smite Gibeon, for it hath made peace with Joshua"
(Chron. 10. 4). They were hated because of their
peaceful connection with Joshua. They were despised
for His sake (John 15. 19). Those who have made
peace with Jesus fare no better now. The world still
hates the Christ of God as much as ever, but He
shall gain the victory. Some are ashamed to confess
their league with Jesus lest they should be despised
by men. The Gibeonites did not seek to hide it, they
rejoiced in it. What cowards, to be ashamed of being
at peace with God!

VII. **Mightily Protected.** In the day of trouble
and threatening danger they send unto Joshua, saying,
"Come up quickly, and save us, and help us" (chap.
10. 6). What a friend they have in Joshua! He is
able to save them to the uttermost. Their saviour
becomes their protector. Is our Saviour less to us?
The sun and moon stood still upon Gibeon, that the
victory might be complete. What honour is now put
upon the trusting Gibeonites! They call on Joshua,
and he conquers for them. They looked unto him and
were lightened. He put their enemies under his feet
(v. 24). The Church of God, like Gibeon, seems about
to be crushed with surrounding enemies, but He who
is the Saviour King shall suddenly come (v. 9). Is your
soul like this city, ready to perish? Let your cry be

to the all-conquering Jesus. These Gibeonites who had taken the place of strangers now claim the privileges of *servants*. Their petition is, "Slack not thy hand from thy servants; come up to us quickly, and save us, and help us." Their prayer was speedily answered. "And shall not God avenge His own elect? I tell you that He will avenge them speedily" (Luke 18. 7, 8; 2 Chron. 16. 9). ———

CALEB.

Joshua 14. 6-15.

"What is the end of fame? 'Tis but to fill
  A certain portion of uncertain paper:
Some liken it to climbing up a hill,
  Whose summit, like all hills, is lost in vapour;
For this men write, speak, preach, and heroes kill,
  And bards burn what they call 'the midnight taper.' "
                                        —BYRON.

IF the worldling's fame ends only in the blinding mists, it is not so with the man of God, for the "path of the just is as the shining light that shineth more and more until the perfect day." The name *Caleb* means *whole-hearted*. In his character he was true to his name, and his fame is still spread abroad as sweet ointment poured forth. His career did not end in the cold vapour of disappointment, like that of the half-hearted Balaam. He "followed God fully," and was rewarded abundantly. Here is a revelation of—

I. His Character. He was—

1. HONEST. He says, "When Moses sent me to espy out the land, I brought him word again *as it was in my heart*" (v. 7). His heart was right with God, so he spoke out what was in it. Solomon saith, "The heart of the wise teacheth his mouth" (Prov. 16. 23). The man with his heart so fixed, trusting in the Lord, is not afraid of evil tidings (Psa. 112. 7, 8). The

hypocrite is a man without *heart*. "The pure in heart shall see God."

2. CHARITABLE. "Nevertheless my brethren that went up with me made the heart of the people melt" (v. 8). Although his companions in the search brought back an evil report, which discouraged the people, dishonoured God, and belied his own testimony, still he speaks of them as "*my brethren*." Charity suffereth long, and is kind; is not easily provoked. Moses cried, "Ye rebels!" and so his tongue hindered his feet from entering the land.

3. DEVOTED. "I followed the Lord my God" (v. 8). Caleb had another spirit within him (Num. 14. 24). He followed the Lord his God exactly in the way in which we should follow Him. By accepting His will, trusting His Word, casting himself into His revealed purpose, and fearlessly standing in the strength of it. As Luther said, "I cannot do otherwise, so help me God." And God did help.

II. **His Faith.** He—

1. RECALLS THE PROMISE. "Moses sware on that day, saying, Surely the land whereon *thy* feet have trodden shall be thine inheritance" (v. 9). "Faith is the substance of things hoped for, the evidence of things not seen" (Heb. 11. 1). Unbelief has a very short memory, but faith remembers the Word of the Lord.

2. BELIEVES THE WORD. The promise of God (Num. 14. 24) is not only remembered, but *trusted*. All along he had been making it the rod and staff of his comfort. Let it be ours also through faith to look not at the things which are seen, but at the things which are *not seen*. "We walk by faith, not by sight" (2 Cor. 5. 7).

3. CLAIMS THE BLESSING. "Now therefore give me this mountain whereof the Lord spake in that day" (v. 12).

The conditions had been fulfilled, and he would enter "now therefore" right into the possession of it. This is not presumption, it is the courage of an honest faith in God that wins His smile, that secures His favour, and gains that crowning benediction—a satisfied soul. Put in your claim. " Now therefore give me this blessing whereof the Lord hath spoken." *Remember* His promise, *believe* it, *claim* the fulfilment of it. " Be it unto me according to Thy Word."

III. **His Testimony.** "I am going to preach Jesus," said one man to another on his way to a meeting. "I trust the Lord will be with you," replied his friend. "Well, if He is *not* I shall speak well of Him behind His back," was his happy answer. Caleb speaks well of God. He testifies to—

1. GOD'S FAITHFULNESS. "Behold, the Lord hath kept me these forty and five years" (v. 10). Kept through these terrible forty years in the wilderness. Kept by the power of God, while the whole multitude melted away through unbelief. Kept by the power of God *through faith* unto this salvation now revealed and enjoyed. He is faithful. Testify according to the proportion of your faith.

2. GOD'S GOODNESS. "I am as strong this day as I was in the day that Moses sent me" (v. 11). If the *joy of the Lord* is our strength there is no reason why the lapse of time should weaken it. Those who lose their first love will also lose their first strength. The trees of the Lord's planting and nurturing are *always* full of sap. Healthy, fruitbearing trees are a good testimony to the wisdom and carefulness of the gardener. A strong, healthy Christian is a continual witness to the riches and goodness of his Lord and Saviour.

3. GOD'S POWER. "If so be the Lord will be with me, *then I shall be able* to drive them out" (v. 12). This

testimony is true. Our ability to gain the victory over our
enemies lies not in our wisdom or strength, but in His
presence with us. Caleb knew that God alone could gird
him with strength sufficient to break the bow of steel
(Psa. 18. 32-34). "Through God we shall do valiantly, for
He it is that shall tread down our enemies" (Psa. 60. 12).
"Thanks be to God, which giveth us the victory through
our Lord Jesus Christ" (1 Cor. 15. 57). It is not surprising
to find that after such a testimony as this Joshua blessed
Caleb and gave him the inheritance (v. 13). "Blessed are
all they that trust in Him."

OTHNIEL'S PRIZE.
Joshua 15. 16-19.

"Anoint our eyes that we below
  The walk of faith, not sight, may know;
  Midst fiercest storms Hope's anchor cast,
  And still in love our Lord hold fast.

Faith! that clings unto the Cross;
  Hope! that looks beyond the sky;
Love! that counts all things but loss,
  To win the *bliss* that is on high."—GROSART.

OTHNIEL'S dare and doing to win the hand of Achsah, the
daughter of Caleb, is a beautiful and unique little episode
in the taking of the cities of Canaan. It would be
perfectly absurd to imagine that an honourable God-
following man like Caleb would offer his daughter to *any
man* who might happen to be the *first* to scramble over the
walls of Debir. A man that could *smite* this fortified city,
and *take it*, could only be the man that could take command
of an army and *lead* them to victory. That worthy man
was Othniel, the brother of Caleb. "All Scripture is given
by inspiration of God, and is profitable for *doctrine*." So
we are quite warranted to look for doctrine even here,
"that the man of God may be furnished unto all good

works" (2 Tim. 3. 16). We always accept this statement
of the apostle as a divine license to seek spiritual teaching
from historical events.

I. **The Hero Mentioned**, OR THE CHARACTER OF CHRIST.
The name of Othniel is significant, the "Lion of God," or
the "Strength of God." This was no misnomer, for in after
years when the children of Israel got into bondage, and
cried unto the Lord, He raised up this same Othniel
as a deliverer to them (Judges 3. 9). Jesus Christ, like
Othniel, is the *"Strength of God,"* sent forth as a Deliverer
for His people. The Lion of the tribe of Judah. If I
speak of strength, lo, He is strong, He travels in the
greatness of His strength, and is mighty to save.

II. **The Task Accomplished**, OR THE WORK OF CHRIST
(vv. 16, 17). Othniel's mission was to *smite* and to *take*,
and he finished the work on which he set his heart to do.
The taking of Kirjath-sepher would doubtless cause him
much effort and agony; but, like the Son of God, he set his
face like a flint to go up. The work of Jesus Christ was also
to *smite* and to *take*. He *smote* the devil with the weapon
of the Word, and spoiled principalities and powers,
triumphing over them (Luke 4. 1-12; Col. 2. 15), and *took*
the helpless prey from the hand of the mighty, making them
prisoners of grace (Luke 11. 21, 22; 2 Cor. 1. 9, 10). In
capturing the citadel of the human heart He has still to
smite with the spirit of conviction before He can *take it* as
an habitation for Himself.

III. **The Reward Offered**, OR THE BRIDE OF CHRIST.
Caleb said, "He that smiteth and taketh it, to him will I
give my daughter to wife" (v. 16). It was a battle for a
bride. The work of conquering the land was a God-given
work; the reward offered in Achsah was a reward of love,
reverence, and service. What a suggestive picture of the
Church, as the Lamb's wife, the reward given Him by

God for His work, and passion, and victory! Purchased at
the sacrifice of His own blood. "He loved the Church, and
gave Himself for it, that He might present it to Himself"
(Eph. 5. 25-27). Caleb's daughter was married to him
who had fought and conquered for her. This is also our
privilege, as sons and daughters have we been given by
God to Him, who lived, and loved, and died, and
conquered for us (John 17. 6). Are we acting the part
of a true wife by giving Him the love of our hearts and
the service of our lives? It is expected of the wife that
"she reverence her husband" (Eph. 5. 33).

IV. **The Dowry Given**, OR THE CHRISTIAN'S PORTION.
"And he gave her the upper springs, and the nether
springs" (v. 19). She asked for springs of water, and
she received them. A spring was a great inheritance
in these days. To possess springs in the hills and springs
in the valleys was to be the heir of an everlasting
source of wealth. These springs are perennial emblems
of the believer's portion in Christ. Since we have
the honour of being part of the bride of Christ, let us,
like Achsah, go in for the springs that are freely given
us of God. Springs for the hills and springs for the
valleys of our daily life. Every promise of God to us
is an unfailing spring of refreshing and comfort. If thou
knowest the gift of God, ask of Him, and He will give you
a spring of living water that shall be in you, springing up
everlastingly (John 4. 10-14). It is the delight of the
Lamb *now* to lead us unto these living *fountains* of water
(Rev. 7. 17). Every child of God may have his or her
dowry of living springs. All is yours, for ye are Christ's.
"Covet earnestly the best gifts" (1 Cor. 12. 31). In the
upper springs we have the promise of supply for all our
spiritual need, in the *nether* springs the promise of supply
for all our *temporal* need. "My God shall supply *all* your
need." "All my springs are in Thee" (Psa. 87. 7).

THE CITIES OF REFUGE;

OR, CHARACTERISTICS OF CHRIST AS A SAVIOUR

Joshua 20.

"I am safe, for Christ holds me;
Comforted, for I hold Him;
Saviour, O thus let it be,
When my dying eyes are dim;
I held of Thee, Thee holding,
Thy strong love me enfolding."

IT takes all the cities of refuge to form a perfect type of the "Man who is an hiding-place from the storm and a covert from the tempest." Observe the—

I. Nature of their Appointment. It was—

1. DIVINE. The Lord said: "Appoint out for you cities of refuge." These cities then were sanctified, or set apart for their sakes, according to the will of God. They undoubtedly point to Christ (Heb. 6. 18), who for our sakes sanctified (set apart) Himself, according to the will of God. It surely would be a consolation to the refugee when he entered the city to know that he was in *God's appointed shelter*. So we may have strong consolation who have fled for refuge. There is no safety but in being where and what God would have us to be.

2. MERCIFUL. They had respect specially to the *murderer*. How gracious is the Lord to think of such, and make provision for all who truly felt their need of *present mercy* and *righteous protection!* These each city afforded, these each sinner sorely needs, and this is what we find in Jesus. Mercy to pardon, grace to help, and the power of justice to protect. He is the Justifier of every one that believes in Jesus. As guilty sinners we need more than mere shelter, we need righteous *justification*, and Christ is *all* this.

II. Significance of their Names. In looking over

the meaning of the names of these cities one is struck
with the distinctive characteristic of each, as showing
forth some particular feature of the character of Christ,
and when taken as a whole illustrating the sufficiency
of Christ as a Refuge to meet all our need and the
need of all.

1. KEDESH (holy place). *A Refuge for the Unclean*. The
holiness of Jesus and the sinfulness of man are at once
suggested here. None of these truths can be denied, both
are alike clearly taught in Scripture. The holiness of Jesus
Christ becomes the hope of the unclean. Only that which
is clean can cleanse. The unrighteous can only find refuge
in the righteousness of God. Christ's finished work affords
a holy hiding-place, for there only are the unclean made
holy. There is no cleansing for the unclean apart from the
fountain opened for sin (Zech. 13. 1).

2. SHECHEM (shoulder). *A Refuge for the Weary*. The
lost sheep found both safety and rest upon the Shepherd's
shoulders (Matt. 11. 28; Luke 15. 5). He is a Saviour, and
a strong one. "The government is upon His shoulders."
We can find no rest in ruling ourselves, but the weary can
find rest under His government. When we *trust* we lean
not only on His merit, but also on His almightiness, or
rather His almighty merit. When on the shoulder the
strength of the carrier is beneath us. What a refuge for the
weary child is the shoulder of its loving father! Christ has
borne our burden upon His shoulder, as Samson carried the
gates of Gaza.

3. HEBRON (fellowship). *A Refuge for the Homeless*.
Man is spiritually a homeless wanderer, like Noah's dove.
Outside the ark, no rest, no fellowship, no safety. The
homeless prodigal found a refuge in the father's house and
in the father's fellowship. "Let us eat," etc. Jesus Christ
is the only Hebron for the soul. No fellowship with the
Father but through Him (1 John 1. 3). This is not the

refuge of a lonely prison, but in the bosom of a loving and beloved one. What a refuge the sailor's home is from a dangerous voyage, or the family ingle to a benighted and bewildered pilgrim. So Jesus is to the soul a refuge of *love* and *communion* (John 17. 21).

4. BEZER (stronghold). *A Refuge for the Helpless.* Man is not only a sinner, he is also *helplessly* sinful. In the case of the manslayer there was to be no such thing as *self-protection*, so is it with us as sinners. We are "without strength." The Name of the Lord is a strong tower, the righteous fleeth into it and are safe. Flee from the justice of God into the mercy of God. The mercy of God in Christ is a stronghold that can never give way. No matter how helpless you are, here you are eternally safe. Jesus is the only Bezer, all other hiding-places will fail and fall like the walls of Jericho, though straitly shut up (Matt. 7. 27).

5. RAMOTH (exalted). *A Refuge for the Hopeless.* By nature we are not only without strength, but without *hope in the world* (Eph. 2. 12). Those who hope *in* the world have no hope. We must hope *out of the world*. He is our Hope, *exalted* at the Father's right hand with a name *above* every name, high and lifted up. Jesus is our Ramoth. If you are downcast, and feeling yourself hopeless in the world, look up. Jesus is a Refuge for you. "I, if I be lifted up, will draw." Flee to Him to hide you, then you are exalted with Him. No mountain could save from the flood; those saved were lifted up in the ark. He is the Ark of hope.

6. GOLAN (separated). *A Refuge for the Tempted.* Many Christians are tempted much in the world because they tamper much with the world; they have not fled to Jesus as their city of separation. They have not become exiles with Him, and for His sake. Although He says, "Come out from among them, and be ye separate, and I will receive

you,'' yet they flee not, and the tempter often overtakes
them. He separated Himself for our sakes, that He might
succour the tempted. Golan is the last city mentioned.
Separation from the world unto God is about the last
refuge that is sought after. Jesus must be our All in All if
we would be perfectly sheltered from the curse, the world,
the flesh, and the devil.

Being enfolded with the arms of His almighty power,
and resting on the bosom of His infinite love, we can sing
with a restful, joyful heart, ''God is our Refuge and
our Strength.''

From these names we may also learn that *in Christ* we
have: (1) Holiness, (2) Rest, (3) Fellowship, (4) Safety,
(5) Exaltation, (6) Separation.

HOW TO POSSESS AND KEEP POSSESSION.
Joshua 23. 1-13.

"The disciples were bow'd by stress of their toil,
The Master was touch'd, and with gracious smile
Said, 'Come to the desert and *rest* awhile.' ''

IT is ever the longing of Christ's gracious heart to give His
beloved ones rest (Matt. 6. 28, 29). Joshua was about to
enter into his rest after a long, busy, and faithful life for
God, being now ''old and stricken in age,'' and in these
verses we have what may be regarded as his dying testimony, and, as we might expect, the predominant features
of his noble life are ''strong in death.'' It is a blessed
sight to see *early* faith ripening into such God-glorifying
fortitude. From his last message to Israel we may learn
how to get into our possessions, and the conditions on which
they may be kept.

I. How this Possession was Secured. There was—

1. A PAST DELIVERANCE. ''As a people they were
saved out of the land of Egypt, and out of the *house of*

bondage. The power that held them as bondslaves had to be broken before they could even set their faces toward the possessions reserved for them in Canaan. So with us, we had to be delivered from the guilt and power of sin ere we could set our hearts on things above.

2. A PRESENT DELIVERANCE. "The Lord had to *fight for* them even while in the land" (v. 3). There were many enemies that sought to *hinder* them from *enjoying* their possessions. But the Lord was able to deliver them from them all. There is also a *present* deliverance needed by all who have been saved from the bondage of sin and the wrath to come. The world, the flesh, and the devil are as bitterly opposed to our entering into our inheritance in Christ as the Canaanites were to the Israelites. We need the power of the same Lord who *brought us out* of the world to *keep us in* the place of blessing. But He is able to keep us from falling out of the blessed land of promise, and to *drive out* every usurping thought from the heart (v. 5).

II. How this Possession was to be Kept. There must be—

1. NO GOING BACK. "If ye do in any wise go back, know for certainty that the Lord your God will no more drive out from before thee" (vv 12, 13). There must be no going back to Egypt nor to the wilderness of sin. The principles that governed the old life must be given up. Put off the old man with his deeds, and let the time past suffice for the will of the flesh (Heb. 10. 38, 39). The *evil* heart will always seek to depart from the living God (Heb. 3. 12). Evil things not driven out of the heart never fail to act as pricks in the eyes (Num. 33. 55).

2. NO FELLOWSHIP WITH THE ENEMY. "Come ye not among them," etc. (v. 7). "Thou shalt make no marriage with them" (v. 12). "Come out from among them, and be

ye separate, and I will receive you'' (2 Cor. 6. 14-17).
To mingle with the Canaanites never improved the
Canaanites, and always brought misery to the people of
God. To become worldly that ye might better the world
is the doctrine of devils, if they should be white ones.

3. No DIVISION OF HEART. ''Take good heed therefore
unto *yourselves*, that ye *love* the Lord your God'' (v. 11).
Love can bear no rival. The *first* commandment is, ''Thou
shalt have no other gods before Me'' (Exod. 20. 2). ''Thou
shalt love the Lord thy God with *all thine heart*'' (Deut.
6. 5). ''This,'' said Jesus, ''is the first commandment''
(Matt. 22. 37, 38). Lot's wife had a divided heart, and
judgment overtook her.

III. **The Consequences of Going Back.** ''Be sure your
sin will find you out.'' The backsliding Christian will
surely be found out by this impoverished life and heartless
testimony. To go back out of the way and will of God
means the—

1. LOSS OF POWER. God would not be with them if
they went back. This is clearly taught in verses 12 and 13.
To turn out of God's way is to grieve the Holy Spirit and
become utterly impotent. It is an awful loss to lose one's
power to live and witness for Jesus Christ. Samson turned
aside, and the Spirit of power left him (Judges 16. 20).
Separation from the Vine entails loss of that sap which is
the power of life.

2. LOSS OF COMFORT. ''Scourges in your sides, and
thorns in your eyes'' (v. 13). These are the results
of disobedience. Miserable failures instead of joyful
conquerors. To turn away from the light is to turn
into the darkness. It is a great mercy that the sins of
God's people pinch the conscience. The most terrible
calamity that can befall a soul is to be comfortable and
happy without God.

3. LOSS OF CAPACITY. "Ye shall perish from off this good land" (v. 13). This *perishing* from off the land of promise, because of disobedience and unbelief, was not the work of a day. When they turned away from God they became day by day more *unfit*, as a people, to keep possession of the God-given land. Backsliding is, of course, a process (Psa. 1. 1), and a process by which our *capacities* for the enjoyment of the spiritual things freely given us of God gradually perish, until we in heart go right out of the land as far as our personal *experience* is concerned. If ye be willing and obedient ye shall eat the good of the land.

BLESSINGS REVIEWED;
OR, MOTIVES FOR SERVICE.
Joshua 24. 1-13

"I place me, Lord, 'neath Thy touch that thrills,
Wilt Thou, O wilt Thou me melt?
Give me the power Thine own arm fills
To impart whate'er of grace I have felt."

IN verse 14 we notice: (1) **That service is demanded.** "Now, therefore, fear the Lord, and serve Him." Every blessed one should arise and serve (Mark 1. 31). (2) **How this service should be given.** "In sincerity and truth." Mere perfunctory service is an abomination (Luke 19. 20-23). (3) **What this service implies.** "A putting away of other gods." The Lord's will *alone* must be the ruling principle of the life. The god, self, must be put away. HIM only shalt thou serve (Rom. 15. 3). "Now, *therefore.*" This word "therefore" suggests some foregoing reasons why this service should be rendered. We observe the following. There had been—

I. **Deliverance.** "I brought you out" (v. 5). They were emancipated through blood (Exod. 12. 13). So are we (1 Peter 1. 18, 19). Once the slaves of sin, now the children of God. Delivered to serve (Luke 1. 74).

II. **Separation.** "The Lord put darkness between you and the Egyptians" (v. 7). The darkness of death still lies between the saved and the unsaved (John 5. 24). The Lord doth put a difference (Exod. 11. 7). No human power will ever be able to bridge the great gulf fixed between death and life.

III. **Victory.** "I gave them (enemies) into your hand" (v. 8). All the enemies of the believer are conquered foes. They need not have dominion over you (Rom. 6. 14; Micah 7. 9). He giveth us the victory through our Lord Jesus Christ (Rom. 7. 25).

IV. **Protection.** "When Balak called Balaam to curse you he blessed you still" (vv. 9, 10). He can turn the counsel of the wicked to naught (Neh. 4. 15). "The Lord is thy keeper; He shall preserve thee from all evil" (Psa. 121. 5, 7).

V. **Possession.** "I have given you a land for which you did not labour," etc. (v. 13). "Not of works, lest any man should boast." What did the prodigal do for the benefits he received? (Luke 15. 22, 23) What have we that we have not received (Eph. 2. 7). "Now, therefore, fear the Lord, and *serve* Him."

CONSECRATION AND SERVICE.
Joshua 24. 14-28.

"How scant and measur'd are our gifts,
 Each on the other duty shifts;
 Upon ourselves we lavish spend,
 And paltry nothings His cause send.
  What cost it Him to save thy soul,
  Ere thou on Him thy sins didst roll?"

IT has been said that "Entire consecration embraces three things—*being*, *doing*, and *suffering*. We must be willing to be, to do, and to suffer all that God requires. It covers body, soul, and spirit. These are to be used *when*, *where*, and *as* God requires, and *only* as He requires. Must be made deliberately for all time coming, without any reserve, and in reliance upon divine strength. This is a faithful and true witness. Here is—

I. A Call to Decision. "Choose ye this day whom ye will serve" (v. 15). Ye cannot serve *two* masters. To halt between the opinions of self and God is to tarry upon the plain of destruction, like Lot's wife (Luke 16. 13). "Know ye not, that to whom ye *yield* yourselves, His servants ye are?" (Rom. 6. 16). Yielding to sin makes us the servants of sin. Yielding to God makes us the servants of God.

II. A Noble Determination. "As for me and my house, we will serve the Lord" (v. 15). The Lord in some way will publicly acknowledge those who, in the fear of God, command their children and their households (Gen. 18. 19). But let this be an individual decision, "As for *me*." "What wilt Thou have *me* to do?" Every man shall give an account of *himself* to God. To *serve* the Lord implies making Him your Master. Not I, but Christ. One is your Master. Who is He? Self or Christ?

III. A Stirring Reflection. The people answered and said, "The Lord our God, He it is that brought us out of Egypt, . . . and did those great signs, . . . and preserved us all the way, . . and drove out the Amorites, . . . *therefore* will we serve the Lord" (vv. 16-18). Their calling to mind the *past* goodness of God led them to a definite surrender of themselves to Him. Shall the memory of Christ's sufferings and victory *for us* not constrain us to yield ourselves in loyal service to Him? "Ye are not your own, for ye are bought with a price, *therefore* glorify God in your bodies and your spirits which are His."

IV. A Solemn Declaration. Joshua said, "Ye cannot serve the Lord, for He is an holy God; He is a jealous God"
H Vol. IV.

(v. 19). It is an easy thing to *say* that we will serve the Lord, but it is a very different thing to put it into daily practice (see Matt. 26. 33-35). The service of God is an holy service, and only holy ones can render it (Lev. 19. 2). "Who shall be able to stand before this holy Lord God?" (1 Sam. 6. 20). Those cleansed by the blood and filled with the Spirit. Ye cannot serve God if Mammon or self has any authority over you, for He is a *jealous* God, jealous because He is Love (1 John 4. 8).

V. A Decided Affirmation. "Nay, but we will serve the Lord. We are witnesses" (vv. 21, 22). They were witnesses against themselves that they had chosen the Lord to serve Him. Peter and the rest of the disciples affirmed that they would rather die than deny their Lord, but they all forsook Him, and fled when danger appeared. Self-confidence is ever the arm of flesh that fails. A strong will may be a blessing or a snare. All depends on whether the *strength* is merely human or divine. Be strong and very courageous (Josh. 1. 7).

VI. An Indispensable Condition. "Now therefore put away the strange gods, and incline your heart," etc. (v. 23). If the Lord is to be served every other usurping god must be *put away*, and the whole heart *inclined leaning* only upon the Lord. Everything that takes the place the Lord alone should have in our hearts is a *strange* god to Him; that with which He can have no fellowship. Service must always be associated with holiness. Work for God is to be the fruit of personal consecration to God. David would not offer to God what cost him nothing (2 Sam. 24. 24). The ministry of the Son of Man was to give His life (Matt. 20. 28). So should we *first* give our own selves to the Lord. "And this they did, not as we hoped, but first gave their own selves to the Lord, and unto us by the will of God" (2 Cor. 8. 5).

THE DEATH OF JOSHUA.

Joshua 24. 29-31.

"When the dangerous rocks are past,
    When the threatening tempests cease.
Oh! how sweet to rest at last
    In a silent port of peace.

Though that port may be unknown,
    Though no chart its name may bear,
Brightly beams its light on One,
    Blest to find his refuge there."

THE spiritual mariner's port of rest has no place on the business charts of earth. Port Death is a haven where those greedy of the world's gain have no desire to cast anchor. Some do rush into it in stress of weather to escape what seems more terrible than the separation of soul and body. The Christian's "port of peace" is the bosom of God. To him death is but the placid waters in the bay that speak of the nearness of the rest that is in the harbour of His all-satisfying presence. To die is gain. The death of Joshua was the final triumph of a conqueror. It suggests—

I. A Great Honour. "Joshua, the servant of the Lord" (v. 29). What a privilege to have one's name and character so closely linked with the Lord! To be known as "the servant of the Lord" is a heritage worth coveting earnestly. It is infinitely better than being known as a successful man or a millionaire. There is no degree that will tell in eternity like this. Of many it may be truly written, "John, the servant of the world." "Samuel, the servant of sin." "Mary, the servant of self." "Martha, the servant of fashion." Such have their reward, their crown of honour is in the dust instead of in the Lord.

II. A Passing Privilege. "It came to pass that Joshua died" (v. 29). Yes, even those who are reckoned indis-

pensable to the success of God's work die. No matter how
great the burden of responsibility it must be put aside.
Life itself, with all its great and eternal possibilities, is but
a passing opportunity. The key-note of Genesis 5 is, "And
he died." "It is appointed unto men once to die." But
this quickly vanishing "little while" is enough to fulfil the
work God has given us to do if the time is redeemed. Did
not our Lord realise this when He said, "I must work the
works of Him that sent Me *while it is day*" (John 9. 4). His
working day was a short one, but, oh, what wealth of labour
was in it.

III. **A Rebuke to Covetousness.** "They buried him
in the border of his inheritance" (v. 30). It does not
matter how large our earthly possession may be, a little
hole *in the border* will suffice when the spirit departs. Those
who pride themselves in adding house to house and land
to land should remember that a few odd shillings will be
enough to pay for their shroud. There are many graves in
the border land. That *lair* in the cemetery may mean *the
border* of your inheritance. The grave is not only in the
border of our earthly heritage, it is also in the border of
eternity. "It is sown a natural body; it is raised a
spiritual body" (1 Cor. 15. 44). The border is the last
point of contact with the old and the perishing before
we touch the new and the eternal. Set your affections
on things above, and not on the things which are on
the earth.

IV. **An Encouragement to Faithfulness.** "Israel
served the Lord all the days of Joshua, and all the days
of the elders that outlived Joshua" (v. 31). Another
evidence of the posthumous influence of a holy life.
"He being dead, yet speaketh." The king that knew
not Joseph dealt hardly with his brethren. The
memory of the wicked shall rot, while the righteous
shall be held in everlasting remembrance. Think of

the posthumous influence of Jesus Christ. The higher the life, or light, the farther will the radiance of its power and glory go. Jesus Christ has been exalted to Heaven, "far above all," that His influence might reach out to the uttermost parts of the earth, and down to the uttermost depths of human need, and on to the uttermost end of the ages. In so far as our lives are lived in the *heavenly* places will they tell with restraining or encouraging power upon those who may come after. The sun may set, but the effect of its healing beams is still felt by every living thing. To me to live is Christ.

"WHY HAVE YE DONE THIS?"
Judges 2. 1-5.

> "If Thou hadst not
> Been stern to me,
> But left me free,
> I had forgot
> Myself and Thee."—BEN JONSON.

THE "angel of the Lord" may mean "the angel of His Presence," that angelic form which makes the *presence of the Lord* a powerful reality. This the Holy Spirit now does. Wherever He is the presence of God is felt. The journey from Gilgal (rolling away) to Bochim (weepers) may in a moral sense be very short. If we do not walk in the light of His will the distance between our successes and failures will never be very great. We observe here—

I. **A Work of Grace.** This grace was manifested in—

1. A MERCIFUL COMPULSION. "I *made you* to go up out of Egypt" (v. 1). It is a blessed thing when salvation becomes a pressing *necessity*. Compelled to forsake our godless ways through the force of constraining grace. It was so with Saul while on the way to Damascus (Acts 9). The compulsion of Almighty love.

2. The Gift of a Rich Possession. "I brought you unto the land" (v. 1). This good land was the land of promise. To Israel it meant freedom, peace, plenty, progress, and power. Typical of the possessions the believer has in Christ Jesus.

3. An Unfailing Assurance. "I will never break My covenant with you" (v. 1). The gifts and callings of God are without repentance. God Himself will not alter the thing that has gone out of His lips (Psa. 89. 34). We may fail, yet He abideth faithful to His own promise. The bargain will never be broken on God's side. He cannot deny Himself.

4. A Needful Warning. "Ye shall make no league with the inhabitants; ye shall throw down their altars" (v. 2). The inhabitants of the land were bitterly opposed to the purposes of God, therefore the children of God must make no covenant with them. The servants of Christ must in no way identify themselves with that spirit that worketh in the children of disobedience. Their false gods must be thrown down, and the Lord alone exalted.

II. A Miserable Failure. "But ye have not obeyed My voice" (v. 2). The failure came in their case, as it often comes in ours, through unbelief. O fools and slow of heart, to *believe all* that He hath spoken! The *voice* of God is still in His Word, because His Word is the breathings of the Holy Ghost (2 Peter 1. 21). The Scriptures are always *living* and *active* (see Heb. 4. 12, R.V.). To turn away from His revealed will is to close our ears to the *voice* of God. Be not deceived, God knows when His voice is obeyed. He is personally interested in every individual child of His. How often have we complained of our failures? May not the cause be here: "Ye have not obeyed My voice?"

III. A Searching Question. "Why have ye done this?" The "angel of His presence" is jealous for the

honour of God. What answer can a disobedient one give
to this personal, pointed inquiry? An honest answer would
be: "I feared man more than God, and was better pleased
with my own thoughts and plans than with His." Paul's
"Not I, but Christ," has been changed into "Not Christ,
but I." Ye know that, apart from the presence and power
of the Holy Ghost within you, ye cannot live or witness
for God as ye ought; yet ye have gone leaning on your own
strength and wisdom, and came away defeated. "Why
have ye done this?" Ye know that to obey His voice is
the secret of heart-restfulness, yet ye have not walked in
this light. "Why have ye done this?"

IV. An Expressive Answer. They answered not by
words, but by deeds. Acts speak louder than words—

1. THEY WEPT. "The people lifted up their voice and
wept" (v. 4). The message from him who represented the
presence of God had gone home to their hearts. "Why have
ye done this?" smote them with the silence of self-condemnation that could only find expression in tears of
repentance. It was a heart question that wrung out this
heart-melting response. The crowing of a cock sent the
same burning question into the heart of self-confident
Peter, and with the very same result. "He went out and
wept bitterly" (Matt. 26. 75). "Godly sorrow worketh
repentance to salvation not to be repented of" (2 Cor. 7.10).

2. THEY SACRIFICED. "And they sacrificed there unto
the Lord" (v. 5). Sacrificing unto God is the only possible
way of *redeeming* what we have lost by disobedience. The
tears that are not followed with self-denying deeds are not
very hot. "The sacrifices of God are a broken spirit"
(Psa. 51. 17). The *broken* spirit allows all that is in it to
flow out for God. "I beseech you therefore by the mercies
of God to present your bodies a living sacrifice, holy,
acceptable to God, which is your reasonable service"
(Rom. 12. 1).

THE SONG OF DEBORAH.

Judges 5.

"Command, Lord, what Thou wilt,
  My way be dark or bright;
Upon the Rock I'm built,
  Thou shalt defend the right;
O look to me, and bring
  Me forth conquering to sing."

"THE song of Deborah," says Dr. Farrar, "is one of the grandest outbursts of impassioned poetry in the Bible." Like the song of salvation, the deep fulness of its harmony depends on the rich variety of its notes. It is a song of triumph. It is wonderful how nicely we can *sing* when we have experienced deliverance from all our enemies through faith in Jesus Christ. Those taken up out of the fearful pit of iniquity have a new song put into their mouth (Psa. 40. 2, 3). This song of the prophetess resembles our song, in that it has in it a note of—

I. **Fellowship.** "Then sang Deborah and Barak" (v. 1). The song of salvation is not a solo, for while the saved one sings for joy there is also joy in the presence of the angels of God (Luke 15. 10). The song of deliverance at the Red Sea was sung by Moses *and the children of Israel* (Exod. 15. 1). Let us exalt His Name together.

II. **Personal Dedication.** "The people willingly offered themselves" (v. 2). This is a sure forerunner to victory. When the people of God willingly offer themselves as instruments of righteousness in His hand, to do His will, the shout of triumph will certainly follow. As with the Church, so with the individual; *personal* consecration to the work of the Lord is the strait gate into the way of success in His service. "They *first* gave their own selves to the Lord" (2 Cor. 8. 5).

III. **Exultant Joy.** "Awake, awake, utter a song" (v. 12). The song of the Lord's delivered ones is so high

pitched that only the saved can sing it, and they need to
be wide *awake* to give it the needed emphasis. The half-
hearted make but a sorry attempt to touch the notes on the
leger lines of this heavenly song. The psalmist was clearing
his throat for it when he said, "Awake up, my glory; awake,
psaltery and harp: I myself will awake early" (Psa. 57. 8).
Ye that dwell in the dust of an unclean and praiseless life,
awake and sing (Isa. 26. 19).

IV. Mutual Encouragement. "Zebulun and Naphtali were a people that jeoparded their lives in the high
places of the field" (v. 18). Reuben could *debate* on the
merits of the war, and create divisions, playing the part of
the "higher critic" (v. 16), and perhaps helping Gilead,
Dan, and Asher in their guilty selfishness and cowardliness
(v. 17). But give honour to whom honour is due. Those
who stand firm on the "high places" in this holy warfare
against worldliness, and every form of sin that works in
opposition to the gracious will of God, let them be mentioned in our prayers and praises to God. All who jeopard
their *lives* for the cause of Christ, and even their own good
name, should have honourable mention before God and
man. This is a very effective antidote for jealousy in the
Lord's work.

V. Faithful Warning. Meroz and the inhabitants
thereof were to be cursed bitterly, "because they came
not to the help of the Lord against the mighty" (v. 23).
The people of Meroz may not have actually hindered the
Lord's warriors, but they did not *help;* in this lay their
guilt. They were cursed because they did *nothing.* Prayer-
less Christian, take note. The fig tree was cursed by the
merciful Christ because it was fruitless. Doing nothing in
the way of helping on the Lord's cause is the sure road to a
withered Christian life, and it may be to a God-dishonouring
posterity. Abigail was well taught in theology when she
assured David that, "The Lord will certainly make my

lord a sure house, because my lord fighteth the Lord's battles'' (1 Sam. 25. 28). Look after His business and He will look after yours.

VI. Solemn Reflection. The mother of Sisera looked out at a window, and cried, ''Why is his chariot so long in coming?'' etc. (vv. 28-30). Deborah's reference to the mother of Sisera watching and wearying for the return of her murdered son is an intensely *womanly* touch. Here is pictured the terrible disappointment that must finally come to those who hope for peace and prosperity while fighting against the purposes and people of God (Exod. 15. 9). While we celebrate our deliverance from the guilt and power of sin in our song of praise, let us not be unmindful of those who are without God and without hope in the world; those who are feeding on vanity, and are as the chaff to the wheat; those who walk in the light of the sparks of their own kindling, and whose light shall suddenly be quenched. The only hymn that we read of Christ ever singing was sung under the shadow of the Cross (Matt. 26. 30).

GIDEON'S CALL.
Judges 6. 11-24.

''Thou art as much His care as if beside
  Nor man nor angel lived in Heaven or earth;
Thus sunbeams pour alike their glorious tide
  To light up worlds, or wake an insect's mirth;
They shine, and shine with unexhausted store—
  Thou art thy Saviour's darling, seek no more.''

—KEBLE.

MANY have lived lives of sorrow and failure because they have mistaken their *calling*. It is not so with those called of God, as was Gideon. The gifts and callings of God are without repentance. Israel did evil in the sight of the Lord, and the consequence was what it always will be when we turn away from the Lord our Redeemer—bondage and oppression under the hand of an enemy (vv. 1, 2). But when they were *impoverished* they "cried unto the Lord" (v. 6), and He saved them out of their distresses by sending them a prophet to warn (v. 8) and a mighty man to save. The cry out of the depths of our impoverished hearts brings an answer out of the depths of His infinite fulness. In seeking to grasp the salient features of this portion let us note—

I. A Sorrowful Plight. "Gideon thrashed his wheat, and hid it from the Midianites" (v. 11). What a picture of a life lived under the *fear of man!* Separation from the ways of God will certainly pervert the motives of life. How are the mighty fallen that the redeemed of the Lord should tremble at the face of man? Elijah, in another sense, thrashed out his wheat fearlessly in the presence of his enemy, because he stood before the Lord God of Israel (1 Kings 17. 1).

II. A Comforting Message. The angel of the Lord appeared, and said unto him, "The Lord is with thee, thou mighty man of valour" (v. 12). This messenger of the covenant preached unto Gideon the Gospel of the grace of God, "The Lord is with thee, thou mighty man." It is His will and purpose to bless you and make you a blessing, therefore arise and put on thy strength. This angel brought to Gideon what the Holy Spirit brings to us—a remembrance of our privileges as His people. He shall take of Mine, and shall show it unto you.

III. An Anxious Question. And Gideon said, "If the Lord be with us, why then is all this befallen us?" etc. (v. 13). All this dishonour and misery came because of sin; but, blessed be God, although we may fall through our iniquity, He does not cast off and for ever deny His people. His great fatherly heart still loves and yearns for the restoration of His erring ones to His bosom. If the Lord is with us, why is our testimony so fruitless and our prayers

so powerless? Just for the very same reason—an evil
heart of unbelief (2 Chron. 15. 2).

IV. **A Great Commission.** The Lord looked upon him,
and said, "Go in this thy might, and thou shalt save
Israel; have not I sent thee?" (v. 14). His *might* un
doubtedly lay in the assurance of *Jehovah's presence* with
him (v. 12). Samson was not a giant; his great strength
lay in the power of the Spirit of God with him. He does
not send us a warfare on our own charges. Depressed and
doubting soul, herein is the secret of might, "Lo, I am
with you alway, and all power is given unto Me." Go
in *this* thy might (Josh. 1. 9; Matt. 28. 18, 19).

V. **A Common Excuse.** "Oh my Lord, wherewith shall
I save Israel? my family is *poor*, and I am the *least*," etc.
(v. 15). It was so also with Moses (Exod. 3. 11) and with
Saul (1 Sam. 9. 21). *Poverty* and *weakness* are no argu-
ments against the exceeding *riches* of His grace and *power*
to usward. Urging *our own* helplessness in the face of His
all-sufficient promise only betrays our lack of faith in His
Word. Still, the Lord expects that His abounding grace
should never beget in us anything like self-confidence or
boasting. The revelation of the glory of His goodness
and of the high calling into which we have been brought
are sure to make us feel keenly the impotency of all
human strength and wisdom (see Luke 5. 8, 9). Our
conscious weakness is one of the best qualifications for
the work of God (1 Cor. 1. 27; 2 Cor. 12. 10).

VI. **An Assuring Promise.** "And the Lord said unto
him, Surely I will be with thee" (v. 16). God meets his
felt need with the promise of His presence. The *presence of
God* means the supplying of all our wants as His servants.
There is no other way whereby the Lord can equip us for
His work than by the power of His presence, by the Holy
Ghost within us. Gideon says, "I am poor, and my

father's house are few in number;" but God's answer to his and our poverty and feebleness is, "I will be with thee." Greater is He that is with us than all that can be against us. "Himself hath said, I will in no wise fail thee," so that with courage we say, "The Lord is my helper, I will not fear" (Heb. 13. 5, 6, R.V.).

VII. **A Confirming Token.** "If now I have found grace in Thy sight, then show me a sign, and there rose up *fire* out of the rock" (vv. 17-21). The God that answereth by fire, let him be God (1 Kings 18. 24; Acts 2. 1-4). Why should a sign be needed after giving His sure word of promise? In infinite grace God adapts His methods to the natural infirmities of man. He adds the seal of the Spirit to the promise of His Word. This holy fire appeared after the offering had been poured out before the Lord. As the fire of the Lord of old had to do with the offerings *on the altar* (Lev. 9. 24), so the Holy Spirit of burning comes now as God's answer and sign to a life consecrated unto Him. Ye shall be baptised with the Holy Ghost and with fire. "Did ye receive the Holy Ghost when ye believed?" (Acts 19. 2, R.V.).

VIII. **An Adoring Act.** "Then Gideon built an altar there unto the Lord, and called it Jehovah-shalom"— Jehovah, send peace (v. 24). Because he had seen the angel of the Lord face to face he feared that he would die. But his fears having been rebuked by His "Peace be unto thee" (vv. 22, 23), he built an altar, and called it the *"Peace of Jehovah."* "My peace I give unto thee." The assuring Word of God's promise ought to be enough to lead us into that adoring attitude of sacrificing restfulness (John 14. 27). This altar, like the altar of the Cross of Jesus Christ, speaks powerfully of the peace of God. The cry of both was, "Jehovah, send peace." And peace has been made. A peace that passeth all understanding. May it garrison our hearts and constrain to adoring worship.

GIDEON AT WORK.
Judges 6. 25-40.

"For as we see the eclipsed sun
  By mortals is more gazed upon
  Than when, adorn'd with all his light,
  He shines in serene sky most bright;
  So valour in a low estate
  Is more admired and wondered at."—BUTLER.

THE apostle Paul has declared that "When I am weak, then am I strong." Judged by the wisdom of the world this is certainly paradoxical. The seeming absurdity is partly explained by his previous utterance. "I will glory in my *infirmities*, that the *power of Christ* may rest upon me" (2 Cor. 12. 9, 10). Gideon in himself was weak and uninfluential; but now that the *presence* and *peace* of Jehovah was with him, and in him, he becomes what God saw that he ought to be: "A mighty man of valour."

I. Where he Began.

1. AT HOME. "Take thy *father's* bullock, and throw down the altar of Baal that *thy father hath*" (v. 25). The command to "honour thy father," etc., has a far-reaching effect, and may be fulfilled by a son in a way that is very painful to the father. Gideon would honour his father, but destroy his father's gods. It takes courage to make a start and take a stand for God and for righteousness among our own kin. "Go home to thy friends, and tell them what great things the Lord hath done for thee" (Mark 5. 19).

2. AT ONCE. "And Gideon took ten men, . . . and did it by night" (v. 27). It would appear that no time was lost. Gideon's ten servants, through his consistent testimony, was fully in sympathy with Jehovah, and ready at once to follow their master in this needed work for God. The call was clear. Why should he put off? Is it not as clear for you? Yet you linger. The Master is come, and calleth for you.

II. What He Did. His work was twofold.

1. A PULLING DOWN. "Throw down the altar of Baal" (v. 25). The altar of Baal represented that which was false, deceptive, and opposed to the will and rule of Jehovah. Every God-usurping thing around us or within us must be overturned and dethroned. "Our weapons are not according to the flesh, but mighty before God to the casting down imaginations and every high thing that is exalted *against the knowledge of God*" (2 Cor. 10. 4, 5, R.V.).

2. A BUILDING UP. "Build an altar unto the Lord thy God" (v. 26). It is not enough to undeceive the worshippers of false gods; the true God must be put in their place. It is not enough to take the pleasures of the world from its votaries; we must be able to put something better in their place. The Altar of God, viz., the *Cross* of Christ, is the divine substitute for the barren and powerless inventions of men. To preach Christ and Him crucified is to build up the Altar of the Lord.

III. What Followed. Such definite action will always be accompanied with very positive results. There came—

1. A CHANGED ATTITUDE. "The men of the city said, Bring out thy son that he may die" (v. 30). Death, in one form or another, is for ever the world's penalty for faithfulness to God. The *men of the city* (who mind earthly things) are always bitterly opposed to those iconoclasts— men of God—who seek first the kingdom of God. But the disciple is not greater than his Master. The first evidence of faithfulness to Christ is the opposition of the ungodly.

2. A CHANGED NAME. "Therefore on that day Gideon was called Jerubbaal" (v. 32). "Let Baal plead," or "*Baal's antagonist.*" It is a blessed stigma to be called "a hater of false gods," an enemy to ignorance and superstition. It is quite becoming for a man to get a new name when he becomes a new creature (Gen. 32. 28).

IV. How He was Encouraged by the—

1. ANOINTING OF THE SPIRIT. "The Spirit of the Lord came upon (clothed) Gideon, and he blew a trumpet" (v. 34). *Fitness* for the service of God can only be found in the Spirit of God. The blowing of the Gospel trumpet by a man clothed with the power of God will surely be effectual in gathering many *after him*. "Ye shall receive power when the Holy Ghost is come upon you" (Acts 1. 8).

2. TESTIMONY OF THE FLEECE. In answer to the prayer of Gideon the fleece was wet with dew, while the earth around was dry; and, again, the fleece was dry while on the ground there was dew (vv. 36-40). A convincing proof that the providence of God in connection with the needs of His people is not the blind workings of chance. The Spirit of God, like the wind, bloweth where it listeth; and, like the dew, it may fall on the fleece or not on the fleece, according to the cry of the man of God. Every servant of God may have this twofold witness: the Spirit within, and the special token of God's workings without. Prayer and providence go together.

GIDEON'S FOLLOWERS TESTED.
Judges 7. 1-8.

"Nor yet conclude all fiery trials past;
　For Heaven will exercise us to the last,
　Sometimes will check us in our mad career
　With *doubtful blessings* and with mingled fear."
　　　　　　　　　　　　　　　　—DRYDEN.

GIDEON had been called of God as a "mighty man of valour." God knows where to find the instrument that is suitable for His work. "Not he that commendeth Himself is approved, but whom the Lord commendeth" (2 Cor. 10. 18). When Gideon blew the trumpet a great many gathered after him (v. 34), commending *themselves*, but whom the Lord had not commended. So the sifting process

had to be applied. They had pitched *beside the well* (v. 1),
and between the water and the warfare the would-be
followers were tested. But note—

I. A Strange Hindrance. The Lord said, "The
people that are with thee are *too many* for Me" (v. 2).
This is "to human *wisdom*, how severe?" An army of
32,000 too *many* for 120,000! (chap. 8. 10). Yes, this
is the Almighty's logic, that no *flesh* should glory in
His presence (Deut. 8. 12-17). Our own strength and
wisdom are always too many for God (1 Cor. 1. 29).
It is to the *faint* that He gives power, and to them
that have *no might* He increaseth strength (Isa. 40. 29).
"When I am weak, then am I strong" (2 Cor. 12. 10).
"Not by might, nor by power" (Zech. 4. 6).

II. An Urgent Call. "Whosoever is fearful and
afraid, let him return and *depart early*" (v. 3). The
presence of the *fearful* and the *self-interested* are always
a hindrance to the work of God (Deut. 20. 8). How
slow we are to learn that our Lord can do without those
doubting and fearful professed followers! We are ready
to be discouraged when *they* turn out of the ranks of
workers for Christ, when *in heart* they never were
really in line with the Spirit of God. They turn *out*,
because *in spirit* they never had turned *in*. "For
if they had been *of* us, they would no doubt have
continued *with* us" (1 John 2. 19).

III. A Startling Revelation. "And there returned of
the people twenty and two thousand" (v. 3). This turn
about made a great gap in the ranks. Only ten thousand
remained. God's warriors have to be weakened and
reduced to bring them up to real efficiency *in His presence*.
When the Church of God and the teaching of Christ are
being assailed by an ever-increasing number of enemies it
is wonderful how many false professors are found out by
their turning away from the faith. Such dissensions

cannot hinder the progress of the kingdom of God any more than the blowing away of rotten twigs by the wind can impede the growth of a tree.

IV. A Second Test. "And the Lord said unto Gideon, The people are yet too many; bring them down unto the water, and I will try them for thee there" (v. 4). When the appeal was made to their *own will* many turned away back, but now the *purging* of those that are left is to be according to the will of God. Much that we would pass for wheat His fan will prove to be only chaff (Isa. 1. 25). The greater the victory to be achieved in the Name of Jesus Christ the hotter the furnace of trial through which we must pass. It was so with Abraham, Joseph, Moses, Daniel, Peter, and Paul. Where are they who have been much used of God who have not had His sifting, purging fire turned upon them? It is one thing *for us* to search ourselves; this will doubtless turn many cowardly things away out of our life, but when God Himself comes by His searching Spirit to try us, then we are brought down to utter hopelessness in our own strength, that *no flesh* may glory in His presence, and that the excellency of the power may be of God, and not of us (2 Cor. 4. 7). "Search me, O God, and try me."

V. A Consecrated Band. "And the Lord said unto Gideon, By the three hundred men that lapped will I save you" (vv. 5-7). A straw may indicate which way the wind blows. Those who *lapped* the water with the hand had evidently a keener sense of and were more alive to the importance and urgency of the occasion. Those who "bowed down upon their knees" were specially eager after their own selfish gratification. We are not fit for the work of God while our own *personal comfort* is our chief concern. No doubt they were all alike thirsty, and the water would be equally precious to both parties as the good and needful gift of God. But we don't live to eat and drink; we eat and drink that we may live to the glory of our God. As the servants of Christ let us lap thankfully of the wells that God in His providence may open before us by the way; but thou shalt not *bow down* to them as a mere hireling, else in the sight of God thou shalt become unfit to join the *victors* in the battle of the Lord. "This one thing I do" is the language of those who have yielded themselves entirely to the doing of the will of God, who partake of the pleasures of this world, as a dog lappeth the waters in passing, but whose *heart* is set on the will and work of the Lord. Consecrated souls lap the waters of earth with their eyes on the Cross of Christ.

GIDEON'S ENCOURAGEMENT.
Judges 7. 9-15.

"Observe the rising lily's snowy grace,
Observe the various vegetable race;
They neither toil nor spin, but careless grow,
Yet see how warm they blush, how bright they glow!
What regal vestments can with them compare,
What king so shining, or what queen so fair?
Will He not care for you, ye faithless, say?
Is He unwise? Or are ye less than they?"—Thomson.

BE not discouraged because of the way. He that hath begun the good work in you and through you will keep performing it until the day of perfection. If Gideon's heart was lifted up with pride when 32,000 gathered around him it would surely sink when he saw the powerful looking army melt away till only a handful of three hundred were left, but this was a "Handful on Purpose." God's handful of separated ones, "ready to do whatever the King would appoint." The divine method is *quality*, not quantity. He desires not appearance, but truth in the *inward* parts. "The Spirit of the Lord came *upon* David, . . . but *departed* from Saul" (1 Sam. 16. 1-7).

Gideon was mightily encouraged by the—

I. **Promise of God.** "Arise, get thee down unto the
host, for I have delivered it unto thine hand" (v. 9). The
battle was already fought and the victory gained in the
purpose of God. Now Gideon is called upon to arise and
enter into that purpose and claim the offered deliverance.
Does not the promises of God in Christ mean as much as
this to us? Is it not the purpose of God that we should be
saved from all our sins and delivered from all our enemies?
Then arise, and in His Name claim the victory. He is
faithful that hath promised (Luke 1. 74, 75).

II. **Presence of God.** The Lord had said unto him,
"Surely I will be with thee" (vv. 6-10). His promise of
victory always brings with it the assurance of His presence
(v. 9). "Lo, I am with you alway." Does this promise
only hold good when we are *conscious* of His nearness?
Are our moral sensibilities to be the criterion of the
truthfulness of His Word? Are we only thankful for His
powerful presence with us when we *feel* it? It is surely an
encouragement that we can continually reckon on our
Lord being with us by His Spirit when we know that
we are doing that which is pleasing in His sight.

III. **Providence of God.** "All things work together
for good to them that *love* God, to them who are the *called*
according to His purpose" (Rom. 8. 28). When our
affections are set on Himself, and while we are walking
according to our high calling, every circumstance in life
is planned for our good by the wonder-working hand of
God. This is part of the great Redemption which we have
in Christ Jesus. See how He wrought for the comfort of
His servant Gideon. There were three different streams of
influence which culminated at one divinely-appointed
moment. There was—

1. A DREAM. "Behold, I dreamed a dream, and, lo, a
cake of barley bread tumbled into the host of Midian,"

etc. (v. 13). Dreams are common, but Jehovah was the Author and Giver of this one. Despair not at the lack of means for getting within touch of those who are the enemies of God and of His Christ while the *ear* of God is open to your cry. He may be causing others to see the little barley cakes overturning their tents and creating dismay even while we are lamenting their utter indifference to the will of God.

2. THE INTERPRETATION OF THE DREAM. "And his fellow answered, This is nothing else save the *sword* of Gideon," etc. (v. 14). When the trembling dreamer told his dream the mighty power of God seemed to take hold of the *hearer* that he could see nothing else but his own and his fellow's doom in this simple vision. Ah, when God is speaking the simple message comes with a self-condemning revelation. Yes, the *cake of barley*, the bread of the Lord's host, becomes the *sword* of the Lord in the camp of His enemies. Gideon's little consecrated band is in the hand of the Lord, and He prepares for them the victory.

3. THE HEARING OF IT BY GIDEON. "And it was so when Gideon heard the telling of the dream, and the interpretation thereof that he worshipped" (v. 15). The whole scene was a divinely-planned coincidence, and another proof of that unerring providence that constrains the faithful servant of God again and again to bow in silent worship. This is the finger of God. It is God's manner to choose the things that are weak and despised to confound the things which are mighty (1 Cor. 1. 27, 28). Although the Lord is often pleased to give us *providential* evidences of the truth of His Word, let us ever remember that His promises are enough without them; what Gideon heard in the tent did not make the Word of God more sure. "All the Promises of God in Him are yea, and in Him Amen" (2 Cor. 1. 20).

GIDEON'S VICTORY.

Judges 7. 16-25.

"'Tis always morning somewhere in the world,
　Thron'd evil yet shall from its height be hurled;
　The nail-pierced hand holds still the 'seven stars,'
　Truth stronger, nobler groweth by its scars."—GROSART.

THE weapons of our warfare are not carnal. Like Gideon,
every *divinely-called* one has a work to do that would be
otherwise perfectly impossible but for the grace of God.
Every regenerated life is a miracle, a new centre of
operation for the spiritual forces of Heaven, and of course
there must be a special manifestation of *supernatural*
and unworldly influences. If a Christian is not in the
eyes of the world an anomaly he is nothing. The
Spirit of God always makes a tremendous distinction
between men. "Ye are a peculiar people." The energy
of the natural man, and that of the Holy Spirit in the
believer, are as different as darkness is from light; as far
apart in character as Judas was from John. Notice the—

I. Strange Preparation. "He put a trumpet in every
man's hand, with empty pitchers, and lamps within the
pitchers" (v. 16). Trumpets, lamps, and pitchers. Those
who have faith in God can afford to use weak things. There
was a great difference between the weapon of Goliath and
that of David (1 Sam. 17. 40-45). Pitchers with nothing
in them but lamps may suggest hearts cleansed and filled
with the *light* of the knowledge of God (2 Cor. 4. 6, 7).
This knowledge to be sounded out with *trumpet* lips
(Rom. 10. 14). When God makes His choice of weapons
they are always weak and base in the sight of the wisdom
of this world (1 Cor. 1. 27, 28). Fools for Christ.

II. Present Example. Gideon said, "Look on me,
and do likewise; as I do, so shall ye do" (v. 17). Each one
must look unto him who is God's messenger, and who goeth
before them. Gideon himself, in his ways and actions, was

an example to each consecrated follower. Christ hath left us an example, that we should follow His steps. Look *unto Him*, and not unto one another. Whatsoever He saith unto you, do it. He pleased not Himself. Look on Him, and do likewise. The Captain of our salvation, like Gideon, desires His followers always to keep *within sight* of Him.

III. **Uniting Battle Cry.** "And they cried, The sword of the Lord and of Gideon" (v. 20). There was only *one* sword among them, but it was enough, for it was the SWORD OF THE LORD, and the hand of Gideon was grasping it. The one glittering blade of divine truth is mightier than all the weapons of darkness The sword of the Spirit is the Word of God. This Word is the sword of the Lord, and of His Christ. It is the *alone* weapon for the whole camp of His followers. It will be a blessed and victorious day for the Church when this is its *unmistakable* cry, "The Word of the Lord and of His Church."

IV. **Peculiar Warfare.** "They *blew* the trumpets, and *break* the pitchers, and *held* the lamps, and *cried*," etc. (vv. 19, 20). Every man, as God's chosen one, had a trumpet, a pitcher, and a lamp, but every one's *faith* was in the "Sword of the Lord." Each soldier *sounded* his trumpet as an individual testimony for God, then the pitchers were dashed together and broken into countless fragments; a broken and a contrite heart is needed if the lamp of heavenly truth is to shine forth in the eyes of the ungodly. Then came the *united* cry, and the great battle was quickly won. Lips telling out the Gospel with clear trumpet tones, and the *light* of the *knowledge of God* shining out of broken hearts, and Christ, the Word of God uplifted. These are the crying needs of to-day, and these are God's means of overcoming the forces of evil. Put on the whole armour of God.

V. **Complete Victory.** "They stood every man in his place round about the camp, and all the host ran, and cried, and fled'' (v. 21). Let us inquire as to the source and secret of such a triumph. They were—

1. UNITED. They were as one man with one sword. When the singers were *as one* then the house was filled with glory (2 Chron. 5. 13). Not only union, but *unison* is needed (John 17. 21).

2. OBEDIENT. "They followed Gideon's example." The wise man is not he that *saith* the will of God, but he that *doeth* it (Matt. 7. 21; see Psa. 81. 13, 14).

3. FAITHFUL. "They stood every man in his place" (v. 21). Only those who truly trust can stand steady (2 Chron. 20. 17). When we take our right place God will take His.

4. TRIUMPHANT. God gave them the victory (Zech. 4. 6). When I sent you, lacked ye anything? They answered, Nothing (Luke 22. 35; 2 Cor. 9. 8). Then the men of Israel said unto Gideon, "Rule thou over us, for thou hast delivered us" (chap. 8. 22).

So may we crown our Deliverer, Lord of all.

GAAL; or, GODLESS EFFORT.
Judges 9. 26-49.

"Ever scorn to be a coward, who stands silent by,
When ill tongues our Lord seek to crucify;
Never be ashamed to *count one for Him*,
Or the lustre of the name of 'Christian' dim."

SCRIPTURAL names are always eloquent of character. "Gaal, the son of Ebed," means the *"loathing son of a slave,"* strongly suggestive of pride and poverty. A man who could not see any one wiser or better than himself. Through his "loathing" eyes he saw others as through a coloured glass. True, Abimelech was a murderer (v. 5), but it is not God's way to overcome evil with *evil*, but to overcome evil with *good* (Rom. 12. 21). Every servant of Christ may find some wholesome food for thought here. Observe his—

I. Hopeful Start. He was—

1. TRUSTED. "The men of Shechem put their confidence in him" (v. 26). The men of Shechem were as blind to true moral greatness as Gaal himself. But doubtless his *self-confidence* would be considerably augmented by this expression of their faith. Whatever helps to *puff us up* helps us to our ruin as workers for Jesus Christ.

2. FEASTED. "They did eat and drink, and cursed Abimelech" (v. 27). Carnal delights make a poor preparation for the service of God. Gideon's men were tested and sifted before the conflict, but Gaal's followers were rested and feasted. Instead of praying they *cursed*. The gladness of the Lord in the heart is greater than that begotten by corn and wine (Psa. 4. 7). Material good does not always mean spiritual prosperity.

II. Courageous Stand. He was—

1. DEFIANT. "And Gaal said, Who is Abimelech, and who is Shechem that we should serve him?" (v. 28). This sounds like the clarion note of a God-raised reformer, but it was nothing but the vain wind of a self-conceited bigot. It is easy even for the Christian worker to *talk* defiantly of the forces opposed to the progress of the soul, and of the kingdom of God amongst men, but everything depends on the *ground* of our boasting (1 Sam. 14. 6).

2. SELF-CONFIDENT. "Would to God that this people were under *my* hand, then would *I* remove Abimelech" (v. 29). O these mighty *my's* and *I's*, the progeny of pride and self-confidence. How would it look to put this language in a more logical form? Would to God that I were God. We naturally shrink from this, but *self-confidence* is a *denial* of God, and the forerunner of destruction (2 Sam. 15. 4). "Pride goeth before a fall."

III. Utter Defeat. "Abimelech chased him, and he fled; and Zebul *thrust out* Gaal and his brethren" (vv. 40, 41). That his work was an ignominious failure need not be wondered at when we consider the God-dishonouring motives that constrained him. Be sure your *secret* sin will find you out in *public* defeat. It was not the *cause* espoused by Gaal and his compatriots that was bad, quite the reverse, but that he undertook it in *his own* name, without the call of God. Jephthah and Gideon accomplished great deliverances because God was with them. The secret of Gaal's failure is still the secret of the failure of many of the Lord's professed servants. There was—

1. No Acknowledgment of God. If we would have His blessing on our work it must be done in His Name. The self-satisfied soul of Gaal had no room for God. It was so different with Moses, David, and Gideon. Some are afraid honestly to acknowledge God lest He should put His foot in all their plans and purposes, so instead of getting their Christless purposes crushed in infancy they get them trodden under foot of God in the full strength of their maturity.

2. No Revelation from God. It is not easy continually to recognise God in our work if we have not had from God a revelation of that work. Gaal had no message from the Lord burning in his heart. Like Absalom, he was self-ordained, and God-deposed. Where there is no vision there is no "Here I am, send me." Where there is no voice from Heaven there is no "What wilt thou have me to do?"

3. No Inspiration by God. The Spirit of the Lord *clothed* both Gideon and Jephthah (Judges 6. 34; 11. 29), but Gaal's inspiration came from the wine cup (v. 27). The one is from above, the other is from beneath; the one is of life, the other of death. "Ye shall receive

the power of the Holy Ghost coming upon you, and ye shall be witnesses unto Me'' (Acts 1. 8). Of how much of our service for the Lord may it be said: There is no *revelation*, no *inspiration*? Of so much may it be said: There is no victory.

_____

JEPHTHAH; or, CALLED TO SERVE.

Judges 11.

"God never meant that man should scale the Heaven
By strides of human wisdom. In His works,
Though wondrous, He commands us in His Word
To seek Him rather where His mercy shines."—COWPER.

THE names of Gideon and Jephthah have honourable mention by the great apostle in his select roll of the faithful who had ''subdued kingdoms, wrought righteousness, and *obtained promises*'' (Heb. 11). The story of Jephthah is the story of every converted sinner—a lifting up ''from the dunghill, and a setting among princes'' (Psa. 113. 7). Observe some things concerning him. He—

I. **Was Born in Sin.** ''He was the son of an harlot'' (v. 1). ''A mighty man of valour,'' but a child of iniquity. Naaman was a mighty man in valour, but he was a leper (2 Kings 5. 1). By *birth* he was disqualified from entering into the *congregation of the Lord* (Deut. 23. 2). ''Except a man be born again, he cannot see the kingdom of God.'' ''That which is born of the flesh is flesh.'' ''Who can bring a clean thing out of an unclean?''

II. **Was Disinherited.** ''They thrust out Jephthah, and said unto him, Thou shalt not inherit in our father's house'' (v. 2). *His* right to inherit by succession was destroyed through his father's sin (Deut. 21. 16). By *one man's* disobedience many have been made sinners. ''The unrighteous shall not inherit the kingdom of God'' (1 Cor. 6. 9). Adam's sin drove him out of his inheritance in the garden of Eden, and all his posterity have been born

outside. If we would have an inheritance among them
that are sanctified it must be by *faith* in Jesus Christ
(Acts 26. 18).

III. **Became a Companion of the Vain.** "Then
Jephthah fled, and there were gathered vain men to him"
(v. 3). Like a sheep gone astray, he turned to *his own way*.
It would appear that he now became a brigand, or free-
booter, an antitype of Rob Roy of modern history. Such
were some of us. When deprived of hope we plunged into
the abyss of a reckless, selfish life. Seeking to drown
remorse with the excitement of sinful pleasures. A man is
known by the company he keeps. "Fowl of a feather
flock together." "And being let go, they went to their
own company" (Acts 4. 23).

IV. **Received an Important Invitation.** "The elders
of Gilead said unto Jephthah, Come and be our captain"
(vv. 5, 6). These elders no doubt saw in this daring son of
the wilds gifts and qualifications that, if rightly directed,
might be of immense value to the cause of God and of His
people—what the early disciples would certainly see in the
gifted, but Christ-hating Saul, and who would doubtless
make many an appeal to Heaven for his conversion. The
call came to Jephthah as the call of the Gospel came to us,
"while we were yet sinners." Like the Gospel call, it
was an invitation to *join* the ranks of the Lord's people,
from whom sin had separated him, and to *fight* the Lord's
battles. Will you come? "Him that cometh to Me, I
will in no wise cast out" (John 6. 37).

V. **Covenanted with the Lord.** "And Jephthah
uttered all his words *before the Lord* in Mizpah" (v. 11).
This unexpected but gracious call that came to him seems
to have had the effect of making him feel his need of being
reconciled to God, and of serving in His Name and strength.
If the Gospel of Christ has not had such a transforming
influence on our lives we have never yet known it. No

matter how unique and outstanding our gifts and abilities may be *before* we turn to the Lord, if we would be used in His service, these must be wholly yielded to Him, or they can only prove barriers to the progress of His kingdom. It is not the *strong* heart, but the *broken* heart that God will not despise. "A broken and a contrite heart, O God, Thou wilt not despise" (Psa. 51. 17).

VI. **Was Endued with Power.** "Then the Spirit of the Lord came upon Jephthah" (v. 29). The Spirit of the Lord did not come upon him *until* he had yielded himself to the Lord, and made full confession, by *"uttering all his words before the Lord"* (v. 11). It is not to the naturally *courageous*, but to the *consecrated* that the gift of the power of the Holy Ghost is given (Acts 1. 8). He who has the gift of the Spirit has a *great gift*, no matter what other gifts he has not. No matter what our needs are—wisdom, strength, holiness, etc.—God's one and all-sufficient provision is imparted by the gift of the Spirit. By Him Christ is made unto us wisdom, righteousness, sanctification, and redemption (1 Cor. 1. 30).

VII. **Gained the Victory.** "And the Lord delivered them into his hands" (v. 32). He is fit now to have them delivered into *his hands*, as he himself is now in the hands of God, that no flesh should glory in His presence. Jephthah is another illustration of God using things which are *despised* (v. 2). There is room enough in the *grace of God* for the most wayward and helpless. There is also sufficiency here for the hitherto barren and unfruitful. We are not saved by our works, neither are we *used* in the service of God because of our superior gifts or past eventful experience. It is all of grace, and His grace is sufficient for all. Without the living energy of the Holy Spirit within we shall achieve nothing. "Be filled with the Spirit" (Eph. 5.18). He hath said "My Grace is sufficient for thee, for My strength is made perfect in weakness" (2 Cor. 12. 9).

SAMSON'S BIRTH
Judges 13. 1-25.

"Choose Thou for me, Lord. O have not me to choose!
I know not what to ask or to refuse;
Thou knowest poverty, Thou knowest wealth,
Langour of sickness, confidence of health;
Choose for me, Lord, I know not what is best,
Thou art too just to wrong—on Thee I rest '

WHEN we trust the Lord to choose our *daily* inheritance for us (Psa. 47. 4) we shall surely have a goodly portion. The gifts of God are all God-like, worthy of Himself. The Lord appeared unto the wife of Manoah, and promised her a son (v. 3). She simply believed the message, and expected that since He had promised He was also able to perform. On the ground of His Word we may confidently expect what humanly speaking is perfectly impossible (Mark 10. 27). The birth of Samson suggests to us an illustration of the new birth of a soul.

I. **He was the Gift of God** (v. 3). What they could not do through the weakness of the flesh, God in grace accomplished. Of the new nature it is said, "Born not of blood, nor of the will of the flesh, nor of the will of man, *but of God*" (John 1. 13). Every regenerated soul is the gift of God to a dark and desolate world, another light in its darkness, another witness for God.

II. **He was Born Free from Hereditary Defect**. The mother was solemnly warned to "drink not wine nor strong drink, and to eat not any unclean thing" (v. 4). The physical body, as the temple of this God-given spirit, must be pure and worthy of it. Those who would travail in birth for souls must take heed to their manner of life, and touch not the unclean. This is the human side; there is another: "That which is born of the Spirit is spirit." The soul that is born from above, born of God, cannot possess any hereditary blemish. Such is made a partaker of the divine nature (2 Peter 1. 4). "Whatsoever is born of God doth not commit sin; for his seed remaineth in him; and he cannot sin, because he is born of God" (1 John 3. 9).

III. His Birth was Connected with Sacrifice and Wonder-working. "The offering was put upon a rock, and the angel did *wondrously*, and ascended in the flame of the altar" (vv. 19, 20). Observe these three things: (1) The *offering*; (2) the *wonder-working*; (3) the *ascension* by way of the altar flame. How suggestive all this is of the *death*, and *resurrection*, and *ascension* of Jesus Christ our Lord, by the virtue of which every child of God is born. His *offering* upon the Cross, the *wonder-working* of His resurrection power and glory, His *ascension* into Heaven, with the *marks* of the Cross in His hands and feet, just as it were *"in the flame of the altar."* "Manoah and his wife looked on, and fell on their faces to the ground" (v. 20). So well may we at this great sight (Ezek. 1. 28).

IV. He was Separated unto God. "The child shall be a Nazarite unto God" (v. 5). His separation was not by vow, but by birth (Num. 6. 5). If we have been "born of God," created anew in Christ Jesus, surely that is enough in itself to teach us that we should be separated in our lives from a world of sin and iniquity. Separation has two aspects. 1. We are separated by the will of God, according to His purpose with us (Lev. 20. 24). 2. We are to be separated by our own definite act, a deliberate and continual *choice* of God's will concerning us (2 Cor. 6. 17). When the precious is separated from the vile, then the testimony will be as the mouth of God (Jer. 15. 19). It was *after* Abraham was separated from worldly Lot that God came with His promise (Gen. 13; 14).

V. He was Blessed by the Lord. "And the child grew, and the Lord blessed him" (v. 24). His name was called Samson—*sunny*. Like the sun. The separated life is a *blessed* life, made sunny with the brightness of His presence. Is all this not needed by us if we are to grow like as our Saviour did, "in favour with God and man?" (Luke 2. 52). Many of Samson's acts and sayings reveal an almost playfulness of spirit that seems to indicate a bright sunny disposition. A sunny life is a powerful life. "The *joy* of the Lord is your *strength*." The separated life is to be a sunny life. Such was the life of our blessed Lord and Saviour—separated, shiny. Though His face was marred, the *light* of His life was unsullied. The blessing of the Lord it maketh rich. It made Samson rich in cheerfulness and strength, and according to Hebrews 11. 32 he was made strong through *faith*. "According to your faith be it unto you."

VI. He was Moved by the Spirit. "The Spirit of the Lord began to move him at times" (v. 25). These periodical *agitatings* of heart by the Spirit of God were premonitory indications of the purposes of God with him, and an inward witness of his separation unto the Lord. It is of the utmost importance that those who have separated themselves unto God should recognise the agitatings of the Holy Spirit in the heart. What may appear to be but a passing thought or feeling may be nurtured into a mighty and far-reaching purpose. The glories of midday splendour are ushered in by what seems to be but struggling rays of light. As soon as Jesus separated Himself unto the will of God as His Servant He was led by the Spirit (Matt. 4. 1). They live a spiritually monotonous life indeed who know nothing of the moving of the waters of the soul, betimes, by the brooding Spirit of God. The victorious Christian can say with Paul "I can do all things through Christ which strengtheneth me" (Phil. 4. 13).

SAMSON'S LIFE AND DEATH.

Judges 14;-16.

"What Heaven bestows, with thankful eyes receive;
First ask thy heart, and then through faith believe;
Slowly we wander o'er a toilsome way,
Shadows of life, and pilgrims of a day.
'Who restless on this world receives a fall,'
Look up on high, and *trust* thy God for all."—CHAUCER.

THE fuller the cup the more easily is it to spill the contents. The higher the spiritual privilege the more need for lowliness of walk before God. The stronger we are the greater the temptation to *trust* in our strength. The more frequently the Spirit of God moves us the more powerfully will the world and the flesh oppose us. The life of Samson alternates with light and shade. A Nazarite who seemed to be partially *unconscious* of the sacredness of his life, a fatal flaw in his character as a servant in the work of God. "*Know ye not* that Christ dwelleth in you?" Let us look at his—

I. **Amazing Exploits.** "He rent a young lion like a kid" (chap. 14. 6). "With the jawbone of an ass he slew a thousand men" (chap. 15. 15). "He carried away the gates of the city of Gaza" (chap. 16. 3). In Samson that promise was literally fulfilled: "*One man* of you shall chase a thousand" (Joshua 23. 10). It is as easy for God to work with *one* man as with three hundred (Judges 7. 7). Samson had no followers; he asked for none. He alone was commissioned and empowered; he alone must do it. In olden times God usually began with *one man*. Jesus began with two (John 1. 37). We will never do exploits for God if we wait on others to help us. One man in the power of the Spirit is always equal to the occasion. "Greater is He that is in you than he that is in the world." The weapons used by Samson were worthy of the mighty Spirit of the Lord. "Foolish and base things" (1 Cor. 1. 27-29).

II. Superhuman Strength. "Delilah said to Samson,
Tell me, I pray thee, wherein thy great strength lieth"
(chap. 16. 6). Samson was not a giant; his great strength
did not, therefore, lie in an arm of flesh. No human
muscle can be developed into spiritual power. The secret
of his great strength lay in the presence of the Almighty
Spirit of God with him, as one consecrated to the will of
God. "Ye shall receive the power of the Holy Ghost
coming upon you, and ye shall be witnesses unto Me"
(Acts 1. 8). This is still the secret of the *great strength* of
any servant of Jesus Christ, and it may be yours. This
great strength cannot be purchased by intellectual wisdom
or social position. It is the gift of God (Acts 8. 18-20),
and should be to our souls what our physical strength is to
our bodies, only in a superhuman degree, the mighty power
of God.

III. Sore Temptation. "She pressed him daily with
her words, and urged him, so that his soul was vexed unto
death" (chap. 16. 16). You will notice that the whole
force of this temptress' energy is brought to bear upon
that *one thing* that distinguished Samson from other men,
"Wherein thy great strength lieth" (v. 15). In falling in
love with Delilah he deliberately steps into the fires of trial.
This was clearly an unequal yoke; from the very first she
sought his ruin as a Nazarite (vv. 5, 6), and proved herself
an enemy to the divine purpose in the life of Samson. It
is a melancholy sight to see one trifling so with the *secret* of
his power for God. Unholy alliances are deadly enemies to
spiritual power. Whatever would mar our relationship
with God must be looked upon as the poison of a serpent.
Our strongest point for God will be the point most incess-
antly assaulted by the devil and the Spirit-resisting world.
"Call upon ME in the day of trouble" (Psa. 50. 15).

IV. Complete Failure. "She made him *sleep* upon her
knees; and he awoke, and said, I will go out, as at other

times, and shake myself. But he wist not that the Lord was departed from him'' (chap. 16. 19, 20). While he slept his locks were cut off, and his strength went from him. He *shakes himself* as at other times, but it is only *himself* he shakes. The mighty enemy-shaking power of the presence of the Lord was gone. He is now but a *withered branch*, fit to be cast into the fire at the hands of *men* (John 15. 6). When the Spirit of God is grieved our defence as servants is gone (Num. 14. 9). When the Spirit of the Lord departed from Saul, at that moment he began to fall (1 Sam. 18. 12). His strength lay not in his locks, but that head that had never felt the touch of a razor was a *witness* of his consecration to the will of God. In losing his hair he lost his *testimony* for God. The power of the Spirit of God alone can make us true witnesses for Christ. Without this we may shake ourselves in feverish effort, but this will only reveal our utter weakness. For a servant of Christ to be as *weak as other men* is doing dishonour to the Spirit of God. Samson is not the only servant of God who has lost his power through worldliness and self-indulgence (v. 19). Much of the powerless preaching of to-day may be traced to the same cause. No one can possibly fail in the work of the Lord who lives and acts in the power of the Holy Spirit (Phil. 2. 13).

V. Terrible Bondage. ''The Philistines took him, and put out his eyes, and bound him with fetters of brass; and he did grind in the prison-house'' (chap. 16. 21). He was betrayed by the woman whom he *loved*, and on whose knees he slept the fatal sleep. The pleasures of sin always deliver over its votaries to spiritual *blindness* and *bondage*. Poor Samson. How are the mighty fallen! Let us take warning, and beware of worldly pleasures that ensnare the soul to the grieving of the Holy Ghost. Is there none among us whose service for God and His Christ is performed under the same conditions as Samson worked in the prison-house of Gaza? *Blind* and *fettered* servants, to whom the house of prayer becomes as a prison, a place to be got out of as soon as possible. We have neither *eyes* to see nor *liberty* to serve, unless we are filled with the Holy Spirit. Apart from this the Lord's work will become a drudgery and a slavery. Prison grinders instead of triumphant warriors.

VI. Final Victory. "And Samson called unto the Lord," etc. (chap. 16. 28-30). Out of the depths of his sorrow and helplessness he cried unto the Lord. This is the only time we read of him acknowledging the Lord. His urgent and pitiful request is granted. "His hair began to grow again" (v. 22); his *separation unto God* began to appear once more. If we have lost our power for God there is only one way whereby it can be restored—confession and fresh consecration. Samson's dying cry was for one more manifestation of the old power, that he might die as a victor; and like Jesus Christ, our *unfailing* Conqueror, by the grace of God he overcame more by his *death* than his life. Our own restoration to God must precede the in-gathering of souls (Psa. 51. 12, 13).

THE YOUNG PROBATIONER.
Judges 17; 18.

> "The highest honours that the world can boast
> Are subjects far too low for my desire;
> Its brightest gleams of glory are, at most,
> But dying sparkles of Thy living fire;
> Without Thee, Lord, things be not what they be,
> Nor have their being when compared with Thee."
> —QUARLES.

"IN those days there was no king in Israel, but every man did that which was right *in his own eyes*" (chap. 17. 6). Our own eyes are about the poorest guides under Heaven. "He that trusteth in his own heart is a fool." These chapters tell a sorrowful tale of social, religious, and moral corruption. What foolish and sinful creatures we are when the guiding hand of God is not with us! Such were some of us, but ye are washed. The old self-life, even *religious* life, is just the doing of that which is *right in our own eyes*. When Saul said, "What wilt Thou have me to do?" he had given up walking in the light of his own eyes. The nameless young man brought before us here is worthy of close study on account of—

I. **Character.** "A young man who was a Levite" (chap. 17. 7). According to Numbers 8 the Levites were *called of God*, separated and sanctified for the work of the Lord. Their work was to look after the different parts of the Tabernacle when the pillar of cloud moved, and to *rebuild* this House of God. They were God's separated ones for His own service (Num. 4. 15-33).

II. **Purpose.** "He said, I go to sojourn where I may find a place" (chap. 17. 9). He is on the outlook for a call; he has no desire to spend the time in idleness. He is an industrious and perhaps conscientious young man; hoping that if he could only find *a place* he might be helpful in some way. It is a sure sign that the House of God is in ruins when the professed servants of God are seeking work at the hands of men. It was otherwise in the days of Moses and Joshua; it was otherwise also in the days of Christ and His apostles. It is the *Lord of the harvest* who is to send out labourers. *Pray ye Him* (Matt. 9. 38). How often young men are pleaded with to go. Why not *pray* the Lord the Spirit to send them? (Acts 13. 2).

III. **First Call** "Micah said unto him, Dwell with me, and be unto me a priest, and I will give thee ten shekels of silver by the year, and a suit of apparel, and thy victuals. So he went in" (chap. 17. 10). Tired of his itinerancy, he accepted the first offer. It was not a large place, only a small congregation (one family), and a small salary. The living was worth about £1 a year with board and lodgings.

He had been doing nothing for a while, "so he went in." Although the loaves were small and the fishes few, there would be connected with the charge some personal dignity and profit. Had he not been a traitor to God he could not have ministered in such a house, for it was full of idols (v. 5), and Micah himself was a superstitious idolater. But doubtless the "ten shekels," etc., shut the mouth of the Levite. He is more concerned about his own personal advantage than the cause of God. A mere hireling (chap. 18. 4).

IV. **Ordination**. "And Micah consecrated the Levite" (chap. 17. 11-13). The root idea of *consecration* seems to be to "fill the hands," so that the worship or service may be abundantly acceptable in the sight of God (1 Chron. 29. 5, marg.). This was the chief aspect in the consecration of Aaron and his sons. Then how could Micah, a worshipper of idols, *fill the hands* of the Levite with that which is pleasing unto God? No more can ye, except ye are filled with the Holy Ghost. But the young minister seemed perfectly satisfied with this hollow and *empty* consecration. What is the value of such empty hands laid on the empty head of him who has an empty heart? "Without *Me* ye can do nothing."

V. **Translation**. Then the Danites said unto him, "Hold thy peace, and go with us; it is better for thee to be a priest to a *tribe* than to *one man*. And the priest's heart was glad, and he went" (chap. 18. 19, 20). This was a call to a larger sphere of labour on the condition that he should "hold his peace" and not expose their criminal craftiness. He accepted the call, virtually promising to keep his mouth shut on the sin of stealing. A man-made minister is only a minister *after man* (see Gal. 1. 10-12). If a man has no revelation from God he has no commission from Him. We must *see* Jesus if we are to be *witnesses* for Him. The *fear of man* bringeth a snare. An enlarged sphere of usefulness did not improve in any way the faithless Levite; it only served to show more fully his godless and time-serving spirit. Higher positions and larger congregations are not enough to make a successful ministry. A self-seeking servant of Christ will always be powerless in the presence of ungodliness and open iniquity.

VI. **Successors.** "The children of Dan set up the graven image; and Jonathan and his sons were priests to the tribe of Dan" (chap. 18. 30, 31). The unprincipled young Levite suddenly drops out of sight as a lifeless, worthless thing. He has wrought no reform amongst the idolatrous Danites; he has left no faithful example behind him. He came as an unclean bird, devoured so much flesh, and flew off we know not where. But *Micah's graven image* still stands in their midst and usurps the place of the God of Israel. His successor was no better than himself. In this instance it was "like people, like priest." The utter worthlessness of an unspiritual ministry is here revealed, the need of being baptised in the Holy Ghost is strongly implied (John 15. 16, 26, 27).

COUNSEL FOR BACKSLIDERS.

"Let us search and try our ways, and turn again to the Lord" (Lam. 3. 40).

1. This is a **needful** work. "Turn again." Implying that we have turned *away* from the Lord (Rom. 3. 12).

2. This is a **personal** work. "Let us." Self-examination needed (1 Cor. 11. 28).

3. This must be a **careful** work. "Search." Search the motives and the *condition* of heart that has fostered them (Psa. 51. 6).

4. This is a **humbling** work. "Try *our ways*" (Psa. 26. 2; 1 John 1. 9).

5. This will be a **profitable** work. "Turn again *to the Lord*" (Heb. 10. 19, 20).

EXPOSITORY OUTLINES.
New Testament.

THE CALL OF JOHN.
Luke 3. 1-6.

> "Pleasure-seeking only,
> Though others be lonely;
> Dressing, drinking, eating,
> The soul madly cheating;
> Scorning the love unpriced,
> So we shall not be missed."

A LIFE is poorly lived indeed that is not missed when gone. Those most anxious to obtrude *themselves* before their fellows seem to leave no gap behind them when they die. John the Baptist sought no place for himself, but God lifted him up as a trumpet, putting him, as it were, to His mouth, and, filling him with His own divine breath, made him the *voice* of God. Luke, as an historian, is very precise in giving us here, in a few words, the outward historical setting of John's life, but we tarry not to look at the framework, beautiful and wonderful as it is. We seek to point out—

I. **When this Call Came.** It came to John while *"in the wilderness"* (v. 2). Into this desert or sparsely peopled part of the valley of Jordan John had evidently gone, that there alone he might learn more fully what the mind of the Lord was concerning him. To *improve* our time we have often to *cease* working and get alone with God, especially when we realise that some definite purpose of God concerning us is breaking in upon our minds and hearts. Take time to be holy. Wait on the Lord. Enter thy closet and shut to the door.

II. **How this Call Came.** "The Word of God came unto John" (v. 2). How the Word of God came to him we are not told. He being filled with the Holy Ghost from his birth, and as his early longings and convictions ripened into settled purposes, the revelation was made to him that this was God's work within him, and God's Word to be uttered through him. How often has the Word of God come to us in this way! When old familiar truths have suddenly flashed up with a new glory and urgency, bringing a fresh message from the Lord to the soul.

III. **The Effect Produced.** "And he came preaching the baptism of repentance for the remission of sins" (v. 3). He was not disobedient to the heavenly vision. When the Word of God burns within the bones the most *unpopular* methods may be adopted, but with sterling success. His mission was not to save, but to preach baptism as the outward sign of a repentant heart, preparing the way of the Lord for their remission of sins. Those who had submitted to his baptism were afterwards pointed to the "Lamb of God, which taketh away the sin of the world" (John 1. 29).

IV. **The Character of his Testimony.** There was—

1. A FULFILLING OF PROPHECY. "As it is written in the book of the words of Esaias the prophet" (v. 4). It is quite clear that John recognised and confessed that this Scripture was fulfilled in him before their eyes (John 1. 23), just as his Master did with regard to Isaiah 61 (Luke 4. 21). Every truly consecrated life is a fulfilling, or filling full, of the Word of God. It shall not return void or empty when our hearts and souls are in it.

2. AN ABANDONMENT OF SELF. "The voice of one crying out in the wilderness" (v. 4). John said, "*I am* the *voice* of one crying," etc. (John 1. 23). John was the Word made *voice*. Christ was the Word made flesh. The message that came through Isaiah over 700 years ago is now *voiced* through John by the power of the Holy Ghost. He who would be a herald of Christ must be content to be

a voice, and that voice not his own. The polluting breath of self-assertiveness must not be in it if its tones are to be pure and heavenly. "Not I, but Christ in me." John's was not a voice singing, but a voice *crying* in the wilderness, as one in an agony for the will of God. Those who so sigh and *cry* will have the divine mark set upon them (Ezek. 9. 4).

3. A GLORIFICATION OF CHRIST. "Prepare ye the way of the Lord," etc. (v. 4). John is not concerned about his own way, but is intensely interested in "the way of the Lord." John honours Christ. 1. As the *pre-eminent* One. The glory of Christ fills the broad horizon of his vision, and occupies both hemispheres of his soul. His *way* and His *paths*. 2. As the *filling* One. "Every valley shall be filled" (v. 5). He fills up the valleys by *exalting* them (Isa. 40. 4). He feeds the hungry by lifting them up into His own fulness. No matter how deep and wide the chasm of our need may be He can fill up out of His own "unsearchable riches." 3. As the *humbling* One. "Every mountain and hill shall be brought low" (v. 5). The lofty pride of Saul was suddenly brought low on the way to Damascus (Acts 9). He brings down that He might raise up. 4. As the *upright* One. "The crooked shall be made straight." Every son of God was once part of a crooked nation (Phil. 2. 15). It takes an upright one to straighten out the crooks in others, and to the crooked this may be, and often is, a painful and shameful process. He suffered, the Just for the unjust, that He might bring us to God. 5. As the *comforting* One. "The rough ways shall be made smooth" (v. 2). *Rough ways* have caused many to faint and be discouraged. Rough ways are very common, and many even of God's children go on sad and wearily. Do we know Christ as the Smoother of our ways? "They looked unto Him, and were lightened." He is the "Breaker up" of our way, and can make the rough places smooth for

us. The Israelites had light in their dwellings, while the Egyptians sat in darkness. He does make a difference. 6. *As the universal One.* "All flesh shall see the salvation of God" (v. 6). The good tidings of the Gospel was for all people (Luke 2. 10). God is not a man that He should lie, and He hath said, "As truly as I live, all the earth shall be filled with the glory of the Lord" (Num. 14. 21). This curse-burdened earth is groaning on, waiting for the emancipating day, when the King Himself shall appear as the "blessed and ONLY Potentate," and when all shall know Him, from the least unto the greatest.

THE PREACHING OF JOHN.
Luke 3. 7-18.

"Some angel guide my pencil while I draw
What nothing less than angel can exceed:
A man on earth devoted to the skies;
Like ships in seas, while in, above the world,
With aspect mild and elevated eye.

Behold Him seated on a mount serene,
Above the fogs of sense, and passion's storm;
He sees with other eyes than theirs. Where they
Behold a Sun, he spies a Deity.
They things terrestrial worship as divine!
His hopes, immortal, blow them by as dust."—YOUNG.

THERE is nothing like the glare of Heaven's light for blinding our eyes to the deceitful things of earth. The eyes of John were on the Son of Righteousness, and his tongue a flame of fire. The pure in heart shall see God, and they that see God shall not fear the face of man. The character of John's preaching has many lessons.

I. **A Burning Question.** "He said, O generation of vipers, who hath warned you to flee from the wrath to come?" (v. 7). There is wrath to come, but *who* hath warned *you* that ye have not fled from it through *repentance*. How can ye flee from the wrath to come if ye are not fleeing

from your sins?   The way of repentance is the way into
the Father's bosom (Luke 15. 20).   From *whom* has your
warning come?

II. An Urgent Demand. "Bring forth therefore fruits
worthy of repentance, and begin not to say within yourselves," etc. (v. 8).   It is easier to *say within ourselves*
than to *show* the *fruits* of repentance towards God in our
lives.   Any tree may shake with the wind, but by their
fruits are they known.   Bringing forth fruit unto God is
the evidence that we have fled from the wrath to come.
This pressing claim of the desert preacher has much need
to be emphasised to-day.   Faith, humility, brotherly
love, and zeal for the kingdom of God are fruits worthy
of repentance.

III. A Testing Crisis. "And *now* also the axe is laid
at the root of the tree," etc. (v. 9).   The message of this
forerunner of Christ was as an axe laid at the root of each
tree, and by which each fruitless tree in due time would be
hewn down.   The *words* of John would judge them on the
testing day.   Every time we hear the Gospel of Christ in
the power of God it is, as it were, an axe laid at the *root* of
our life that will be used by the hand of the Judge in cutting
down the fruitless impenitent.   Hath Jesus not declared
that "the *Word* that I have spoken, *the same* shall judge
him on the last day?" (John 12. 48).   "Take heed therefore
how ye hear" (Luke 8. 18)..

IV. A Practical Doctrine. "The *people*, the *publicans*,
and the *soldiers* asked him, saying, What shall we do?"
(vv. 10-14).   The man whose eyes are on the coming Christ
is the most practical man on earth.   Here were three classes
of anxious inquirers.   To the first he preached *brotherly love*
(v. 11), to the second *honesty in business* (v. 13), to the
third *forbearance and contentment* (v. 14).   John's preaching of righteousness led to repentance, but culminated,

as all such preaching ever should, on pointing to the "Lamb of God, which taketh away the sin of the world" (John 1. 29). The repentance that does not lead to the Cross is a repentance that needs to be repented of.

V. A Self-Humbling Confession. "John answered, saying, One mightier than I cometh, the latchet of whose shoes I am not worthy to unloose" (v. 16). John was mighty in righteousness, but Jesus was mightier in grace. The might of a servant of Christ lies in the mightiness of his Master. "One mightier than I *cometh.*" The knowledge of the nearness of the mighty *coming One* filled the heart of John with courage and comfort. The great Spirit and Fire-baptiser was at hand, and the herald is already lost in the brightness of His coming. Present-day preachers crying like a voice in the wilderness of this Christ-rejecting and pleasure-loving world have much need, like John, to know the sustaining power of this heart-bracing truth. "The Lord is at hand." The Almighty King will soon appear. Behold He cometh.

VI. A Soul-Inspiring Proclamation. "He shall baptise you with the Holy Ghost and with fire" (v. 16). The marginal rendering of the Revised Version is *"in"* instead of *"with."* John baptised with water as an outward evidence of repentance. Jesus Christ baptises with the Holy Ghost as an *inward* assurance of for-. giveness and acceptance (Rom. 8. 16). To be baptised with or in the Holy Ghost means the entering of the soul into a holy, heavenly, illuminating atmosphere, where the things of God and eternity are clearly seen. It is a passing from darkness into *His marvellous light.* To live in the Spirit is to live in the glowing fire of the divine presence. Here spiritual things become more real than the visible things of earth; here all believers are made to drink into one Spirit (1 Cor. 12. 13). This baptism cannot come through the works of the flesh; it is the gift of the Mighty Ascended One. *"He* shall baptise you." Are *you* so baptised?

VII. A Solemn and Timely Warning. "Whose fan is in His hand. He will gather the wheat; He will burn the chaff" (v 17). He who baptises with the Holy Ghost and fire carries the *fan* in His hand. He who *unites* and enriches with spiritual blessings also *separates* and judges. To come into contact with Christ is to come under the power of His fan. He carries it in His hand, and in a very real sense the purging process is going on now in the lives of those who have come into the baptism of the Holy Ghost. But the time will come when He will thoroughly purge the Church as *"His floor,"* the sphere in which He has in grace been operating by the Holy Spirit, and where the lifeless chaff and the precious wheat meanwhile lie mingled in a confused heap. The fan is *in His hand,* so that He Himself must come before the final sifting can take place. He shall separate the precious from the vile (Mal. 3. 3). The wheat and the tares are allowed to grow *together* until the harvest (Matt. 13. 30). His wheat is gathered into "His garner," but the empty chaff He will not own, but appoints it to the "fire unquenchable" (Matt. 25. 46).

THE CHRISTIAN LIFE.
Luke 4. 1-13.

"We mourn, Lord, that our wav'ring will
So oft invites the tempter's skill;
We must confess that still we find
Some fleshy lusts war 'gainst the mind;
O break our chain, Lord, set us free,
Thou tempted once, us tempted see."

JESUS CHRIST was tempted on all points like as we are. How He met the tempter in the wilderness reveals to us some of those principles that lie at the root of every Christ-like life, also teaching us something of what is meant by the "armour of God" (Eph. 6. 11). We shall look at these *sayings* of our Lord as a summary of the characteristics of a Christian life. It is—

I. A Life not of this World. "Man shall not live by bread alone" (v. 4). *"Bread alone"* may stand for all that goes to satisfy the natural cravings of man. It is possible to possess all that this world can furnish, and yet be destitute of *life* in this deep and divine sense. That which is "born from above" must also be supplied from above. We must ever distinguish between soul and spirit. Material things will satisfy the soulish life, but not the spiritual. You hath He quickened, who were dead.

II. A Life of Faith. "Man shall not live by bread alone, *but by every word of God."* The words of God are spirit and life, and so become food for the inner man (John 6. 63). "Thy Word hath quickened me" (Psa. 119. 50). "Thy words were found, and I did eat them, and Thy Word was unto me the joy and rejoicing of mine heart" (Jer. 15. 16). The Word of God is always sweet to the taste of faith. While we feed on the Word of God faith itself will be fed, for faith cometh by hearing, and hearing by the Word of God (Rom. 10. 17).

III. A Life of Adoration. "Thou shalt *worship* the Lord thy God" (v. 8). This was our Lord's answer to the devil when he offered Him the glory of "all the kingdoms of the world" on condition that He worshipped him. The *glory* of this Christ-rejecting world is only the mirage of the devil. Any one who worships him may easily have the promise of it. The glory of this world *passeth away.* Whoever or whatever has the worship of our hearts is by us crowned as Lord of all we are. "Thou shalt have no other god before ME."

IV. A Life of Service. "Him only shalt thou serve" (v. 8). "One is your Master, even Christ" (Matt. 23. 8).

The will of God ought to be supreme in the life of every Christian. "Ye call Me Master and Lord, and ye say well: for *so I am.*" He can take no other place than that of being "Head over all." In our daily work and calling are we conscious that we serve Him only? Doing all as for Him will lift the commonest drudgery into a work so holy that angels might covet. This is the cure for a grumbling spirit, and an unfailing remedy for the prevailing sin of discontent.

V. A Life of Humble Obedience. "Thou shalt not tempt the Lord thy God" (v. 12). The Lord charged His people in the wilderness with tempting Him "ten times" by *not hearkening unto His voice* (Num. 14. 22). Our unbelief and disobedience sorely tempt the loving kindness of our God. What could try a true mother's heart like the doubting of her love? How would a faithful husband feel if treated by his wife like an untrustworthy stranger? Let us cease to tempt the Lord our God by hearkening unto other voices and walking in the light of our own eyes. Has He not declared, "This is My beloved Son, in whom I am well pleased?" "*Hear ye Him.*" Thou shalt not tempt the Lord thy God with thy discontent, thy doubtings, and thy unbelief.

VI. An Overcoming Life. "The devil departed from Him" (v. 13). The victory was gained by the sword of the Spirit, which is the Word of God, "It is written." The Word of God is the sword of the Spirit, not only because He uses it, but also because He is the Maker of it. "Holy men of old spake as they were moved by the Holy Ghost" (2 Peter 1. 21). Jesus fearlessly used the *written* Word against the archenemy of souls. We may as confidently use it against all his modern little angels. "In all these things we are more than conquerors through Him that loved us" (Rom. 8. 37). "Thanks be to God, which giveth us the victory through our Lord Jesus Christ" (1 Cor. 15. 57).

A POWERFUL SERMON.
Luke 4. 14-30.

"Nazareth, O Nazareth!
Tho' a name of evil holding,
Here was brought 'The Undefiled,'
Like a dove a serpent folding,
Here grew up 'The Holy Child.'
Nazareth! Cross—like we see
Thy stained name from all stain free."

IT was said, "Can any good thing come out of Nazareth?" But ever since these words were uttered the name has become sacred because of its association with Jesus Christ. In fact, there is a heaven-born principle here, viz., *everything* with which Jesus Christ identifies Himself becomes holy, no matter how small and disreputable it may be in the sight of men. Palestine is called the Holy Land just because the feet of the Holy One trod upon it. A sinner out of whom no good thing could ever come may become holy in the self-same way by coming into *contact* with Jesus. If Nazareth lost its stain of sin through the Name of Jesus, so may we.

"Take the Name of Jesus with you,
Child of sorrow and of woe;
It will joy and comfort give you,
Take it then *where'er* you go."

Anywhere and everywhere His Name is a *saving* Name. Let it be then as the "new cruse" of salt to sweeten every bitter spring in our lives (2 Kings 2. 20, 21). The picture before us is beautiful and impressive.

I. **The Preacher.** "Jesus *returned* in the power of the Spirit into Galilee" (v. 14). Jesus had gone out of Galilee, as others had gone, to the baptism of John, but the coming of the Holy Spirit upon Him and the assault of the devil in the wilderness had wrought a marvellous change upon His public character. "There went out a fame of Him through all the region." He was an obscure

L Vol. IV.

man till He was baptised with the Holy Ghost. So was Peter and the rest of the apostles. The man or woman who *returns* to his or her work in the *power of the Spirit* will not be without manifest tokens of the blessing of God.

II. The Place. "He came to Nazareth, where He had been brought up" (v. 16). He began at home. "Go home. to thy friends, and tell them how great things the Lord hath done for thee" (Mark 5. 19). The first example of piety is to be shown at home (1 Tim. 5. 4). The *home* field is often the most barren. "Neither did His brethren believe in Him." Nevertheless His faithful testimony led many to say, "Whence hath this Man this *wisdom* and these *mighty works?*" (Matt. 13. 54). Wisdom and mighty works characterise all those who are filled with the Spirit.

III. The Text. "And when He had opened the book (roll) He found the place," the place where the lesson was for that day (v. 17). The place was Isaiah 61. 1. The text He found was the prophetic counterpart of *His own experience*. As preachers we may be assured of this, that it is not the will of God that we should preach from texts that have not had their *fulfilment* in our own experience. "We speak that we do know" was the testimony of Jesus (John 3. 11). He had just received the anointing of the Spirit, now He declares it to them.

IV. The Sermon. He began with the application, saying, "This day is this Scripture fulfilled in your ears" (v. 21). The Scripture here referred to is a fountain of living waters (v. 18). Streams of blessing from the *Anointed One* to the *poor*, the *broken-hearted*, the *captives*, the *blind*, and the *bruised*. It was a sermon suited for the needs of all. This is the Gospel of Christ, but it was also heart-searching and convincing. His reference to the Sidonian widow and the Syrian leper (vv. 25-27) magnified the grace of God, while it cut at the roots of their pharisaical pride. He did not plead for their favour or forbearance, but boldly declared that "No prophet is accepted in his own country." The man who has a message from God does not preach to please the people. One of the best things that could happen many Gospel hearers is that they should be tremendously offended.

V. The Results. "That there will be definite results of some kind is a moral certainty when the preacher is anointed with the Holy Spirit." They—

1. WONDERED. "They wondered at the gracious words which proceeded out of His mouth" (v. 22). Men are still more inclined to wonder at *gracious* words than mere philosophical words. The tongue of the divinely learned knows how to speak a word in season to him that is *weary* (Isa. 50. 4). The wisdom that cometh from above is always practical. Those filled with the Holy Ghost have grace poured into their lips (Psa. 45. 2). Gracious words are seldom out of season.

2. WERE FILLED WITH WRATH (v. 28). Their wonder was turned into hate when the searchlight of truth was turned in upon their own hearts. These synagogue members, like many modern Gospel hearers, were quite pleased to hear beautiful words of grace as long as their own personal sins were allowed to remain hidden and untouched. Christ is the Truth as well as the Way.

3. CAST HIM OUT (v. 29). Those who have bad eyes are inclined to blame the sun. There is not much sometimes between man's admiration and disgust. Those who sacrifice the truth of God for the sake of their own proud and selfish ends show that they are animated by the grossest form of tyranny. Oh, the riches of His grace! He whom they cast out has said, "Them that cometh unto Me, I will in no wise cast out."

4. FAILED TO HINDER HIM. "But He passing through

the midst of them *went His way*" (v. 30). Oh, the peerless
dignity of Christ the Truth! He went *His way*, not hindered by the wrath of man any more than the clouds of the
sky could impede the progress of the sun in the heavens.
Sin-blinded man máy thrust the Christ of God out of his
life, but His eternal purpose will still go on its way. Be
not deceived, God is not mocked.

A SCENE IN A SYNAGOGUE.
Luke 4. 33-37.

"O ignorant poor man! what dost thou bear
Lock'd up within the casket of thy breast?
What jewels and what riches hast thou there?
What heavenly treasure in so weak a chest?

Think of her worth, and think that God did mean
This worthy mind should worthy things embrace;
Blot not her beauties with thy thoughts unclean,
Nor her dishonour with thy passion base."
—SIR JOHN DAVIES.

THEY were not all saints who attended the synagogue;
unclean devils are regular hearers. But when Jesus Christ
speaks with power (v. 32) the unclean spirits are sure to
"cry out." There is never much real work done for God
without the roaring of the adversary. The lion roars when
robbed of its whelps. In examining this interesting scene
we shall look at—

I. **The Enemies of Jesus.** There was, first, "the *spirit*
of the unclean devil;" and, second, the *man* who was
possessed of this spirit (v. 33). This "unclean spirit"
uses the will and the mouth of the man for his devilish
purposes, and speaks of the man as one with himself.
"Let us alone. What have *we* to do with Thee?"
Those at enmity with the work and purposes of Jesus
Christ are in league with the devil, and unless there is
a divorce of will and interest the doom of the devil will
be theirs. Listen to their language. They—

1. ACKNOWLEDGE HIS TRUE CHARACTER. "I know Thee who Thou art, the Holy One of God" (v. 34). The confession of this fallen and unclean spirit might put to shame all Unitarian infidels who deny the divinity of Christ. This demon from the pit, in acknowledging Him as "Jesus *of Nazareth*" and the "Holy One *of God*," made confession both of His *humanity* and *divinity*. Christ as the Son of God was *given* (John 3. 16), but as the Son of humanity He was *born* (Isa. 9. 6).

2. QUESTION HIS MISSION. "Art Thou come to destroy us?" (v. 34). Does this unclean devil judge Jesus Christ to be like himself, "coming only to steal and to kill?" How far the purposes of God's grace are above the thoughts of the unclean and the sinful! Although He had come to destroy *us*, devil-polluted ones, who could have charged Him with injustice? But, thank God, "He came to seek and to save" (Luke 19. 10). Ponder this demon-possessed one's question in the light of Isaiah 53 and the glory of His Cross." "Sin is of the devil."

3. SHUN HIS PRESENCE. "What have we to do with Thee?" (v. 34). There is certainly nothing in common between the "Holy One of God" and an "unclean devil." "What communion hath light with darkness?" (2 Cor. 6. 15). Satan and all who are his servants will for ever hate the light because it reproves their deeds (John 3. 21). This question, "What have we to do with Thee?" might be profitably turned into "What hast Thou to do with us?" "He *loved us*, and gave Himself for us!" Better have to do with Him now in mercy than delay till we have to do with Him in judgment.

4. SEEK REST IN THEIR SINS. "Let us alone" (v. 34). This is still the cry of those wedded to the devil and uncleanness. All the Heaven such desire is just to be allowed to lie peaceably on the bed of their carnal pleasures, and when the Gospel of salvation comes knocking at their door

they cry, "Trouble me not, for I am in bed." If Jesus had
come to give men peace in their sins the godless world
would have gladly received Him.

II. The Word of Jesus. The Word of God is quick and
powerful. It is—

1. A Convicting Word. "Jesus rebuked him, saying,
Hold thy peace" (v. 35). The first work of Jesus Christ is
to *silence* the sinner. Such foul mouths must be stopped
(Rom. 3. 19). In the presence of this heart-searching One
every clamorous devil must be speechless. The Word of
Christ turns self-justification into self-condemnation. To
see sinfulness in the light of His holiness is enough to shut
us up to the cry of the leper, "Unclean! unclean!"

2. A Converting Word. Jesus said to the unclean
spirit, "Come out of him." This is the Gospel of Christ,
which is the power of God unto Salvation. There is no
spirit too evil for the overcoming power of Jesus, no soul
too *unclean* for His cleansing blood (1 John 1. 7). No
thought, however proud or polluted, that He cannot cast
out. This Almighty Deliverer can make prisoners of every
enemy that wars against the highest interests of the soul
(2 Cor. 10. 5).

III. The Work of the Devil. "The devil threw him in
the midst" (v. 35). This helpless demon-possessed man
got his *last throw* of the devil in the very presence of the
Saviour. The prince of darkness will never let his subjects
go without a desperate effort to render them useless by
throwing them down. The *hour* and *power* of Satan is sure
to be manifested when the Great Deliverer is at hand; even
at the very *feet of Jesus* the devil will dare to throw a man
down, but this proves his last throw. This bull of Bashan
only threw the man at the feet of the Saviour.

IV. The Victory of Jesus. Jesus said, "Come out of
him," and he came out of him, and hurt him not (v. 35).

If unclean spirits are not exorcised by the word of Jesus Christ, then for man Paradise is lost. Who but He can bring a clean thing out of an unclean? The unclean spirit *came out*, so that *man's soul* was rescued as a prey from the destroying power of the mighty. Ye are *clean* through the *word* which I have spoken unto you. When an unclean devil hears the word of Christ he must obey because he is under *law*. Shall we be less obedient because we are under grace? God forbid!

V. **The Astonished Onlookers**. "They were all amazed, saying, What a word is this" (v. 36). It is possible to be amazed at the "authority and power" of Christ, and yet not be amended. Many are confounded at the manifest power of the Gospel of God who are not converted. Better is it to be a devil-driven soul at the *feet of Jesus* than a mere amazed self-righteous onlooker. To gape and wonder at the overcoming power of the grace of God in others who were worse than ourselves is no token of grace. There are many who devoutly talk about churches, ministers, and religious affairs who are in heart far from the Kingdom of God. "Marvel not that I say unto thee, Ye must be born again." ———

LAUNCH OUT INTO THE DEEP.
Luke 5. 1-10.

"Thy love, O Christ, is boundless,
   More boundless than the sky;
To deepest plummet soundless,
   For Thou for me didst die.
Thy love is 'grace abounding,
   With fulness like the sea;
Still, still it is forth-sounding,
   Glad tidings unto me."

"That ye may know what is the *breadth* and *depth* of the love of Christ" (Eph. 3 18). "Launch out into the deep."

BLESSED light, to see the people *pressing* to hear the Word of God. Oh, that to-day we could witness this soul thirst for the message of life! Blessed anxiety that presses the people to Jesus. He knows how to speak a word to the weary. Grace and truth flow from His lips. Notice here—

I. Devoted Possession. "He entered into Simon's ship, and taught the people out of it" (v. 3). His ship was *ready* for the Master's use. Oh, what an honour to be the means of helping Jesus to reach the pressing crowd! He did this through Simon's ship. How is this same Jesus to reach and teach the heathen millions? Much in the same way, through your possessions. But how few are willing to lend *their all* to the Lord. Simon's loan was abundantly rewarded, even in this life, by the marvellous draught of fishes. Let us not talk boastingly nor think presumptuously about *our* possessions; if we are withholding them from the cause of Christ we are robbing God and our own soul, and what shall it profit? etc.

II. A Gracious Commission. "Launch out, and let down" (v. 4). When Christ takes possession He also gives commission. If you have been sitting fretting over your own *weakness*, "Launch out into the deep" of divine strength. If you are despairing over your own *unworthiness*, launch out into the deep of God's infinite love (Eph. 3. 18, 19), and let down the net of restful trust. If you are floundering in the shallows of your own *feelings*, launch out into the deep of God's faithfulness. The great fishes are in the deep, and those who *launch out* may hope to find them. God's footsteps are in the deep, and there His wonders are seen (Psa. 107. 24). Are you a preacher? Then, like Paul, you will be all the better of being a "night and a day in the deep" before coming forth to the people. Come with a heart filled with the *treasures of the deep*, the deep things of God (1 Cor. 2. 10).

III. A Humbling Confession. "We have toiled all night, and taken nothing" (v. 5). It is always very trying after honestly and earnestly toiling and struggling all the night to catch men to find you have taken nothing But this is not all *loss*, for even *then* we are in a better condition for giving God the glory when *He* gives the blessing. Are you ashamed to confess your failure in the past? Would you fain hide the fact that your labour has been fruitless? Surely not! Like Simon, confess it to Jesus, for this is necessary before the launching out on the tack of faith. Tell Him all that is in thine heart, keep nothing back. He has a remedy for your weakness and failure. He can turn your mourning into dancing (Psa. 30. 11).

IV. **A God-honouring Resolution.** "Nevertheless at *Thy* word I will" (v. 5). The way to victory is the pathway of faith. Simon's *feelings* said, "It's no use; I've toiled all *night*, the most likely season, and taken nothing;" but Simon's *faith* says, "Nevertheless." This was not a point to be *reasoned*, but simply *believed*. Christian toiler, let not the past hinder the present. Like Simon, make a fresh start on *the authority of Jesus*. Peter knows now *where* to find "launch out." He knows now *how* to find "*At Thy word*." Those who go out at *His word* will have good cause to praise Him. Unbeliever, your case is sad, toiling and struggling in the darkness of night, thinking by your own efforts to gain God's blessing and taking nothing. Here is the more excellent way, "*At Thy word I will*."

V. **An Amazing Satisfaction.** "They inclosed a great multitude" (v. 6). This time they are more successful "*out of season*" than they were before "in season." The word of Christ believed made all the difference. They had the *habit* of fishing at night; but sometimes our *old forms* have to be broken through before we can see the power of Jesus manifested. If Simon had contended for the form he would have lost the haul. Ah, yes, soul-satisfying fulness through the power of Christ can only be enjoyed in the way of doing His will in His presence. Let not habits, forms, or customs, however good, stand in the way of doing what now plainly appears to be the will of your Lord. Follow Him, and He will satisfy the longing soul (Psa. 107. 9).

VI. **A Brotherly Co-operation.** "They beckoned unto their partners, and they came and *filled* both ships" (v. 7). Had they not invited their brothers to co-operate, how much would have been lost? Alas, how much is still being lost in Christian work for lack of union! What hinders it? Pride and selfishness. The blessing came to Simon's boat, through faith in Christ, but He did not mean it all to remain there. Others were needing as well as he, so he beckoned his brethren to come and help. Notice, it is the *helpers* that share the results. If pastors do not come to help in the times of blessings they need not wonder although they should not gather much of the fruit. When will churches, like these boats, *come together*, and gather the fruits of the promise of Christ?

VII. **An Unfeigned Humiliation.** "I am a sinful man, O Lord" (v. 8). This is always the effect where His greatness and goodness are realised. The *goodness* of God leads to repentance. God forbid that success should ever lead to pride and self-sufficiency. And yet sometimes it **does** on the part of Christian workers. Has the goodness of God, as seen on the Cross, ever led you to cry "I am a sinful man?" If so, you need not say, like Simon, "Depart from me," when He says "Come unto Me." If you are a sinful man, Jesus is the sinful sinner's Saviour. In bidding *Him* depart you know not what ye do.

VIII. **A Complete Consecration.** "They forsook *all*, and followed Him" (v. 11). You would have thought that they had as much here as would have satisfied them for a long while, but, no, they "*forsook all.*" We are not to *live* on our *experience*, no matter how wonderfully gracious it may be. We must forget the things that are behind, and press on to follow and to know. We cannot feed on the souls we win for Jesus, however precious or numerous. We must learn to follow Jesus for our joy and strength; our life is in Him only. Friend, where art thou? Are you still sitting by your boat gloating over your good works and past accomplishments, loving *these* more than Christ; or are you sitting mending the meshes of broken resolutions after much fruitless effort? In either case, hear the Master's call, and arise and follow Jesus (Phil. 3. 7, 8).

THE LEPER CLEANSED.
Luke 5. 12-15.

"What though my harp and vial be
Both hung upon the willow tree?
What though my bed be now my grave,
And for my house I darkness have?

What though my healthful days are fled,
And I lie numbered with the dead?
Yet I have hope by *Thy great power*,
To spring—though now a withered flower.'"

—HERRICK.

"I AM the Resurrection and the Life; he that believeth on Me, though he were dead, yet shall he live." This is Heaven's jubilee note of hope for the inmates of this great, needy world. Man's withered hopes are resurrected at His touch, and the leprous breath of the unclean made sweet by His grace. He can turn the dolorous cry "Unclean" into joyful songs of praise. He is as merciful and mighty on the lonely sea (**v. 8**) as in the crowded city (**v. 12**). Wherever the presence of Jesus Christ is there is *"the power of God."* Observe his—

I. **Miserable Condition.** "A man full of leprosy" (v. 12). His terrible disease had reached its final stage; he was now *full* of leprosy. Like sin, this loathsome malady may work slowly, but its course is irresistible and deadly. It poisons the blood, and so the whole physical being becomes polluted. Sin affects the heart, out of which are the issues of life   In the early ages the Church of Rome regarded lepers as dead, and had "the rites" said over them. There is a law in France that such shall be disinherited. A man living in sin is a man dead to God, and disinherited of Heaven's love and peace.

II. Inspiring Revelation. "Who seeing Jesus" (v. 12). *Seeing Jesus* will never fail to awaken hope in the darkened, sin-crushed heart. He had doubtless heard of Christ's "mighty works" without ever uttering a prayer; but now those dull, despairing eyes suddenly brighten with a new light as they gaze upon the living Person of the merciful Wonder-worker. He believed the report, and faith has been turned into *sight*. What a contrast is here between the Man "full of compassion" and the man "full of leprosy;" between a seeking Saviour and a seeking sinner!

III. Humble Position. "He fell on his face" (v. 12). Seeing the face of God always makes us hide our own. It is the outward expression of a deep inward conviction. It was so with Isaiah (chap. 6), with Job (chap. 42. 5, 6), with Peter (Luke 5. 8), and with John (Rev. 1. 17). They are only lip-professing Pharisees, who *stand* afar off. We have never seen ourselves as in His sight if we have not been overwhelmed in the dust through shame.

IV. Earnest Petition. "Lord, if Thou wilt, Thou canst make me clean" (v. 12). The prayer of this poor outcast was more to the point than that of Peter the disciple (see v. 8). This prayer reveals—

1. A KNOWLEDGE OF THE CHARACTER OF CHRIST. Out of this knowledge there springs up an intelligent faith in His power. "If Thou wilt *Thou canst*." "Is anything too hard for the Lord?" (Gen. 18. 14). To doubt His divinity and almightiness is to knock at a locked door. He that cometh to God must believe that He is a rewarder of them who diligently seek Him (Heb. 11. 6)   This petition brings out also—

2. THE ONE BURNING DESIRE OF THE LEPER. "To be made *clean*." He frankly confesses his need, and pleads for personal cleansing. It was the work of the High Priest of old to make atonement, that the people might be clean from *all their sins* before the Lord (Lev. 16. 30). If we confess our sins He is faithful and just to forgive us.

V. Instant and Perfect Salvation. "He put forth His hand, and touched him, saying, I will: be thou clean. And immediately the leprosy departed from him" (v. 13). Every miracle is linked on to the "*I will*" of Jesus Christ. Before the critics can eliminate the miraculous from the Bible they must turn out the "I wills" of the Son of God. These few words of our Lord are weighted with precious meaning. There was the—

1. ATONING TOUCH. "He touched him." The holiness of God comes into contact with man in all his defilement. But the Holy One, like the light which shineth in darkness, is not in any way defiled by the touch. He who bore our sins was no sinner. As never man spake like this Man, so never man *touched* like this Man. All the resources of the Godhead are in the touch of Christ.

2. ASSURING WORD. "I will: be thou clean." With His healing touch comes His word of assurance. We are saved by His blood, and assured by His word. His touch of love is accompanied with His word of power. He speaks, and it is done.

3. COMPLETE DELIVERANCE. "Immediately the leprosy *departed* from him." *Where* the leprosy went would not trouble him. The joy of salvation was now his. Our sins are said to be cast behind His back and buried in the depths of the sea. Where God's back is, or how deep the sea is, need not concern us, since they have departed from us through the almighty grace of God.

VI. Special Commission. "Go and show thyself unto the priest, and offer" (v. 14). In showing *himself* unto the priest, and *offering* according as Moses commanded, he was bearing "a testimony unto them" that Jesus Christ came not to set aside the law, but to fulfil it. The work of Christ can stand the minutest inspection, not only of the law and the prophets, but also of the world and the devil. Go, show thyself, if so be that *thyself* hath experienced His perfect cleansing from the power of sin. Every saved soul should be a testimony unto Him.

STRANGE THINGS.
Luke 5. 17-26.

"The Lord lacketh nothing; yet maketh—
　　Maketh power in weakness;
　　So that this fallen race of ours basketh—
　　Basketh in His meekness."

"WE have seen strange things to-day," was the language of some of those who were eye-witnesses to the healing and forgiving of this poor palsied sinner. Christianity will always be a "strange thing" to a gaping, godless world. The saving, healing power of Christ will never cease to awaken amazement in the minds of men. Christ Himself is to many the most perplexing wonder of all. The mystery of the divine working in the soul of man is the mystery of the incarnation. It is as easy for Christ to create a world as to forgive a sinner. Each is equally *strange*. But what were some of the "strange things" that they saw that day?

I. An Unlettered Man Teaching. Those who heard Him in the synagogue said, "Whence hath this Man this wisdom?" (Matt. 13. 54). While He taught in the Temple the Jews marvelled, saying, "How knoweth this Man letters, having never learned?" (John 7. 15). Here we have Him teaching in the presence of "doctors of the law." Christ, who is the wisdom of God, said of Himself, "I am from *above*, ye are from *beneath*." A man may be "lettered" and "scholarly," and yet blind to the wisdom that comes from above through the eyesalve of the Holy Ghost (Rev. 3. 18). To be *taught of God* is the heritage of every soul that has been born from above.

II. A Sick Man let Down through a Roof (v. 19). Those who really believe in Jesus will some way or other bring their burdens to His feet, as those four men brought the helpless paralytic. Whatever *burdens* us should lead to the breaking up of everything that stands between us and Jesus. Such roof breaking is sure to appear as needless waste to those who stand unconcerned, with no burden of grief, no pressing request on behalf of a wasted life. If we have no burden of our own, let the need of others bring us into His presence.

III. A Man Forgiving Sins. "He said unto him, Thy sins are forgiven thee" (v. 20). What? A *Man* forgiving SINS! "Who can forgive sins but God alone?" This is a strange thing. Yes, it is. Had not JEHOVAH said, "I, even I, am He that blotteth out thy transgressions, and will not remember thy sins?" (Isa. 43. 25). Who is this that forgiveth sins also? Let those who deny His divinity answer. The Man Christ Jesus *forgiving* sins is the crowning act of the matchless grace of God, and will be one of those "strange things" at which we shall marvel through all eternity.

IV. A Man Receiving Forgiveness Through Faith. "When He saw *their faith* He said" (v. 20). The faith of the four men who carried, as well as the faith of the anxious man lying sick on the couch. To the self-righteous scribes and Pharisees a man receiving the forgiveness of all his sins through *believing* in Jesus was indeed a startling sight. By the *works* of the law shall no man be justified in the sight of God (Rom. 3. 28). It is of faith that it might be by grace. He *saw* their faith. The eyes of Jesus are always quick to discern the trust of the heart, and His hand is equally quick to help.

V. A Man who could Read their Thoughts. "Jesus perceived their thoughts" (v. 22). While they were reasoning in their hearts the Lord was reading their thoughts. "All things are naked and open unto the eyes of Him with whom we have to do" (Heb. 4. 13). Thus saith the Lord, "I know the things that come into your mind, every one of them" (Ezek. 11. 5). In the workshop of men's minds there are many weapons forged secretly against the people and purposes of God, but they shall not prosper, for our Lord and Master *perceives* their thoughts. "Be not deceived, God is not mocked."

VI. A Man Perfectly Healed at Once. "And immediately he rose up before them, and departed to his own house glorifying God" (v. 25). This was another "strange thing" seen that day. This is not after the fashion of men, but it is very God-like. His work is perfect. No man will ever be able to add a finishing touch to the saving work of Christ. The work of healing and forgiving was done suddenly and completely. It was such a blessed work wrought on him that he could *rise up* and go *to his own house* glorifying God. That man is well saved who can glorify God in his own house. Man's chief end is to glorify God, but until he is healed and forgiven through the grace of our Lord Jesus Christ the *chief end* is lost.

VII. Scribes and Pharisees Filled with Fear. "They were all amazed, and filled with fear, saying, We have seen strange things to-day" (v. 26). When the worldly-wise and those stuffed full of religious pride confess their amazement and fear at the sayings and doings of Jesus Christ it is in itself a "strange thing." Why should the exhibition of sovereign *mercy* fill religious men with *fear*? What has worldly-wiseman to say to this? Self-satisfied souls can never be the recipients of the saving *grace* of God. They that be whole need not a physician. "I am not come to call the righteous, but sinners to repentance." It is possible to see these "strange things" performed on others, and to be for a time both amazed and fearful, yet never profit personally by the healing power of the Redeemer (Psa. 103. 1-5). "He that believeth not shall not see life."

BLESSINGS AND WOES.
Luke 6. 20-26.

> "Methinks we do as fretful children do,
> Leaning their faces on the window pane
> To sigh the glass dim with their own breath's stain,
> And shut the sky and landscape from their view;
> And thus, alas! since God the maker drew
> A mystic separation 'twixt those twain,
> The life beyond us, and our souls in pain "—BROWNING

THESE words of our Lord, though in substance the same as those spoken by Him on the mount, were not delivered on the mount, but "on the plain" (v. 17). They were spoken with "His eyes on His disciples" (v. 20), as if the teaching was specially meant for them first of all, and through them by their lives and teaching to the generations that were to follow. The *blessings* and the *woes* are equal in number (four), as if every blessing had its corresponding woe. Every privilege neglected brings its woe of remorse. There is no *via media* between blessing and woe. All who are not in this marvellous light are in darkness.

I. Here are Four Conditions of Blessedness.

1. POVERTY. "Blessed be ye poor, for yours is the kingdom of God" (v. 20). Of course poverty *in spirit* must be meant (Matt. 5. 3), for with respect to material things a man may be as poor as Lazarus and yet be as proud as the devil When a man is really sensible of his personal destitution before God he has entered into a blessed state, "for to this man, saith the Lord, will I look, that is poor and of a contrite spirit, and trembleth at My Word" (Isa. 66. 2). Such poor ones in this world God hath chosen *rich in faith* and heirs of the kingdom (Isa. 2. 5)

2. HUNGER. "Blessed are ye that hunger now, for ye shall be filled" (v. 21). This is the hunger that cannot be appeased with the things of earth and time. It is not goods, but *goodness*, that alone can. fill the hungry soul (Psa. 107. 9). "He filleth the hungry with good things" (Luke 1. 53). Spirit hunger is the cry of real need, the silent language of a soul in distress; a feeling never felt by those who are *dead* in trespasses and sin.

3. SORROW. "Blessed are ye that weep now, for ye shall laugh" (v. 21). The *blessedness* of being able to weep in the presence of Christ is utterly unknown to the world of frivolity and fashion. Such sorrow is not the result of disappointment through the blasting of selfish hopes or the upsetting of one's own personal interests. It is the sorrow of Christ begotten in the heart through sympathy and love. "Unto them that mourn *in Zion* He shall appoint beauty for ashes, the oil of joy for mourning" (Isa. 61. 3). The sorrow of crucifixion shall be turned into the joy of resurrection (John 16. 20). As the sufferings of Christ abound in us, so our consolation also aboundeth in Christ (2 Cor. 1. 4-7; Rev. 21. 4).

4. PERSECUTION. "Blessed are ye when men shall hate you, separate you, reproach you, cast you out for the Son of Man's sake. Rejoice, for your reward is great in Heaven" (v. 22). Persecution is part of the promised heritage of the Christian (Mark 10. 29, 30). It is blessed, because it lifts the sufferer into closer fellowship with the Saviour (John 17. 14). The early disciples rejoiced that they were counted worthy to suffer shame for His Name (Acts 5. 41).

II. Here are Four Conditions of Woefulness.

1. A WOE FOR THE RICH. "Woe unto you that are rich, for ye have received your consolation" (v. 24). There is no sin in having abundance of riches any more than in having abundance of health, but if not used for the glory of God, verily ye have your reward. The woe of laying up

treasure for *ourselves* is poverty towards God (Luke 12. 21). In the rush of life the pre-eminent object of many is to be rich in the sight of men, while they are utterly indifferent and insensible to their abject poverty in the sight of God. Like the inhabitants of Bashan, "God spake unto them in their prosperity; but they said, I will not hear" (Jer. 22. 21). Here is a Heaven-sent epitaph for their tombstones: "Thou in thy *lifetime* receivedst thy good things, *now* thou art tormented" (Luke 16. 25).

2. A WOE FOR THE FULL. "Woe unto you that are full, for ye shall hunger" (v. 25). A life *stuffed full* of worldly pleasures and possessions, but not *satisfied*. They are like drunken men craving for drink. The iniquity of Sodom was pride and *fulness* (Ezek. 16. 49). A heart *filled* with the love and enjoyment of earthly things has done its very best to shut out God, as every corner of the being has been already crammed with Christless interests. "Have you any room for Jesus?" The woe of graceless fulness is the gnawing of eternal hunger.

3. A WOE FOR THE MERRY. "Woe unto you that laugh *now*, for ye shall mourn and weep" (v. 25). This *now* implies the time of our Christ rejection. The Lord fills the mouths of His people with laughter when He turns their captivity. When the prodigal came home they "began to be merry," but the mirth of fools is folly (Eccles. 7. 6). The mirth of the ungodly shall die away into everlasting mourning. Frivolous worldly minds hunt after the latest joke, and when it is found they immediately gape after the next. Their mirth is like the crackling of thorns beneath a pot, there is more noise than heat. The woe of Christless mirth is the tears of eternal shame.

4. A WOE FOR THE APPLAUDED. "Woe unto you when *all men* speak well of you" (v. 26). The maxim, *Vox populi, vox Dei*, is another failure here. The teaching of Scripture is tremendously emphatic on this point, and so

contradictory to the wisdom of this world. "The friendship
of this world is enmity with God." "Whosoever will be
a friend of the world is the enemy of God" (James 4. 4).
The world loves its own; if it loves you, then you are of the
world. If ye have been *chosen out* of the world the world
will hate you (John 15. 19). It is our highest wisdom
to choose, like Mary, that good part that shall not be
taken from us. The woe of the applauded worldling is
everlasting contempt. _____

BE MERCIFUL AS YOUR FATHER.
Luke 6. 27-38.

"Constant Faith and holy Hope shall die,
    One lost in certainty and one in joy,
    Whilst thou, more happy power, fair Charity,
    Triumphant sister, greatest of all the three.

Thy office and thy nature still the same,
    Lasting thy lamp and unconsumed thy flame
    Shall stand before the host of Heaven confessed
    For ever blessing and for ever blessed."—MATT. PRIOR.

TRUE charity is the love of God shed abroad in the heart
by the Holy Ghost. Love is of God. God is love. He
that loveth not knoweth not God. These words of our
Lord, "Love your enemies," "Bless them that curse you,"
come with greater force as they do after the "blessings"
and the "woes" that go before. This Great Teacher come
from God rightly divides the Word of Truth. Let us
look at—

I. **The Precepts.** These Heaven-made laws laid down
here for us by Jesus Christ are mirrors that reflect the
merciful character of our Father in Heaven, and their
purpose is to help us into His likeness. "Be ye therefore
merciful as your Father also is merciful." These precepts
touch us in a fourfold manner.

1. CONCERNING LOVING. "Love your enemies" (v. 27).
Of course this does not imply that we should not love our

friends, but that our love should be God-like, who, while we were yet sinners, gave His Son to save us (John 3. 16). If thine enemy hunger give him bread to eat, for this thy Father did for thee in the time of thine enmity, and so heaped such coals of fire upon thy head as melted thy heart (Prov. 25. 21, 22).

2. CONCERNING BLESSING. "Bless them that curse you" (v. 28). You will bless the reviler by reviling not again. This is after the divine example (1 Peter 2. 23). The apostle Paul obeyed this command to the letter (1 Cor. 4. 12). "Not rendering evil for evil, but contrariwise blessing" (1 Peter 3. 9), will evidence that we are possessed by the Spirit of the Father.

3. CONCERNING PRAYER. "Pray for them that despitefully use you." To be able to pray for our enemies in the Spirit of Christ is a notable triumph for the grace of God. Christ gained such a victory when He prayed, "Father, forgive them, for they know not what they do" (Luke 23. 34). This grace abounded also in Stephen (Acts 7. 60). This love springs from the mercifulness of the Father.

4. CONCERNING GIVING. "Give to every man that asketh of thee" (v. 30). This does not teach that we are to give *all* that every man may ask of us, but to every petitioner we are to *give*. This is after the mercifulness of the Father. A drunkard may ask you for a sixpence, but instead of that you *give* him a word of warning. If giving to the poor is not an evidence of the *love of God* dwelling in us, withholding is a certain proof that it does not (1 John 3. 17).

II. The Examples. The mercifulness of our Father in Heaven is here contrasted with the natural kindness of ungodly men. The world loves its own. This comes before us in a threefold *negative* aspect. Our mercifulness is not to be like the sinner's, but like the Father's. The one is like a muddy pool, the other like a river clear as crystal.

1. *Let not your* LOVE *be like the love of sinners*. "If ye love them that love you, what thank have ye? for sinners also love those that love them" (v. 32). The love of the unregenerate heart only goes out to those who love in return. The love of God embraces even those who hate Him without a cause. "Be ye therefore merciful, as your Father also is merciful."

2. *Let not your* WORKS *be like the works of sinners*. "If ye do good to them which do good to you, what thank have ye? for sinners also do even the same" (v. 33). The motives of the Christian worker must be infinitely higher than those who are mere time-servers. The ungodly will show kindness to those who are *kind to them*. But our Father is kind even to the unthankful. "Be ye therefore merciful, as your Father also is merciful."

3. *Let not your* GRACE *be like the grace of sinners*. "If ye lend to them of whom ye hope to receive, what thank have ye? for sinners also lend to sinners to receive as much again" (v. 34). Unbelievers will show grace and lend to their sceptical brethren in the hope of receiving as much again. But our Father in Heaven gives to the evil and the unjust, "hoping for nothing again" (Matt. 5. 45). "Be ye therefore merciful, as your Father also is merciful." Your righteousness must exceed the righteousness of the scribes and Pharisees, because it is not ye that act, but the Spirit of the Father which is in you (Matt. 10. 20).

III. **The Promises.** If the love of God is shed abroad in our hearts, so that we can love our enemies and do good to them, hoping for nothing from them, then your Father which seeth in secret will reward you openly.

1. YOUR REWARD SHALL BE GREAT (v. 35). It will be great in this life in that the *divine* nature will be manifestly ruling in our being. It will be great in the life which is to

come, because that in the midst of a wicked and perverse generation you have glorified your Father in Heaven by letting your light shine before men.

2. YE SHALL BE THE CHILDREN OF THE HIGHEST (v. 35). The God who ruleth over all shall claim you as His own children, and as the sons of the HIGHEST your life shall be *lifted up* in Him who is *"far above* all principality, and power, and might, and dominion, and every name that is named, not only in this world, but also in that which is to come" (Eph. 1. 21-23). "Be ye therefore merciful, as your Father also is merciful." _____

THE TREE AND ITS FRUIT.
Luke 6. 41-45.

"O gracious Lord, when Thou didst give
   By Thy divine prerogative,
   Warning that men bear fruit for Thee,
   I bless Thee it was thro' a tree."—GROSART.

THIS great Teacher come from God uses the simplest and most common illustrations in pressing upon the hearts of men the profoundest truths of revelation. In these verses He speaks of the "mote," the "beam," the "good tree and the bad tree," "thorns," the "bramble bush," "figs and grapes." All nature, like the burning bush, is ablaze with flaming thoughts of the divine. But, like Moses, we have to *turn aside* to see this great sight, and for this the beam had better first be taken out of our own eye. Christ here deals with the state of the *eye* (uncharitableness), and the condition of the *heart* (unfruitfulness). The corrupt heart has much to do with the marred eye. The clean in heart have always a merciful eye, for the pure in heart see God. When the beam of prejudice or envy is in our own eye then the motes of weakness and failure are easily seen in the eyes of others. Let us see that there is no *beam* marring our own spiritual vision while we talk of the *motes* which hinder the eyesight of others. The only remedy for a beam or a mote in the eye is to *pull it out*. It is a great mercy and a very blessed ministry to be able to take a mote out of a brother's eye, but it must needs be done very gently, for the eye is a most tender and sensitive member. It takes the tenderness of Christ to deal with mote hindrances in the doctrine and life of a brother. This is no work for hypocrites.

In this parable of the good and evil tree there is brought before us—

I. Two Classes of Character.

1. THE GOOD TREE OR THE GOOD MAN. A good tree is one which serves the purposes for which it was made. It is a reflection of the goodness of God, and constrains to thankfulness and praise. So with a good man, he is the image of God whose name is GOOD. The goodness of a tree is the gift of God through nature; the goodness of a man is the gift of God through grace. "There is none good but God." The *good* man is in perfect harmony with the mind and will of God. The chief end for which he was made is fully achieved through His abounding grace.

2. THE CORRUPT TREE OR THE EVIL MAN. A rotten or bitter tree is the likeness to which the Holy One compares the *evil man*. The evil does not lie so much in appearance as in character. A tree whose root is bitter or whose heart is rotten and corrupt may still have a beautiful and attractive exterior. This rottenness of heart is the result of a hidden disease. The Lord looks upon the heart. The *evil* man in the sight of God is he whose heart is still in the gall of bitterness. A heart not right with Him who is both Creator and Redeemer. He is one in whose heart the corrupting power of sin has unbridled sway like rottenness in the bones. He may be learned, courteous, fashionable, and even religious, but if the *heart* is not right he is an *evil* man. Jesus Christ says nothing about that large class of

people who are neither good nor bad, but just *"middling."* In these latter days we are called upon to try, not only the professions, but the *spirits* whether they be of God (1 John 4. 1).

II. Two Classes of Fruit.

1. THE GOOD FRUIT OR GOOD TREASURE OUT OF THE HEART. Fruit is the visible outcome of the inward *character.* This is a universal and unalterable law. "The good tree *cannot* bring forth evil fruit; neither can a corrupt tree bring forth good fruit." The *acts* of a good or godly man come *out of his heart*, and so partake of his real character; they are called "good treasure," because they are precious and go to enrich others. "Poor, yet making many rich." If the heart is not sound and filled with the goodness of God good treasure will never come out of it. The fruit of the Spirit in us—as the unpolluted sap is in the good tree— is love, joy, peace, etc. (Gal. 5. 22). The wisdom that is from above is pure, full of mercy, and good fruits (James 3. 17). The good man *bringeth forth* the good treasures of his heart just as naturally as the tree brings forth fruit. There is no conscious effort, no thought of self-display, just that sweet constraining of love that makes giving a delightful necessity. We have this treasure in this earthen vessel because God hath shined in our hearts and given us the knowledge of the glory of God in the face of Jesus Christ (2 Cor. 4. 6, 7).

2. THE CORRUPT FRUIT OR THE EVIL TREASURE OF THE HEART. The evil man bringeth forth the evil treasure out of his heart just in the same way that a rotten and polluted tree brings forth bad fruit. The poisoned fountain of the carnal mind will never send forth the refreshing waters of spiritual thought. It seems strangely paradoxical to speak of the evil *treasure* of an evil man. He heaps up wrath against the day of wrath, while imagining that he is the

heir of precious things. The character of the fruit reveals the condition of the *heart* of a tree. "Out of the heart are the issues of life." The evil is not only in the eyes or the lips, but deep down in the core of the being. "As a man *thinketh* in his heart, so is he." "Son, give Me thine heart."

DIGGING DEEP.

Luke 6. 46-49.

"Methinks it is good to be here,
　　If thou wilt let us build; but for whom?
Nor Elias nor Moses appear,
　　But the shadows of eve that encompass the gloom,
　The abode of the dead and the place of the tomb,
　　Shall we build to ambition? Ah, no!"—KNOWLES.

THERE are three words here that characterise a wise man in the eyes of Jesus Christ. "Whosoever *cometh* to Me, and *heareth* My sayings, and *doeth* them" (v. 47). To come to Him as a Saviour, to hear Him as a Teacher, and to obey Him as a Master is an evidence that we have been and are being taught of God and made wise in Christ. These two builders are representatives of two great classes or conditions of men—those who live by faith on the Son of God, and those who walk in the light of the sparks of their own kindling.

I. **The Wisdom of the Obedient.** Our Lord says, "He is like a (wise) man which built an house, and digged deep, and laid the foundation on a rock" (v. 48). He is like such a man—

1. BECAUSE HE BELIEVED IN THE ROCK. He had no faith in the sandy earth as a foundation, and because he believed in the rock he would do nothing in the way of building until he found it. Jesus Christ is the Rock. "Apart from Me," He says, "ye can do nothing." Dost thou believe on the Son of God?

2. BECAUSE HE SPARED NO TROUBLE TO GET AT THE ROCK. "He digged deep." These are most suggestive

words. A life that is to be pleasing to God by resisting temptation and finally triumphing over all the assaults of the world, the flesh and the devil must not begin in any *superficial* fashion Its foundation will be *deeply* laid. There is much that may lie between the seeker and the Saviour Much pride, prejudice, and false teaching. It is no loss of time for a man to examine himself and to dig deep down through everything until the strong and mighty Christ stands revealed before him. Every builder knows that even dust will hinder the stones from being cemented together Let there be "nothing between."

3. BECAUSE HE BUILT HIS HOUSE UPON IT AFTER HE DID FIND THE ROCK He was not satisfied with merely finding a good foundation, he sought the rock for the purpose of *building* thereupon How many there are who seem perfectly satisfied in that they have found Christ as the Rock of Salvation, as their Atonement for sin, but who are utterly indifferent as to what they build thereon. They *rest* on the foundation, but they do not *build on it* They are saved, but their lives do not *reveal* the structure of faith (1 Cor 3 12). Peter tells us how this building is to be done. Add to faith virtue, etc (2 Peter 1. 5-7). We are labourers together with God. Ye are God's building.

4. BECAUSE HE WAS NOT DISAPPOINTED WITH THE RESULTS. "The flood arose, the stream beat upon that house, and *could not shake it*, for it was founded upon a rock." Christianity is no failure. The life that is built on Jesus Christ will be found as stable as the Eternal Throne. "He is able to *keep that* which I have committed unto Him against that day." He is able also to *keep us* from falling The Church or soul that is built upon this Rock "the gates of hell shall not prevail against it" (Matt. 16. 18). "The foundation of God standeth sure" (2 Tim. 2. 19).

II. The Foolishness of the Disobedient. "He that heareth, and *doeth not*, is like a man that without a foundation built an house upon the earth'' (v. 49). The foolishness of this man is seen in that—

1. HE DISREGARDED THE ROCK. He no doubt believed about the rock, but he imagined that he could get on equally well without it. He is a type of those who have been spoiled through false philosophy and vain deceit (Col. 2. 6-8). ''Woe unto them that are wise in their own eyes'' (Isa. 5. 21). The scribes and Pharisees went on with their building, although they had rejected ''the Chief Corner Stone.'' If we wish to end with Christ we must *begin* with Him.

2. HE COMMENCED BUILDING TOO SOON. He began to plant the stones of hope before he had found the rock of safety. He would be saved by his works before he found *rest* on the Eternal Rock. What a picture of many modern religious builders! They set to the rearing of a strong and beautiful life before they have ever come into contact with the saving strength of Christ the Rock. They begin *building* when they should be *digging*, so anxious are they for something pleasing to the eyes of men.

3. HE BUILT WITHOUT A FOUNDATION. ''He built an house upon the earth.'' The loose sandy earth beside the rolling river was treacherous ground. He felt the need of a house of refuge for his soul, but he did not realise his absolute need of an infallible rock for his house. We need salvation, but we need an Almighty Christ to save. ''Other foundation can no man lay than that is laid, which is Jesus Christ'' (1 Cor. 3. 11; Isa. 28. 16).

4. HIS HOPES WERE SUDDENLY CUT OFF. ''The stream did beat vehemently, and it fell, and the ruin of that house was great.'' ''He that believeth shall not make haste.'' But this man made haste because he trusted not the rock, and his earnestness only hastened on his ruin. Earnestness in religious life availeth nothing where the foundation of atoning blood is awanting. He did not perish because he

was lazy or indifferent to his need of a shelter. He did his very best, but it was his best without the "one thing needful." Your works may be many and beautiful, but if Jesus Christ is not at the *foundation* of all, "one thing thou lackest," and the lack of this "one thing" renders useless and fruitless every other thing It is too late to build another house when the flood has come (Mal. 4. 1; 2 Thess. 1. 8).

> "My hope is built on nothing less
> Than Jesus' blood and righteousness,
> I dare not trust the sweetest frame,
> But wholly lean on Jesus' Name,
> On Christ the solid Rock I stand,
> All other ground is sinking sand."

A SOLDIER'S FAITH.
Luke 7. 1-10.

> "Dim as the borrow'd beams of moon and stars
> To lonely, weary, wandering travellers
> Is reason to the soul.
> And as those nightly tapers disappear,
> When day's bright lord ascends our hemisphere,
> So pale grows reason at religion's sight,
> So dies, and so dissolves in supernatural light."
> —DRYDEN.

"FAITH is a courier swift and sure who will carry us to the absent." All things are possible to him that believeth. In this Roman centurion we see a thoroughly practical man in ethical and spiritual warfare. His matter-of-fact manner in dealing with the Lord Jesus Christ is like a refreshing breeze from the mountains of Lebanon. Is his servant sick? He does not *talk* about his pity; he sends at once for the physician (v. 3). Does he love the Jewish nation? Then it is not in *word* but in deed "he builds them a synagogue" (v. 5). He does not *speak* of his faith, but he *shows* it in a way that makes the Lord Himself marvel at its simplicity and greatness (vv. 8, 9). How beautifully simple is his holy logic! "Say the word, and my servant shall be healed, for I *also* am a man under authority, and I say, Go, and he goeth.'' Soldier-like he believes that the Great Commander has but to speak and it shall be done. Such a compliment from a Gentile army captain could not pass without special mention.   He said, ''I have not found so great faith, no, not in Israel.'' Lord, increase our faith. This incident is full of Gospel to us. Observe—

I. **The Servant's Need.** He was in a condition of—

1. UTTER HELPLESSNESS. ''He was sick'' (v. 2). Although a bondslave, he may have been surrounded with many mercies and favours, but he was unable to help himself. A picture of every one under the spirit-sickening power of sin. The helplessly sick have no thought of earning anything by their *works*. This hope has died away.

2. GREAT MISERY. ''He was grievously tormented'' (Matt. 8. 6). One may be helpless and yet unconscious of it, but this servant was in sore distress. When a man is deeply convicted of his guilt and utter inability to help himself he will be grievously tormented. But such timely *torment* is infinitely better than the fatal insensibility that will inevitably result in the eternal scourge of remorse. Fools make a mock of sin.

3. IMMEDIATE DANGER. ''He was ready to die'' (v. 2). He was just at the point of dying. His disease had brought him to the very brink of eternity, and all the wisdom and power of man were vain and impotent to deliver. The danger of perishing at any moment should add to the torments of every unsaved one.

II. **The Centurion's Petition.** He made intercession for his devoted servant ''when he heard of Jesus,'' clearly implying that he had believed what he did hear. Faith cometh by hearing. The *manner* of those elders who came to Jesus with his request shows the character of the centurion's prayer. It was—

1. EARNEST. "He sent unto Jesus, *beseeching* Him" (v. 3). Real anxiety and heart-felt sympathy are the parents of earnestness. When Peter's wife's mother was sick they kept continually telling Jesus of her (Mark 1. 30). His servant was *dear unto him*, so *love* warmed up his prayer. All coldness and formality in prayer means heartlessness on the part of the petitioner. Where there is love for those "ready to die" there will be earnest beseeching on their behalf.

2. HUMBLE. "I am not worthy," said he, while the Lord was on the way to his house (v. 6). The elders said, "He is worthy, for he loveth our nation, and hath built us a synagogue." But this good man did not believe that his *good works* could merit such worthiness as having the Son of God beneath his roof. Nothing we can do will make us worthy of having Christ dwelling in us. This humility of spirit, like the self-unconsciousness of a little child, is the very breath of Heaven, and is refreshing to the soul of Jesus. In the sight of God unworthiness felt is worthiness shown. When Saul was little in his own sight the Lord exalted him (1 Sam. 15. 17).

3. BELIEVING. "Say in a *word*, and my servant shall be healed" (v. 7). Faith has always to do with the *Word* of God, and is satisfied with that, knowing that He is faithful who promises. His Word cannot fail. How many are serving the Lord in sorrowful bondage, looking for signs and feelings instead of acting confidently on His Word. The Lord has already spoken many words that exactly suit our case, and they are as valid for us now as they were of old. "The words that I speak unto you are spirit and life" (John 6. 63). Come believing.

III. The Saviour's Response. It was—

1. PROMPT. "Then Jesus went with them" (v. 6). The grace and truth that comes with Jesus Christ never comes too late. The prayer made urgent through intense

love will speedily find a response in the love of God. "In *due time* Christ died for the ungodly;" how will He not also in due time answer the cry of faith?

2. ENCOURAGING. "I have not found so great faith, no, not in Israel" (v. 9). These faith-honouring words were spoken to the people that followed Him. He marvels at his faith, but He does not rebuke him for expecting too much. He is marvellously pleased with great faith. Without faith it is impossible to please Him. "O ye of little faith, wherefore do ye doubt?" Why have we not the faith of God in His own Son? (Mark 11. 22, margin).

3. EFFECTUAL. "His servant was healed in the self-same hour" (Matt. 8. 13). He sent His Word, and healed him (Psa. 107. 20). "As thou hast believed, so be it done unto thee." This "*so be it done*" is the Amen of Christ to the prayer of faith. Christ Himself is God's AMEN to the agonising, trustful cry of humanity (Rev. 3. 14). Little faith belittles the Christ of God and narrows up the channel of blessing. Doubting hearts may call Him great, but they trust Him little; they are like the soldiers who cried, "Hail, King!" then put on Him the mock robe.

THE WIDOW'S SON.
Luke 7. 11-16.

"The valley of dry bones,
Insensate as the stones,
Beneath Thy quickening breath
Rose up a living host.
O midst our sin and death
Come stir, Thou Holy Ghost."
—GROSART.

IT is a hope-quickening thought that the Holy Spirit, that "other Comforter," who is the gift of the risen Saviour, possesses the *resurrecting* power of Jesus Christ. It is the Spirit that quickeneth. The raising of a dead body demonstrates His power to raise a soul dead in sin into a new life.

Who has not seen a funeral? Who has not buried a friend? We can easily lift the hat off our head as the mournful cortege passes; but Jesus Christ alone can lift the load of grief from the aching heart of the bereaved. As D. L. Moody used to say, "Jesus spoiled every funeral that He went to." The darkest night of gloom He can turn into midday brightness. We have here—

I. An Afflicted Woman. Her circumstances reveal a—

1. SORROWFUL PAST. "She was a widow" (v. 12). The scene of her husband's death-bed, the heart-rending parting, the mournful funeral, and the dread loneliness that followed; these were bygone sorrows, but perhaps merciful time had somewhat rubbed off their keen edge. It may be that we have had deep convictions of sin in the past when the pleasures of the world partly lost their savour, and by and by that spirit-wound got healed.

2. BITTER PRESENT. "Now her dead son is being carried out." Another season of trial has come; again the thick dark pall of sorrow has been spread over her sky. Once more she is face to face with death. Learn that if the Spirit awakens a second time the *past* will greatly aggravate the misery of the present.

3. HOPELESS FUTURE. This was the funeral of "the *only son* of his mother" (v. 12). The alone source of her comfort and *help* has been cut off. She is now without hope, having no promise, utterly cast down, but to such Jesus draws nigh. It is only when we are "without strength" that the power of God is manifested on our behalf. They that be whole need not a physician, but they that are sick. All her future prospects, like the centurion's servant, were "ready to die." But the Resurrection and the Life are at hand.

II. An Almighty Friend. "A friend in need is a friend indeed." The nearer she comes to the grave the nearer does she come to the life-giving Saviour. The darkest hour is the hour before daybreak. The sorrow that endures for a night shall be turned into joy in the morning when Jesus comes. Jesus meets the funeral, life and death come into contact, earthly weakness, sorrow, and disappointment in this woman are met by heavenly strength, consolation, and hope in Jesus Christ. Sin's ruin and God's remedy have come together. What are the results?

1. AN EXPRESSION OF SYMPATHY. "When the Lord saw her He had compassion on her" (v. 12). As soon as the Lord saw her the love of His heart flowed out to her. Although as yet she is a stranger to His sympathy He is no stranger to her sorrow. Surely the sting of human suffering is the *unconsciousness* of divine compassion.

2. AN UNUSUAL WORD OF COMFORT. "He said unto her, Weep not" (v. 12). Weep not? Does she think these words spoken in mockery? Does He not know that this is the "only son of a widow?" He knew Himself what He would do. We may dry our tears at His bidding, no matter how bitter they may be. But perhaps it is not your tears so much as your *cares* that He bids you put away, saying, "Take no thought for your life," etc. (Matt. 6. 25), as He Himself knows what He will do.

3. A TIMELY ARREST. "He touched the bier, and they that bare him stood still" (v. 14). This was the arresting touch of the mercy that saves. A little while longer and he would have been buried out of sight. Who shall arrest that soul which time, like a death-car, is carrying off to the grave of eternal doom if Jesus Christ is not met on the way?

4. A STRANGE COMMAND. "Young man, I say unto thee, Arise" (v. 14). Who is this that commands the dead to rise up? This is He who speaks as one *having authority*. As the coming of the light commands the darkness to vanish, so does the coming of His Word

imply the power to overcome. Ignorance may cavil where faith is blessed. He is the mighty to save, who speaks and it is done.

5. A WONDROUS CHANGE. "He that was dead sat up, and began to speak" (v. 15). An example of one *begotten again* by the Word of God. What a change His life-giving Word brings! He who was a minute ago cold, helpless, silent, and corrupting is now aglow with the warmth of a new life, and able to testify by *speech* to His resurrection power. He is now a new creature, old things have passed away, all things have become new.

6. A HAPPY REUNION. "He delivered him to his mother" (v. 15). Oh, praise Him for His tenderness, He not only saved the son from death, but delivered him (gave him back as *His own*) to the comforting of the broken-hearted widow! She could truly say, "This my son was dead, and is alive again." A foretaste of Heaven's reunited fellowship and joy was hers. Death has been conquered, and loved ones meet each other again in the presence of the living Son of God.

7. A GOD-HONOURING RESULT. "There came a fear on all, and they glorified God" (v. 16). Those who follow Jesus (v. 11) will always have good cause for glorifying God, for they shall see great and mighty things done by Him. Yes, Jesus will be glorified in *every word* that He speaks. All His words and works shall praise Him. It will be for ever to the praise of His grace that "He saved others," but because of the might of His love for us "He could not save Himself" (Matt. 27. 42).

THE TWO DEBTORS.
Luke 7. 41-43.

THIS little pithy parable was spoken in Simon's house, who desired Jesus to eat with him, and Jesus did not refuse. He *never does*. Then Simon sat in judgment on Him in

allowing this woman to touch Him.(v. 39). Simon's cold
heart was a stranger to the love of Christ. Like many a
modern Pharisee his religion was an outward form. But
Jesus had a meat to eat that Simon knew not of. The
woman's *love* was more precious to Him than Simon's feast.
It is the *heart* He seeks. Giving can only grieve Him when
it is heartless. There are many Simons who show *outward*
respect to religion, but who have no heart sympathy with
Jesus Christ in His saving mission.

I. **The Certain Creditor** (v. 41). The great Creditor,
no doubt, represents God Himself. There is something
graciously beautiful about this thought, because—

1. A creditor is one who is supposed to have A GOOD
REPUTATION. Can God deceive? Is His character not
trustworthy? He cannot lie.

2. A creditor is one who has SUFFICIENCY FOR OTHERS.
Our sufficiency is of God. Human need can be fully met
only in Him. "All my *salvation* and all my *desire*." The
sinner's needs are deep and many, but the fulness of His
mercy is enough. "Come unto Me."

3. A creditor is one who looks for SOME RETURN FOR
HIS OUTLAY. He gives only on loan. God gives His best,
and expects our best; but, alas, we have returned Him evil
for good. Evil is poor payment for good; hatred is a
miserable return for love. Could you reckon up the good
He has given? How much owest thou my Lord?

II. **The Different Debtors.** "Two" (v. 41). The 500
and the 50. Representing two classes of *actual* trans-
gressors, the great and the little, and implying all the
grades that lie between. The fifty pence debtor is the
religious moralist who lacks "one thing." The five
hundred pence debtor is the open profligate that lacks
everything. But there is the hundred pence debtor, who
has been *somewhat indifferent* to the goodness of God. The

two hundred pence debtor who has been wholly indifferent
to the gifts of God, and the three hundred pence debtor
who questions His love and mocks at His people, and the
four hundred pence debtor who denies God and despises
His mercy, yet whose outward character is counted respectable. But *all* with whom the Great Creditor has been
dealing in grace are His debtors. "*All* have sinned," "all
have come short." He that offendeth in one point is
guilty of *all*.

III. **The Helpless Bankrupts.** "They had *nothing* to
pay" (v. 42). The great and the little debtor were both
alike in the same insolvent condition. "No difference."
Just so with every sinner in God's sight. Our responsi-
bilities to God may be different, but the hopelessness of
our *condition* in His sight is the same. By nature all are
alike, "without strength." Where there was no sprinkled
blood Jehovah could make no difference (Exod. 12. 13).
All outside of the ark were treated alike in His judgment.
They had NOTHING. Who but God only can create out of
nothing? We can only make nothing out of nothing.
Then *payment* is impossible. There is no other creditor
from whom we can borrow. So one of two things must
follow—a pardon or a prison.

IV. **The Happy Deliverance.** "He frankly forgave
them both" (v. 42). These few words reveal the heart of
God as big with abounding grace. Notice—

1. WHAT HE DID. "He forgave." He did not
compromise. How suited *His* way was to their sad
circumstances! *Forgiveness* is God's gracious remedy
for the sinner's debt. "I believe in the *forgiveness*, not
the *payment* of sins" (Luther). Oh, that men would
believe God's willingness and readiness to forgive!

2. WHOM HE FORGAVE. "Both." Both alike needed
it. The self-righteous moralist and the respectable
church-going fifty pence debtor need *forgiveness* just the

same as the five hundred pence ne'er-do-weel. One can
have no more claim than another, both are debtors.

3. How HE FORGAVE. "Frankly." In a free, liberal,
loving manner, not grudgingly, just as the father forgave
the prodigal, with open arms and joyful heart. "He
delighteth in mercy." He keepeth mercy for thousands.
When God pardons a sinner He does it as Joseph forgave
his brethren, with a heart ready to burst with deep,
unutterable compassion.

4. WHEN HE FORGAVE. "When they had *nothing to
pay*." It was when the prodigal had spent all that he had
that he came and was accepted. When Joseph's brethren
had nothing to eat, *then* they were enriched by him whom
they had despised. The young ruler came with a great
price in his hand, and he went away sorrowful. The
Laodicean Church "had need of nothing" while Christ
stood outside. "Blessed are the *poor* in spirit." "Jesus
paid it all." Accept His settlement. Buy *without money*.
"Nothing to pay."

V. The Grateful Evidence. "Love." Which of them
will *love* Him most? "He to whom He forgave most,"
says Simon. "Thou hast *rightly* judged," says Jesus. It
is right judgment, then, to expect the *forgiven* to manifest
in some way or other their love for Him who frankly
forgives *all*. The poor woman had been forgiven *much*,
and she loved *much*, and showed it.

1. Much love WEEPS (v. 44). Not only tears of regret
for the past, but of deepest gratitude toward God, and
of tenderest sympathy toward the perishing. The
world needs such tears. Christ shed them, so did Paul
(Phil. 3. 18).

2. Much love WASHES. "She hath washed My feet"
(v. 44). Many a dusty foot and life *love* has washed. "He
loved me, and washed me." Love covereth a multitude of

sins. Christ, as our Head, is in Heaven; we, as His feet, are on earth.

3. Much love STOOPS. "She wipes His feet with her hair" (v. 44). She puts her glory at His feet. If He is to increase, I must decrease. The heart must bow if Jesus is to be served.

4. Much love KISSES. Her lips of affection are pressed to His feet (v. 45). The feet of the body of Christ, the dusty, naked members, are often neglected. Love seeks contact with them.

5. Much love ANOINTS. The Father anoints His head, but the forgiven one must anoint His feet (v. 46). "Do as I have done unto you."

6. Much love FOLLOWS. She followed Him into Simon's house. She heeded not the reproach of others. Love constrained her (1 John 4. 19).

7. Much love GIVES. "She brought her box of ointment" (v. 37). This was all her treasure, and she laid it at His feet, not only her ointment, but *herself*.

Lovest thou Me? How much? Let the life testify.

Contrast the three characters: (1) The *proud-hearted* Pharisee. (2) The *broken-hearted* sinner. (3) The *loving-hearted* Saviour. ———

THE QUESTION OF JOHN.
Luke 7. 17-35.

"Though vexing thoughts may seem to last,
  Let not thy soul be quite o'ercast;
  Soon will He show thee all His wounds, and say,
'Long have I known thy name, know thou My face
    alway.'" —KEBLE.

THE raising of the widow's son had evidently produced a profound impression; the rumour went throughout "all the region round about," and was carried also to John while lying in his dismal prison. Every resurrected soul is a mighty testimony to the saving power of Jesus Christ (Eph. 2. 1). By reason of such many have believed on Him (John 12. 10, 11).

I. The Question. "Art Thou He that should come, or look we for another?" (v. 19). It does seem strange that such a question should come from John Baptist; from him who saw the Spirit descend like a dove upon Him, and who bore record that *this is the Son of God*, and who said, "Behold the Lamb of God" (John 1. 32-36). Yes! But why should this almighty Deliverer allow His forerunner to pine away in a dark and loathsome dungeon? It may be as easy for us as for John to say, "He must increase, I must decrease," but when the *decreasing* goes on and on till we almost question our relationship to Christ it is a trial of faith. But the trial of your faith is precious.

II. The Answer. Christ's reply shows no displeasure at the question of John. Our Lord is very gracious, and knows the frailty of our frame. "Go your way, and tell John what things *ye have seen and heard*" (vv. 21-23). Those who would speak for Jesus and comfort the tempted must speak what they have *seen and heard*. Christ never sends any one to tell what they *think*. "We speak that we do know" (1 John 1. 1-3). And what a story they had to tell: "The blind see, the lame walk," etc. Such a Gospel is enough to drive away all doubts and fears.

III. The Testimony. As soon as the messengers are gone Jesus bears witness to the true character and divine mission of John (vv. 24-30). He was no silly reed shaken with every wind of doctrine that may blow; he was no city dandy in soft raiment seeking to make a display of himself; he was more than a prophet, in that he *prepared the way* of the Lord Christ. Even John's martyrdom prepared the way for the Crucifixion. If John's faith had not been tested we would not have had this beautiful testimony to his noble nature. "All things work for good," etc.

(Rom. 8. 28). To reject the testimony of His servant is to reject the testimony of God (v. 30).

IV. **The Application.** "Whereunto shall I liken the men of this generation?" etc. (vv. 31-35). The children in the market place often played at funerals and marriages; at the one they mourned, and at the other they piped and danced. "This generation" had been called upon by the austere life of John to mourning and repentance, and by the gracious, winsome life of Jesus to joy and gladness; but they charged John as being possessed with a devil, and Jesus as being a "gluttonous man, a friend of publicans and sinners." The testimony of both was rejected. If the warnings of the law and the wooings of the Gospel fail to bring us to God, how shall we escape? "But the wisdom of God is always justified in the children of such wisdom" (Prov. 8. 35). ⸻

SAVED BY FAITH.
Luke 7. 36-50.

"Triumphant Faith!
Hers is a conquering path to Heaven,
With feet fire-shod, because her hand is placed
Immovably in God's; her eye doth rest
Unchangeably on His."—Miss TATHAM.

THIS Pharisee desired Jesus that He would eat with him, but he did not desire this woman, branded with the name "sinner," to come into his house. Her faith in the pity and compassion of Christ must have been strong when it constrained her to follow Him into such a house and at such a time. Such sorrowful sinners are never found weeping at a Pharisee's feet. There is a holy, winsome magnetism in the love of God, as manifested in the Person of Jesus Christ; the vilest may draw nigh and find the blessing of "eternal redemption."

I. **The Character of this Woman.** "She was a sinner" (v. 37). Evidently a great sinner, for the Lord speaks of "her sins which are *many*" (v. 47). The Pharisee called her *a sinner* with emphasis (v. 39). Such a sinner as should not be touched; but Christ had to designate the Pharisees themselves as hypocrites (chap. 11. 44). She was a sinner, so was Simon, but she had this advantage, that she *knew* it, while he was proudly unconscious of it. The one owed five hundred pence, the other fifty, but in their relation to God they were both alike, "having nothing to pay." "All have sinned, and come short of the glory of God. There is none righteous, no, not one."

II. The Workings of Her Faith. "Even in a spark there is fire." Little faith may cling to an almighty Saviour. Faith is an operative energy of the soul that will not rest till the object desired has been grasped and enjoyed. Observe how it wrought in this woman. It constrained her to—

1. COME TO JESUS (v. 37). Perhaps the sneer of the self-righteous Pharisees had awakened hope in her heart. "Behold a gluttonous man, and a winebibber, *a friend of publicans and sinners*" (v. 34). Her faith constrained her to draw near to Him without any personal invitation. Does such an act not put to shame the many who are still refusing the call of God? (John 5. 40).

2. REPENT OF HER SINS. "She stood at His feet behind Him weeping" (v. 38). When one stands at His feet and contrasts his own life with His the bitter tears of contrition are sure to fall. Seeing ourselves in His light is always a humbling revelation. Such tears are precious jewels in the sight of God; they tell of mountains of guilt flowing down at His presence (Isa. 64. 1). What effect has your faith had in this direction?

3. SHOW THE TOKENS OF HER LOVE. "She kissed His feet, and anointed them with the ointment" (v. 38). Hers was the faith that *worked by love*. The *kiss* spoke of the *affection* of her heart, while the precious ointment

poured out told of a willingness to *consecrate* her all to Him. The faith that does not work in this fashion is a dead faith (James 2. 26). The lips of love must come into contact with Christ as well as the hands of faith. With the *heart* man believeth unto salvation.

III. The Blessed Results. She was—

1. APPROVED. "Seest thou this woman?" (vv. 44-46). These words spoken to Simon would fall on the poor, sin-smitten soul of the woman as the music of Heaven. Jesus Himself knew the joy of being "a man approved of God" (Acts 2. 22). Study to show thyself approved unto God (2 Tim. 2. 15). Her manner of approach had His most gracious welcome, although she had no promise to plead. But what a solace to her heart that HE commended her!

2. FORGIVEN. "Thy sins are forgiven" (v. 48). She was forgiven much, for she *loved* much. There was a great difference between the cold, calculating belief of Simon and the simple, loving, heartful faith of the woman. She came, and with her tears and kisses she reasoned together with her Lord, and her sins, which were as scarlet, were made white as snow (Isa. 1. 18). What encouragement for the wicked to forsake their ways is found in His abundant pardon! (Isa. 55. 7).

3. ASSURED. "Thy faith *hath* saved thee" (v. 50). Faith in Christ not only saved her from the guilt of sin, but also from the tyranny of its power. She was now freed from the very *love* of sin. His *grace* saved her, His *Word* assured her. It was not the tears of her eyes nor the kisses of her lips that saved her, but the *faith* of her heart. By grace are ye saved through faith, and by the *record* given are we assured (1 John 5. 11-13).

4. COMMISSIONED. "Go in peace" (v. 50). Go in peace with God, because justified by faith (Rom. 5. 1). Go in the peace of God, because now a child of God and an

heir to the kingdom. Go and publish the Gospel of peace,
as an ambassador for Him, who is the Prince of Peace, and
who has made peace by the blood of His Cross. Go in
peace back to your home and to your associates in sin as a
messenger of mercy, telling them what great things He hath
done for thy soul. Thy faith hath saved thee, go!

THE MAN WHOSE NAME WAS "LEGION."
Luke 8. 26-39.

> "Love it was that first created light,
> Moved in the waters, chased away the night
> From the rude chaos, and bestow'd new grace
> On things disposed of to their proper place."
>
> —EDMUND WALLER.

LOVE is the mightiest moral force in Heaven, Earth, or
Hell. It was *love* that constrained God to give up His Son
(John 3. 16). It was *love* that constrained His Son to speak
such words of grace, to perform such miracles of mercy, and
to give His life a ransom for many. "God is love."
Behold, what manner of love the Father hath bestowed
upon us, in that through His Son He hath delivered us
from the power of the devil and from this present evil
world. In the salvation of this demoniac we have a
grand exhibition of that divine power which worketh
by love.

I. His Dreadful Condition. He was—

1. SHAMELESS. "He ware no clothes" (v. 27). Naked,
and he knew it not. He was so completely *possessed* and
occupied by evil spirits that he was utterly unconscious of
his own nakedness. When Adam and Eve sinned they
knew that they were naked, and sought to cover themselves.
To be *insensible* of our nakedness before God is an evidence
of satanic possession and delusion.

2. FRIENDLESS. "Neither abode he in any house, but
in the tombs" (v. 27). Being in league with the devil,

he was cut off from all his relatives and friends; he could have no fellowship with the inhabitants of the tombs, although the abodes of the dead are always more congenial to such than the houses of the living. No *man* could help him. While we are the slaves of sin vain is the help of man.

3. HELPLESS. "He was *driven* of the devil" (v. 29). He could in no wise help himself. He was driven like a beast by the powerful impulses wrought in him by the wicked spirits. Led captive by the devil at his will because his mind was blinded by that god of this world. Christ was driven by the Holy Spirit (Mark 1. 12). Which is your master?

II. His Attitude Towards Christ. It was one of—

1. FEAR. "He cried, and fell down before Him" (v. 28). When a soul comes face to face with the Son of God the inner thoughts and intents of the heart are sure to be revealed. Those who live under the dominion of sin, while they may know that they cannot escape the presence of Christ, yet they dread Him, although He is the most merciful of all. They fear a separation from their sins.

2. OPPOSITION. "He said, What have I to do with Thee, Jesus, Thou Son of God Most High?" (v. 28). It is quite true that devil-possessed have nothing in common with the Holy Son of the Most High, any more than the darkness of the pit of hell has to do with the glory of Heaven. Where is the link of connection between the sin-driven sinner and the sin-hating Saviour? It is only found in the love of God in Christ. There is absolutely nothing in us but what is opposed to His holy will. "What have I to do with Thee?" I am animated by a spirit that is at enmity with Thine. You are from above, I am from beneath.

3. ENTREATY. "I beseech thee torment me not" (v. 28). In this prayer there is the confession of an inner

conviction that the final judgment is in the hands of Jesus the Son of God, and that the last end of a sin-governed life is *torment* (Jude 6). The way to be saved from the eternal torment of sin is to be washed in the blood of the Lamb. "He hath loved us, and loosed us from our sins by His blood" (Rev. 1. 5, R.V.).

III. **His Perfect Deliverance.** Let us note the process. There was—

1. CONFESSION. "Jesus asked him, saying, What is thy name? And he said, Legion" (v. 30). Some think that a legion was a company of 6666. It was a confession at any rate that *many* demons had influence over him. In making such a statement he was simply declaring the truth. No good can come through seeking to hide our true state from the saving Son of the Highest. If our sins and our iniquities have carried us away like a legion of devils, let us say so in the ears of Him with whom we have to do.

2. EMANCIPATION. "They found the man out of whom the devils were departed sitting at the feet of Jesus, clothed, and in his right mind" (v. 35). The devils *departed* out of him. The salvation of Jesus Christ implies the deliverance of the man from the grip and tyranny of evil. It is a *loosing* from the dominion of sin, a translating of the soul out of the kingdom of darkness into the kingdom of God's dear Son. It is a homeless, restless soul finding a refuge in the loving heart of Jesus, and rest at His conquering feet. The *driving* of the devil has now given place to the *leading* of Jesus.

3. WITNESS-BEARING. "He went his way, and published throughout the whole city how great things Jesus had done unto him" (v. 39). The Lord had indeed done great things for him. He had lifted him out of a *horrible pit*, and put a new song in his mouth. To be the slave of sin and the devil is to be in a horrible plight. Let the redeemed declare what the Lord hath done for their souls

(Psa. 66. 16). The tongue of testimony will surely be loosened when the bands of iniquity are broken. "Lazarus, come forth. Loose him, and let him go." Deliverance, then liberty. ———

THE VIRTUE OF CHRIST.
Luke 8. 43-48.

"In having all things and not Thee, what have I ?
Not having Thee, what have my labours got ?
Let me enjoy but Thee, what further crave I ?
And having Thee alone, what have I not ?"

—QUARLES.

THE riches of the glory of Christ are like the riches of the glory of the sun. Just as every flower finds its beauty and variety of colours in the sunshine, so may each soul find in Christ that very blessing and adorning that becomes them. He met the need of the one who came for Him to heal another (v. 41) as well as this woman who touched Him for herself. In the sunshine of His grace there is all-sufficiency for all. It does not matter much *how* we come into the fresh air of His healing presence if we are only there; the health of His countenance will revive and strengthen. Let us learn here that—

I. **There is Healing Virtue in Christ.** The soul-healing power can be found nowhere else. Why? All the virtue of the Eternal God is in Christ for the purpose of healing the sin sores and woes of the world. This virtue is threefold. There is: (1) The virtue of a holy, blameless, God-pleasing *life*. (2) The virtue of an all-atoning substitutionary *death*. (3) The virtue of an all-conquering *resurrection*. There is none other name under Heaven that has such virtue. Through sin man has lost the virtue of holiness. If this virtue is to be restored it must be wholly through another than himself. This virtue or saving health is in Christ as the fragrance is in the flower, as the light is in the sun, or as the electricity is in the cloud; and He can shed it forth just as easily.

**II. This Virtue is Sufficient for the Most Desperate
Case.** This woman's disease had lasted for "twelve
years," and she had "spent all her living; neither could be
healed of any" (v. 43). Her disease, like the workings of
sin, was a secret life-wasting malady. But even for
such there is hope in Christ, for God *is in Christ*. While
she was *spending* her all she met with many a disappointment. "Nothing bettered, but rather grew worse." In the
anguish of her soul, as she stood on the border of despair,
her faith looked to Jesus, muttering, "If I could but
touch His garment I would be made whole."

III. This Virtue goes out at the Touch of Faith.
"She came and touched the border of His garment" (v. 44).
Sin, with all its consequences of impurity and misery,
came by coming into *contact* with the forbidden thing
through *unbelief*. "Eve *took* of the fruit thereof, and did
eat" (Gen. 3. 6). To *touch* the dead made a man cere-
monially unclean (Lev. 5. 2). The fringe of blue on the
border of the garment spoke of *obedience* (Num. 15. 38-40).
In touching the *border* of Christ's garment was she thinking
of His obedience unto death for her sake? This thought
must be uppermost if our touch is to bring the healing life
of Christ into our diseased and wasted souls. Her needs
were fully met by the incoming of His strength and power,
so that the life she now lived was the life of Christ in her
(Gal. 2. 20)

**IV. This Virtue is Consciously Given and Con-
sciously Received.** Christ said, "I *perceive* that virtue is
gone out of Me" (v. 46). As for the woman, "she *felt* in
her body that she was healed" (Mark 5. 29). Her thirsty
soul had received a cup of cold water out of the ocean
fulness of His saving grace. She did not steal the cure.
The virtue was deliberately *given* by Jesus Christ in answer
to her practical faith. She believed, and therefore she
touched, and her touch was rewarded with the assurance of

perfect deliverance. Is it not always so? (Matt. 15. 28).
The virtue of Christ, imparted at the touch of faith,
vaccinates the soul against the plague of sin and the
contaminations of this present evil world. The law of
the "survival of the fittest" does not hold good here,
for the virtue of Christ makes the most helpless and
hopeless to survive. This battle is not to the strong.
Christ's life is always an overcoming life (Acts 14. 8-10).

V. **The Thronging Multitude need not Hinder from
such a Healing Touch.** "Master, the multitude throng
Thee and press Thee, and sayest Thou, Who touched Me?"
(v. 45). The *throng* and the *press* of earthly cares and duties
are often made the excuse for not seeking personal contact
with the Saviour of men. The "more convenient *season*"
is tarried for, which seldom comes. "The kingdom of
Heaven suffereth violence, and the *violent take it* by
force." If this poor, bloodless, dying woman had waited
till the throng and the press were over she would have
waited till Jesus the Saviour had passed beyond her reach.
Behold, now!

VI. **This Virtue when Received should be Publicly
Acknowledged.** "Who touched Me?" The woman came
and declared *before all* for what cause she had touched Him,
and how she was healed immediately (v. 47). Before
them all she testified of two things: (1) For *what cause* she
had touched Him. She had touched *Him* because every
other physician had failed, and because she wanted to be
healed at once. (2) How she was *healed immediately.*
Blessed testimony to the infinite grace of God. Healed
perfectly, and in a moment of time. Her open testimony brought to her His additional word of *assurance.*
"Daughter, be of good comfort, thy faith *hath* made thee
whole" (v. 48). Tradition says that she declared Christ's
innocence before Peter, and wiped His face while He
was on the way to Golgotha. At anyrate, such faithful

testimony and loving service surely become those who
have been saved with so great salvation. Made partakers
of the divine nature. ———

THE TESTING PRESENCE.
Luke 9. 18-27.

"Ye scorners in your wild unrest,
  O would that ye would turn to Him,
  Far, far above the seraphim;
  And of His mercy make request;
  (Christ is)—
  Most hidden, yet most manifest."

In gathering up the most salient features of this portion we
observe that they all centre on the Lord Himself. We
have here—

I. **Christ and Private Prayer.** "He was alone
praying" (v. 18). Many there be who don't like to be
alone, because they have no delight in prayer. Jesus
often sought for solitude that He might be alone with
His Father whom He loved so much. If the holy and
sinless Jesus found it needful and blessed to pray in
secret, how much more do we need it? Those who pray
in *secret* will have their *open* reward (Matt. 6. 6).

II. **Christ and Public Opinion.** "Whom say the
people that I am?" etc. (vv. 18, 19). Common reports
are not always to be trusted. "The voice of the people"
is not always "the voice of God." In this case it was
the voice of wilful ignorance and unbelief, for had He
not been publicly declared to be "THE LAMB OF GOD,
which taketh away the sin of the world" (John 1. 29),
and had not His Word and works declared Him to be
the Son of God with power? It is always more easy
for us to say what *others* think of Christ than to say
honestly what we ourselves think of Him.

III. **Christ and Personal Conviction.** "But whom
say *ye* that I am?" (v. 20). It will not satisfy the Saviour

to tell Him what our fathers, and mothers, and teachers said about Him. This question is one that we have all to answer individually for ourselves. "What think ye of Christ?" Peter's answer, "Thou art the Christ (anointed, of God," reveals more than natural wisdom (Matt. 16. 16, 17). "If thou shalt *confess* with thy mouth the Lord Jesus, and *believe in thine heart*, thou shalt be saved" (Rom. 10. 9).

IV. **Christ and Substitution**. "The Son of Man *must* suffer," etc. (v. 22). As the Captain of our Salvation Christ was made perfect through suffering. He was "*rejected* by the elders and chief scribes," showing that the carnal mind, even though religious, is enmity against God. With wicked hands they put Him to death, but by the authority of the Father He *laid down* His life and took it again (John 10. 18). It was according to the Scriptures that He died *for our sins*, and rose again *for our* justification.

V. **Christ and Discipleship**. "If any will come after Me, let him deny himself, and take up his cross daily" (v. 23). Our sinful *self* ever plays the part of the elders and chief priests in *rejecting* Christ. Self must be denied if we would follow the steps of Him who "pleased not Himself." The Cross of Christ will ever be a shameful thing in the eyes of the world, but God forbid that we should glory, save in the Cross of our Lord Jesus Christ, by which we are crucified unto the world. This cross of discipleship is not thrust upon us, we are to *take it up* daily. It is absolutely necessary to a life of fellowship with Him (2 Tim. 2. 11, 12).

VI. **Christ and Service**. "Whosoever shall lose His life for My sake shall save it" (v. 24). This losing our life by saving it, and saving our life by losing it, is very paradoxical to all who are strangers to the Power of Christ's Cross. The life that is spent in the service of Christ is a saved life; the life that is spent for self is a lost life. We may

have a saved soul by trusting the Cross of Christ, and yet
have a lost life through not living for Christ (1 Cor. 3. 15)
All the riches of this world will bring us nothing worth
calling *an advantage* unless we ourselves are saved (v. 25).

VII. **Christ and His Coming Glory.** "Whosoever is
ashamed of *Me* and *My words*," etc. (vv. 26, 27). Christ
and His Word stand or fall together. We cannot trifle with
His words without trifling with Him. He who emptied
Himself that He might become obedient unto death for us
shall yet come in *His own glory* to reward all who have been
faithful to Him in the days of His rejection (2 Cor. 5. 10).
Are we able to say with Paul, the bond-servant of Christ,
"I am not ashamed of the Gospel of Christ?"

FEATURES OF THE KINGDOM OF GOD.
Luke 9. 27-36.

> "Courage! though the skies are clouded,
> Blackest clouds will pass away;
> Courage! though the future's shrouded,
> All is clear to Him as day;
> And 'His purpose' shall endure,
> Ever faithful, ever sure."—GROSART.

WHAT did Jesus Christ mean when He said, "There are
some standing here which shall not taste of death till they
see the kingdom of God?" (v. 27). This question is not
easily answered. Some think that the kingdom of God
came, in judgment, at the destruction of Jerusalem,
although we fail to see the *kingdom* then or there. Others,
that this prediction was fulfilled at Pentecost by the
coming of the Holy Spirit, when that kingdom, which
is not of this world, was set up *in the hearts* of those who
believed in Jesus. Perhaps so; but how did Jesus speak
of some *seeing* it instead of knowing it experimentally?
Looking carefully at what happened eight days after on
the Mount, when *some* of them that stood by were with

Him, do we not *see* visible characteristics of that invisible kingdom of God which is now within us? There was—

I. **A Changed Countenance.** "As He prayed, the fashion of His countenance was altered" (v. 29). If we take the *countenance* as the outward expression of the inward condition of the soul, then we cannot be in the kingdom of God without having an altered countenance. Those in the kingdom of God have passed out of darkness into His marvellous light. The outward effect of this inward change must be "as the shining light." "Except ye be converted, and become as little children, ye cannot enter into the kingdom of Heaven" (Matt. 18. 3).

II. **Glistering Raiment.** "His raiment was white and glistering" (v. 29). *White* (bright, margin) raiment is emblematical of the *righteousness* of the saints (Rev. 19. 8). This is a whiteness that no fuller on earth can produce (Mark 9. 3). All our righteousnesses are as filthy rags. In the eyes of God the Father the raiment of Christ's righteousness was always white and glistering (Matt. 3. 17), but now the glory of His hidden life is made *manifest*, and they were "eye-witnesses of His majesty" (2 Peter 1. 16). The kingdom of God is not meat and drink, but *righteousness*, and peace, and joy in the Holy Ghost. Such will be Christ's appearance when He shall come the second time without sin unto salvation (Heb. 9. 28).

III. **Heavenly Fellowship.** "There *talked* with Him two men, Moses and Elias" (v. 30). Communion with the unseen (Father and Son) is a marked characteristic of the kingdom of God. Those in the kingdom are in perfect harmony with the law and the prophets, as represented by Moses and Elias, and will be fellow-partakers of the *resurrection* and the *translation* which they both represent. Spiritually we have already been resurrected from the dead (Col. 2. 13), and translated into the kingdom of God's dear Son (Col. 1. 13), and made to sit together in heavenly

places (Eph. 2. 6). At the coming of Christ in that glory
which was revealed on the Mount there will be with Him
those who, like Moses, have been raised from the dead
(1 Thess. 4. 14), and also those who, after the manner of
Elijah, have been *caught up* to meet the Lord in the air
(1 Thess. 4. 15-17). The kingdom of God is the kingdom
of His saving glory.

IV. A Particular Interest in the Death of Christ.
"They spake of His decease" (v. 31). Another special
feature of the kingdom of God is that the DEATH OF CHRIST
is the centre of profound and unfailing interest. All those
in the kingdom should ever realise that they are there by
virtue of His Cross and Blood. Let us learn from the
talk of the glorified on this Mount that the atoning death
of the Lamb of God should be uppermost in our hearts
and minds in the midst of our greatest privileges and
blessings. The Cross is the key to the glory; it is the
foundation of the kingdom of grace.

V. A Glorious Overshadowing. "There came a
cloud and overshadowed them" (v. 34). This cloud,
called "the excellent glory" (2 Peter 1. 7), was the *visible*
symbol of the all-enveloping presence of God, in which the
children of the kingdom live, and move, and have their
being. *Abiding in Him* is another distinguishing feature of
those who are in the kingdom of God (1 John 2. 28). As
they *entered into* the cloud, by the cloud overshadowing
them, so may we by faith enter into "His marvellous
light" by the overshadowing of the Holy Ghost. The
surrounding, all-enveloping glory of His presence may be
ours now through that other advocate who dwells in us, and
of whom Jesus said, "He shall glorify Me" (Rom. 8. 28).

VI. A Christ-Honouring Voice. "There came a
voice out of the cloud, saying, This is My beloved Son:
hear Him" (v. 35). That clear, "still small voice" that

acknowledges Jesus as the eternal Son of God is another well-defined characteristic of the kingdom. This voice from Heaven still speaks in the hearts of all those who have through grace come under the blessed rule of the Lord as King. It was first heard when Jesus took the place of a sinner, and *yielded* Himself to the perfect fulfilment of the will of God (Matt. 3. 17). Jesus sought the honour that comes from God only, and He got it. Are we seeking only the honour that comes from *one another*? (John 5. 44).

VII. **A Joyful Experience.** "Peter said, Master, it is good for us to be here" (v. 33). When Peter said "Let us make three tabernacles" he was speaking foolishly and in ignorance, for the glorified cannot abide in temples made with hands; but when he said "It is good for us to be here" he was uttering the deep and happy feelings of his soul. It is good for us to be in such company as this, to hear such a voice, and to be surrounded with such a glory. Blessed are such, for theirs is the kingdom of God. "Except a man be born again he cannot see the kingdom of God." ———

GRACE AND GRUDGE.
Luke 9. 51-56.

> "I would not angered be but grieved
> When I do find myself deceived;
> I would be kind to ignorance,
> Rememb'ring Thy long sufferance;
> I would Thy gentleness approach,
> On Thy Name never bring reproach."

A STRAW may indicate which way the wind blows or in what direction the river runs; a trifling event may have a tremendous significance. One had been casting out devils in the Name of Jesus, and some of His disciples forbade him (vv. 49, 50) "because he followeth not *with us*." Observe the grace of the Master in allowing a stranger so to use His Name and the grudge of the disciples in forbidding him.

The marked contrast between the spirit of the Master and that of His followers will become more apparent as we consider further the—

I. Saviour's Devotion. "He steadfastly set His face to go to Jerusalem (v. 51). Now that it has become the *fixed purpose* of His heart no power on earth or hell can hinder. "The time was come that He should be received up." He will go to Jerusalem that He might suffer and die in obedience to the Father's will, and that He might overcome him that had the power of death, that is the devil (Heb. 2. 14). Blessed be His Name, His *heart* was in His great self-sacrificing work. He went on steadfastly, like a warrior to the battle, confident of victory. He knew that the time was at hand when He would be *received up* (v. 51).

II. Samaritan's Bigotry. "They did not receive Him, because His face was as though He would go to Jerusalem" (v. 53). The Samaritans had their temple on Mount Gerizim, but because He was making for the city of His Father's House they would honour Him not. This Christ-rejecting bigotry manifests itself in many ways. There are still those who will not receive Christ.

1. BECAUSE HE DOES NOT HONOUR THEIR WORKS. They have, like these Samaritans, built a temple of their own, fashioned after their own thoughts and opinions, and unless the Lord Jesus Christ compliments them in some way for their good works they will receive Him not (Rom. 10. 2, 3; Luke 18. 9).

2 BECAUSE HE WILL NOT GO WITH THEM IN THEIR WAYS. They had made up their minds to do their worship at Gerizim, and unless Jesus Christ would condescend to meet with them *there* they would have nothing to do with Him. The self-righteous devise their own plans, determine their own ways, and if Christ does no acknowledge such they simply receive Him not, and go on with their Christless work and worship.

3. BECAUSE HE SEEMS TO FAVOUR THOSE WHOM
THEY DESPISE. "His face was as though He would
go to Jerusalem." The Jews had no dealings with the
Samaritans. They were like some High Churchmen who
will have nothing to do with the Christ that blesses
Dissenters. In setting His face toward Jerusalem He
was setting His face to the Cross which still makes Him
an offence to many.

III. **Disciples' Intolerance.** "When His disciples
saw this they said, Lord, wilt Thou that we command fire
to come down from Heaven and consume them?" (v. 54).
Perhaps James and John remembered that it was hereabout
where Elias had wrought such a miracle of judgment
(2 Kings 1. 10). The sudden outburst of this ungracious
and odious spirit reveals at least three things: Their—

1. FAITH. They believed that the Heavens would
answer their call, and that fire would come down at their
bidding. Such faith is not to be lightly esteemed. Men of
like passions with ourselves have wrought by faith such
mighty works (James 5. 17).

2. ZEAL. Their indignation was hot at the insulting
attitude of these Samaritans toward their Master. They
could not stand by, as perhaps some of us can, and see the
Lord being despised and rejected without any *moving* of
the soul, either with divine pity or selfish rage.

3. IGNORANCE. They knew not what manner of spirit
they were of, neither did they know the manner of their
Master's spirit, nor the great deep purpose of His mission.
"I am not come to judge the world, but to *save* the world"
(John 12. 47). The devotion of which ignorance is the
mother is both blind and merciless.

IV. **Master's Rebuke.** "He turned and rebuked
them, and said, Ye know not what manner of spirit ye are
of" (v. 55). Zeal without knowledge is bigotry. It was

this *manner of spirit* that kindled the fires of Smithfield and soaked the Scottish heather with the blood of Covenanters. It is this "manner of spirit" that still reveals itself in such prayers as this: "Lord bless me, and my wife, my son John and his wife; bless us four, and no more, Amen." It is this same manner of spirit that does not, and cannot, rejoice and praise God for the good work done *by others*. In this connection study James 3. 16, 17.

V. Gracious Explanation. "The Son of Man is not come to destroy men's lives, but to save them" (v. 56). While in the days of His humiliation He made Himself of no reputation, being reviled He reviled not again. He remained true to His divine character and mission, to LOVE, to SUFFER, and to DIE (John 3. 17). Behold now, not the judgment time, but the *accepted* time; hence the long suffering patience of God. If any man have not the spirit of Christ he is none of His, "As He is so are we in this world." Our mission, then, like His, is not to destroy men's lives, but *to save them*.

SENT ONES.

Luke 10. 1-20.

"Man hath his daily work of body or mind
Appointed, which declares his dignity,
And the regard of Heaven on all his ways,
While other animals inactive range,
And of their doings God takes no account."

—MILTON.

THESE seventy were *appointed* by the Lord, and *sent* forth, two and two, and surely it was a great comfort for them to know that they were going *"before His face,"* and into the very places *"whither He Himself would come"* (v. 1). May not every *sent one* now rest in this same assurance, that wherever they go, at His will and in His Name, *there* shall He manifest His presence. But there is to be no selfish monopolising of this work on the part of the sent ones, for it was to them the Lord said, "Pray *ye* the Lord of the harvest, that He may send forth labourers" (v. 2). In this spirit of prayer, begotten by real love for the Lord and His work, we do become "co-workers together with Him." There are precious lessons here for all who seek to do the will of God.

I. A Great Commission. "Go your ways; behold, I send you forth" (v. 3). They went as—

1. LAMBS. "Behold, I send you forth as lambs among wolves" (v. 3). They were not sent as *rams* to fight their way by the power of their *heads*, but as lambs, entirely under the protection of the ever-watchful Shepherd, and as such they represent *heart* life more than head life. The influence of love is always more powerful than that of reason. The wolves represent those who live the grossly selfish life—men of the world.

2. FORERUNNERS. "They went whither He Himself would come" (v. 1). As such they were to "salute no man by the way." Their coming into any city or place was a testimony that the King Himself was coming. Have we, as sent ones (chap. 20. 17, 18), been animated by a like faith in the promise and power of Christ? Do we expect Him to follow up our word and work in His Name with His own convincing presence?

3. HERALDS. Saying, "The kingdom of God is come nigh unto you" (v. 9). From that time Jesus began to preach and to say, "Repent, for the kingdom of Heaven *is at hand*" (Matt. 4. 19). The kingdom itself was brought near by the very presence of the heralds of it. If the kingdom of God is *within you* (Luke 17. 21; Rom. 14. 17), then when you come into contact with those who know not God, nor His Christ, does not the kingdom come near to them *in you*?

4. AMBASSADORS. Jesus said of them, "He that heareth you heareth Me, and he that despiseth you despiseth Me"

(v. 16). "Now then, we are ambassadors for Christ, as though *God did* beseech you *by us*; we pray you *in Christ's stead*, be ye reconciled to God" (2 Cor. 5. 20).

II. **A Joyful Testimony.** "They returned with joy, saying, Lord, even the devils are subject unto us through Thy Name" (v. 17). Those who go at His bidding and in His Name will always have a *joyful* testimony to bear. They will be more than conquerors. "We wrestle not against flesh and blood, but against principalities, against powers, against *the rulers* of the darkness of this world, against *spiritual wickedness* in high places" (Eph. 6. 12). Our foe is not in the form of *"flesh and blood"* (human), but in the character of wicked spirits which rule the kingdom of darkness—invisible demons—that possess the hearts of men, and that can only be cast out through the power of the Name of Jesus (Eph. 2. 2). The works of the devil are still being destroyed *in* those to whom the Son of God is being manifested (1 John 3. 8). Thus, the lifting up of the Son of God is still the power to bring the devils of doubt and uncleanness into subjection (John 12. 13).

III. **A Suggestive Comment.** "Jesus said unto them, I beheld Satan as lightning fall from Heaven" (v. 18). What a strange and startling statement, coming as a reply to their exultant account of *"devils* being *subject* to them." It appears that Satan shot down from the heavenlies with lightning speed when he saw that his angel demons were being routed and overcome by those seventy messengers of the Son of God. The more we triumph in the *Name of Jesus*, the more intensely will we be tried and opposed by the powers of darkness. The *wrestling* mentioned in Ephesians 6. 12 implies a real and desperate struggle in very close quarters—wrestlers grip each other.

IV. **An Assuring Promise.** "Behold, I give you power to tread on . . . all the power of the enemy" (v. 19). Although Satan hath come down like lightning in all his power to·oppose the mission of Christ through you, I *give you power* to tread all his power beneath your feet. The sphere of Satan's work is now on the earth. Let us treat all "criticisms" and "teachings" that are opposed to the mind and purposes of Jesus Christ as the "doctrines of devils" (1 Tim. 4. 1). Take courage from His promise, "I give unto you power" (Acts 1. 8). The time has come when the God of peace can bruise Satan under your feet (Rom. 16. 20). One of the signs of *faith* in His Name is the casting out of devils (Mark 16. 17).

V. A Source of Joy. "Rejoice not that the spirits are subject unto you, but rather rejoice because *your names are written in Heaven*" (v. 20). To have our names written there is a guarantee of deliverance (Dan. 12. 1). Overcoming devils is, in the mind of Christ, a comparatively small matter, but to have our names written in the Lamb's Book of Life (Rev. 21. 27), and to belong to the General Assembly and Church of the Firstborn, which are written in Heaven, is something to *rejoice* over, as it is a privilege that will be fruitful of joy and honour through all eternity, for a man may cast out devils and yet himself be a castaway (Matt. 7. 22, 23). _____

THE GOOD SAMARITAN.
Luke 10. 30-37.

> "He is bound to me,
> For human love makes aliens near of kin."
> —INGELOW.

THIS lawyer, being "willing to justify himself, said unto Jesus, And who is my neighbour?" (v. 29). The world has never seen anyone better fitted to answer such a question than Jesus. "He knew what was in man." There are but few who are not *willing* to justify themselves in their neglect of that *mercy* (v. 37) which constitutes true neighbourliness. This is a parable, beloved, for the Samaritan's sake. A beautiful reflection of the mercy of God in Christ

Jesus, unexpectedly coming into contact with a destitute and alien heart. Observe here—

I. A Threefold Misery. He was—

1. STRIPPED of his raiment (v. 30). This certain man in going down from Jerusalem to Jericho, a distance of about eighteen miles, fell among thieves and was stripped. Ever since the fall of Adam this world has been a den of thieves. Every man's business, more or less, is just to get out of others all he possibly can. Only those taught of God can look, not at their own, but at the good of others. All who fall into the clutches of sin and iniquity are sure to be stripped of their raiment of righteousness and of their "garment of praise." The devil is still seeking whom he may devour.

2. WOUNDED (v. 30). He in all likelihood received His wounds in His desperate attempts to withstand the robbers. Our own strength and wits are a poor defence against the sudden onslaughts of evil. The morally wounded and disabled in the battles of life are found lying everywhere along the highways of human concourse. Their name is legion who have sunk into the ditch of a city slum through being stripped of their reputation and having their hopes and prospects wounded to the death (Isa. 1. 6).

3. HALF DEAD (v. 30). In this wretched condition he could do nothing but *wait* and pray. Waiting for the compassion of some loving heart and the kindly touch of some neighbourly hand. To be half-hearted about anything is to be half-dead to the matter. With regard to the things eternal, how many are half-dead and quite unconscious of it. Backsliders in heart (Rev. 3. 16). But let us not in our pride condemn this poor outcast, for if we had gone the *same way* we might have been in the same plight. If we had gone the way of those who are born and reared in the city slum, or in dark heathendom, what better would we be than they are?

II. A Threefold Attitude. In the Priest, the Levite, and the Samaritan we see three different attitudes toward the helpless and unfortunate. That of—

1. PERFECT INDIFFERENCE. "The priest passed by on the other side" (v. 31). This priest was doubtless on his way home from the Temple service. In the discharge of his ceremonial duties he is very punctilious, and would pass by nothing, but a needy, dying brother by the wayside is unworthy of his notice. "Weighed in the balance and found wanting." No hope can on the *Law* be built.

2. INTERESTED CURIOSITY. "The Levite came and *looked*, and passed by on the other side"(v. 32). This man is a type of those who are not a little inquisitive, but who are not even a little compassionate. They want to *know*, but they don't want to *help*. This Levite could tell a story about this poor man when he went home, and justify his heartless conduct by saying that the place was too dangerous for him to tarry and lift the fallen. He also by his act is "weighed in the balance and found wanting" (1 John 3. 17).

3. PRACTICAL SYMPATHY. "The Samaritan came where he was, and had compassion on him," etc. (vv. 33-35). Although the Jews had no dealings with the Samaritans, this Samaritan in mercy would have dealings with the half-dead Jew. This is *the point* in the parable. A despised one, compassionates, shows mercy, and saves one who was living at enmity with him, thus manifesting that love of God in Christ Jesus which stoops to show mercy with a self-sacrifice that slays the enmity (Eph. 2. 16).

The Good Samaritan bears the features of the despised Nazarene, who comes to seek and save the lost.

(1). *"He came where he was."* Christ comes to us right where we are. In our stripped and wounded condition we could do nothing for ourselves (Rom. 5. 6).

(2). *"He had compassion on him"* (v. 33). His *heart*

was moved toward him. The Salvation of Christ was heart work. "He loved us, and gave Himself for us."

(3). *"He bound up his wounds, pouring in oil and wine."* Although we are full of wounds and bruises (Isa. 1), Christ can bind up and heal (Luke 4. 18). This He does by the oil of His Spirit and the wine of His Word.

(4). *"He set him on his own beast."* Those whom the Lord lifts up are also set in His own place. "Now are we the *Sons* of God."

(5). *"He brought him to an inn."* The saved of the Lord also find shelter and new friendships.

(6). *"He took care of him."* In the Salvation of Christ there is not only a great deliverance, but also a special providence (Rom. 8. 28). He careth for you.

(7). He left a promise concerning him (v. 35). Our Great Shepherd has also left enough for our need during His absence in "the exceeding great and precious promises." "And inasmuch as ye did it unto these, ye did it unto Me." "When I come again I will repay thee."

The Great Lesson.

Christ has suffered for us, leaving us an example that we should follow His steps. "Go thou and do likewise" (v. 37).

"MARTHA, MARTHA."
Luke 10. 38-42.

"Nor can the vain toil cease,
Till in the shadowy maze of life we meet
One who can guide our aching, wayward feet,
To find Himself our Way, our Life, our Peace;
In Him the long unrest is soothed and stilled;
Our hearts are filled."—F. R. HAVERGAL.

THE heart that is only half-conquered by Christ's peace will be easily tossed about when assaulted with the "cares of this world." Martha comes before us here as one cumbered and troubled about her work. A weary, burdened servant, just at the point of breaking down. What to her was *duty* has become drudgery. There is wholesome food for thought here for every servant of Christ. Martha—

I. Received Jesus. "Martha received Him into her house." Being perhaps the oldest in the home the right of receiving guests into the house would be hers. Her *receiving* Him was the proof of her *faith* in Him. It is vain and presumptuous for us to talk about our *faith* in Christ if we have not actually *received* Him into the house of the heart (see John 1. 12).

II. Sat at His Feet. "She had a sister called Mary, which ALSO sat at Jesus' feet and heard His words." This word *also* surely proves that Martha had sat and listened to His words as well as Mary. The faith that received Christ will certainly desire to know His will. This is the second step in the Christian life—learning. "*Come* unto Me, and I will give you rest. *Learn* of Me, and ye shall find rest" (Matt. 11. 28, 29).

III. Was an Active Worker. She busied herself with "*much serving.*" She was none of those spongy Christians who can do nothing but drink in. There are many whose sole conception of the Christian life is to *hear*. Martha was not only a hearer, but a doer. She had listened to His words, and she would minister to Him.. Her service, too, was no ordinary service. She had planned to do *much*. The honest, earnest design of her generous heart was to accomplish much for the honour of Jesus.

IV. Became Worried over her Work. "Martha was *cumbered* about much serving." Tersteegen has said: "We are not always to be seeking, we must sometimes have found Him. The seeker works actively; the finder enjoys quietly." Whenever work for the Lord brings upon us the worry of "carefulness and trouble," we may be assured that we have somehow got out of Christ's

yoke, for He says, "My yoke is easy, and My burden is
light. Take My yoke upon you, and ye shall find *rest*
unto your souls."

V. **Began to Complain.** "Lord, dost Thou not care
that my sister hath left me to serve alone? Bid her therefore that she help me." The worried and cumbered worker
will soon be found in the ranks of the grumblers. Martha's
big task of "much serving" was self-imposed, and she, like
all those in similar circumstances, soon got burdened and
wearied. God-given work will never be cumbersome when
done in His strength. But let it be noted to Martha's
credit that she made her complaint, not to her sister, but
to her Lord. Those cumbered and grumbling workers who
are continually pouring their grievances into the ears of
their fellow-servants ought to be shamed out of their
cowardliness by the straightforward heroism of Martha.
Dare to be honest, and say as she did, "Lord, dost Thou
not care?" Have the question of worry settled with your
Master. Find out in His presence whether your harassing
anxiety about His service is pleasing to Him, or whether
there is not some one that He might bid come and help
you, or whether you are not "careful and troubled" about
things which the Lord has no interest in.

VI. **Was Rebuked by the Lord.** "Jesus said unto her,
Martha, Martha, thou art careful and troubled about
many things, but one thing is needful." It is no honour to
the Prince of Peace that His servants' hearts should be
filled with restless solicitude about His business. "My
peace I give unto you. Let not your heart be troubled,
neither let it be afraid" (John 14. 27). "I would have you
without carefulness" (1 Cor. 7. 32). "Take no thought
(anxious concern) for your life." Your Father knoweth
(Matt. 6. 25; see also v. 8). If the Lord had bidden Mary
go and help Martha He would have partly justified her in
her complaint, but, no, He said in substance, "You take

too much upon you. The one thing you need is not a *helping* hand, but a *restful heart*."

Mary had chosen that good part, and He will not take it from her. There are many Matthews as well as Marthas, whose countenances bear the traces of a worried and troubled heart, even while they are seeking to serve Jesus. "Cumbered about much serving." Cast all your care upon Him, for He careth for you. Rest in the Lord.

PRAYER: ITS PRIVILEGE AND POWER.
Luke 11. 1-13.

"LORD, TEACH US TO PRAY" (v. 1).

"The prayers I make will then be sweet indeed,
If *Thou* the spirit give by which I pray;
My unassisted heart is barren clay,
That of its native self can nothing feed."—M. ANGELO.

IT would appear that while the Lord was praying in a "certain place" His disciples heard Him, and were deeply moved, as never man prayed like this Man. What calmness of spirit, what assurance of faith, what holy familiarity with the unseen Father of Spirits, what an overawing reality and power there was in these simple utterances of their Master! No wonder that when He ceased they came with tear-filled eyes, saying, "Lord, teach us to pray." The power of prayer lies more in what we *are* than in what we say. They pray well who have *"holiness unto the Lord"* written across their lives. Prayer, wrote a deaf and dumb girl, is "the *wish* of the heart." If the heart is right with God, then the desires of the heart will be granted (1 John 5. 14, 15). *Desires* are plentiful in human hearts, but how few are confidently breathed into the ear of God. Notice here—

I. Need of Prayer. "Lord, teach us to pray" (v. 1). All men pray in the way of *wishing*, or earnestly *desiring*, but not to the living.God. "Before I was converted," said one, "I said my prayers to nobody, now I pray to God." We have never learned to pray if we have not learned to speak personally to a personal God, and to know that He hears us. Intercourse with God is a crying need of the soul of man. We need more than *human* sympathy. We need a greater than human help. DIVINE power and compassion are the counterparts of human weakness and need. "Lord, teach us to pray."

II. Teacher of Prayer. *"Lord,* teach us." Surely this "Teacher come from God" is well able to instruct us in the way to God. His whole life was lived in the atmosphere of prayer. He constantly breathed the breath of Heaven. In His every act we hear the voice of His pleading on our behalf. His incarnation, His holy life, His agony in the garden, His atoning death, and His rising again from the dead were all mighty voices of supplication unto God. He who spent whole nights in prayer had too much to do to be in a hurry or to neglect secret communion with His Father. "Lord, teach us." He teaches us to pray by giving us a deep insight into the poverty of our own natures that we may *hunger* after righteousness (Rom. 8. 26). He teaches us to pray by revealing to us, through His Spirit, of His own unsearchable riches that we may covet earnestly the best gifts (Heb. 4. 16).

III. Spirit of Prayer. In answer to their requests the great Prayer Teacher said, "When ye pray, say, Our Father which art in Heaven," etc. In putting this prayer into their mouths our Lord was not only teaching the *order* in which our prayers should be formed, but, we think, the very spirit and *condition of heart* necessary to true prayer. Looked at in its subjective aspect this prayer implies a condition of—

1. SONSHIP. "Our Father." Before we can say "Our Father" in any real sense we must have received the Spirit of adoption (Rom. 8. 15). We must be made sons

through receiving His Son ere we can honestly say Father (John 1. 12).

2. SANCTIFICATION. "Hallowed be Thy Name." His *Name* stands for all that He is in His holiness, righteousness, love, and almightiness. How can an unsanctified soul *hallow*, set apart as holy, the great Name of God in the daily life? What communion hath light with darkness? If His Name is to be hallowed in us we ourselves must be hallowed to His Name.

3. SUBJECTION. "Thy kingdom come." How can we utter this petition if we are not willing that our own hearts and thoughts should be subject to His rule? So, to be able to pray, there must be entire submission to the will of God (Rom. 14. 17).

4. CONSECRATION. "Thy will be done." To pray *"Thy will be done"* there must needs be a willingness *to do* His will.

5. BROTHERLY LOVE. "And forgive us *as we forgive every one*," etc. Our prayers may often be hindered for lack of tender-heartedness toward those who may be indebted to us (Eph. 4. 32). Does this reveal the spirit in which we pray?

IV. **Manner of Prayer.** "Because of his *importunity* he will give him as many as he needeth" (vv. 5-8). The word importunity here stands for "*shamelessness*," and this is the only time it is used in the New Testament and employed by our Lord in connection with prayer; it is exceedingly expressive. It means that in offering our requests to God for things *needful* we should take no denial; turn not aside through any seeming providential rebuff, being utterly shameless in our persistent, confident waiting (Exod. 17. 11).

V. **Simplicity of Prayer.** "Ask, and it shall be given you," etc. (vv. 9-12). The child in its own way begins to ask as soon as it is born, and the mother has no difficulty in interpreting its cry. As long as we maintain the child-like spirit prayer will be a simple, delightful, and soul-strengthening exercise. The more we get conformed to the image of Christ the nearer do we come to the very presence of God. And the nearer we approach to Him in our real soul likeness to Him the more simple and childlike will our prayers be. "Ask, and ye shall receive."

VI. Efficacy of Prayer. "If ye, . . . how much more shall your heavenly Father give the Holy Spirit to them that ask Him?" (v. 13). The Father will give the Holy Spirit to them that ask Him, and in *giving* the Spirit He is putting within the reach of each child of His EVERY SPIRITUAL BLESSING (Eph. 3. 14-19). Many of us have yet to learn what our gracious Father is willing to do for us, and through us, by His gift of the Holy Ghost. As workers together with Him we beseech you that ye receive not *this* grace of God in vain. "If ye ask anything in My Name I will do it" (John 14. 12-14).

THE STRONG AND THE STRONGER.
Luke 11. 16-22.

"If we were not weak,
Should we be less in deed than in desire."—SHELLEY.

How strange that they should seek "a sign from *Heaven*" (v. 16) when they see *devils* being cast out. But men will yet try to ignore the divine character of Christ while there are infallible proofs of it before their eyes in the changed *lives* and *hearts* of men. They are like owls sitting in the dark, and crying, "Where is the sun?" Every *evil* overcome is a proof of the existence of a holier power. Evil cannot expel evil. This principle leads to God. "There is none *good* but God." If *sin* has been conquered and hated, and the heart changed and filled with love to God, then this is not of man. This is the finger of God. In these verses we have two great princes representing two

great kingdoms. To one or other all belong, and peace
and safety can only be enjoyed by the subjects of the
greatest, as the one is most bitterly antagonistic to the
other. Here we see the warriors described, the battle
fought, the victory won, and the spoil divided. Consider then—

I. **The Great Enemy.** "Satan," the chief of the devils
(v. 15), and his chief end is to deceive and destroy. His
deadly campaign commenced in Eden, and goes on still
(Gen. 3. 1). Notice—

1. His CHARACTER. "A strong man" (v. 21). The
strength of the devil is in his cunning and deceit. In the
garden we have a revelation of the *wisdom* of this serpent.
He is strong because he knows exactly where human
weakness lies. He enters the citadel of man's soul as a
pledged friend when he comes as an angel of light; how
few can discern him in his real malignant form. He is
strong to overcome the righteous scruples of the young,
and also to deceive the Godward longings of the old.
Too late, too late, he whispers, or, you are too great a
sinner. But although he is strong he is but a strong
man; his is limited strength, not almighty. Yet his
"wiles" are innumerable and his darts are fiery.

2. His CONDITION. "Armed" (v. 21). His is the
armour of darkness; he loves the darkness rather than the
light. "While men slept he sowed tares, and went his
way" (Matt. 13. 25). He is the prince of darkness, and
those who are in darkness are under his power (Eph. 2. 2).
His armour is just the opposite of God's. 1. His *girdle* is
the girdle of falsehood—a liar from the beginning, and so
his children go speaking lies from the womb. 2. His
breastplate is that of wickedness, for wickedness is in his
heart. 3. His feet are shod with the preparation of the
gospel of enmity. 4. His *shield* is the shield of doubt. 5.
On his head is the *helmet* of damnation. 6. His *sword* is

the imaginations of the evil heart, and with this he slays
the word of truth that darkness and death might reign
(compare Eph. 6. 11-18).

3. His Occupation. "Keepeth his palace" (v. 21).
His palace is the dungeon of the unrenewed heart, where
every window is glazed with perverting glass, so that
things can never be seen as they really are. Here the
occupant is a prisoner of darkness and ignorance. He may
boast of what he knows of the world of light, truth, and
liberty outside, but he knows nothing as he ought to know.
Did he but know the truth he could abide no longer in
bondage. This his vigilant keeper knows right well, so he
keepeth his palace that his goods may have peace. This is
the "peace, peace, when there is no peace." The more
anxious the soul is to escape the more closely is he kept.
If fair promises will not do, the iron fetters of despair will
be applied.   Notice some of the ways in which he keepeth
his palace. "I can read my Bible at home." "You can
tell me nothing new." "I go regularly to Church." "I
do as well as I can." "You make too much ado," etc.

4. His Possession. "Goods" (v. 21).   He who occupies the palace of the heart also possesses the powers and
faculties of the whole being. These powers and faculties
are *valuable* "goods," their intrinsic worth, who can cal-
culate?   The precious blood of Christ speaks volumes as
to the value of these "goods." These "goods," generally
speaking, may represent *all* who are under Satan's keeping.

Let us look at the character of an individual article,
the qualities of a single soul. There is—

(1). *Reason*, the Governor.

(2). *Understanding*, the Receiver.

(3). *Memory*, the Recorder.

(4). *Conscience*, the Discerner.

(5). *Will*, the Decider.

(6). *Affection*, the Distributer,

All these are prisoners to Satan under his power, used for his dark, devilish purposes. *"His* goods," not even your own free will! Ah, "strange liberty."

II. The Great Deliverer. "Christ."

1. His CHARACTER. "Stronger than he" (v. 22). Not merely a stronger *man,* but one whose strength is almighty. "If I speak of strength, lo, He is strong." The strength of hills is His. "I will send you a Deliverer and a strong One." "Help has been laid upon One that is mighty." How mighty is the sun to overcome darkness; how strong are the hills to bear the crushing tempest. So man's deliverer must be strong both to bear and to *overcome.* His arm is strong; it upholds the universe and guides the helm of providence. His *Word* is strong, none can gainsay it, none can hinder it from working. His *work* is strong, His foundation stands sure. Neither time nor eternity, nor the powers thereof can ever displace one single stone of His building. Hallelujah! One has come to seek and to save, with whom *nothing is impossible.* No enemy too strong for His power, no difficulty too monstrous for His strength. "The Lord shall fight for you, and ye shall hold your peace" (Exod. 14).

2. His ENCOUNTER. "He shall come upon him" (v. 22). The Prince of Life and the prince of darkness must come into close combat according to Genesis 3. 15. David must go out to Goliath, come upon him, strip him, and overcome in behalf of Israel, for he fought not for himself, but them, and love constrained him, although, like Christ, his brethren despised and rejected him. Yet he had the King's favour, and in overcoming the enemy he secured for himself a bride (1 Sam. 17. 25). Beautiful picture of our Deliverer who came forth from the Father, like David, to conquer the great enemy and purchase the Church as His bride. He "came upon the wiles of the devil" in the wilderness, upon his *enmity* and hate

in the Pharisees, upon his *works* in the demon-possessed, upon *himself* on the Cross. Then was the *hour* and *power* of darkness; dreadful conflict!

3. HIS VICTORY. "Overcome him, and taketh from him *all* his armour" (v. 22). Goliath is slain with his own sword. "Through *death* Christ destroyed him that had the power of death." His helmet was broken and his head bruised; his whole armour of darkness wherein he trusted has been destroyed, and the "true light now shineth." None need now be under his power as He came to set the prisoners free. But, alas, men love darkness rather than the light, and the bondage of Satan rather than the liberty of Christ, saying, "I love my master, and I will not go free." And so become a slave for ever. Jesus Christ is the rightful owner of the soul. "Thou hast ascended on high, Thou hast led captivity captive: Thou hast received gifts in the man" (Psa. 68. 18, *marg*.).

"The number of them was ten thousand times ten thousand, and thousands of thousands; saying . . worthy is the Lamb that was slain" (Rev. 5. 11, 12).

4. HIS GRACE. He divideth His spoils as the fruit of His warfare. He possesses pardon, peace, power, and paradise. These He willingly divides with the mighty *many* (Isa. 53). *All* who believe shall share in His victory. *All* is yours, for ye are Christ's (1 Cor. 3. 22). This great battle was substitutionary. Man had been spoiled of his goods by the devil, but Christ overcomes and recaptures the possession, as Abraham overcame the kings and brought back *all* the goods, and also his brother Lot (Gen. 14. 16). *Thou* shalt *keep* him in *perfect* peace whose mind is stayed on *Thee*. None can pluck them out of His hand. Will you share Christ's victory or the devil's overthrow? If the Son make you free, ye shall be free indeed (John 8. 36). The spoils of Calvary's Cross hath made many rich.

SINGLENESS OF EYE AND FULNESS OF LIGHT.
Luke 11. 33-36.

> "Earth's crammed with Heaven,
> And every common bush afire with God;
> But only he who sees takes off his shoes,
> The rest sit round it and pluck blackberries,
> And daub their natural faces unaware,
> More and more from the first similitude!"
> —BROWNING.

"LIGHT is sweet, and it is a pleasant thing for the eyes to behold the sun." So is it also with the light of truth that beams from the Son of Righteousness. It is in His light that we see light clearly. Blessed are such eyes that see. Our Lord Jesus Christ, who is here teaching us the blessedness of the single eye, bad in Himself in a pre-eminent degree the single eye; so His whole body was full of light. His light was not put in a "secret place" nor "under a bushel" (v. 33), but was "lifted up" on the lampstand of the Cross that all in the house of this world may see it. "There was the true Light which lighteth every man coming into the world" (John 1. 9, R.V.). Ye are the light of the world; let your light *so* shine. In examining this portion we would note—

I. The Medium. "The light (lamp) of the body is *the eye*" (v. 34, R.V.). The eye is—

1. PASSIVE. It does not, and cannot, create the light, neither can it form or transform any object. It is simply a *receiver* and a *reflector* of outward objects to the inner consciousness of man, a channel through which visible things are revealed to the invisible spirit.

2. VERY SENSITIVE. A little thing mars the vision of the eye. It is very easily offended. So with a tender conscience. They are blessed indeed who are as careful

about their conscience as they are about the apple of the
eye (Acts 24. 16). Oh, that our spirits were as sensitive
to the things of the Spirit of God!

II. **The Means.** "LIGHT." The light was made for
the eye, and the eye for the light. The successive
waves of light that lash with infinite tenderness upon
the eye prove the divine adaptation of the one to the
other. But light is not more suitable to the eye than
Christ is to the soul of man. There is a deep meaning
in the words of Goethe, "Were thine eye not sunny,
how could it ever see the sun?" So were thy soul not
God-like, how could it ever enjoy God? No one would
be foolish enough to say "I have an *eye* of my own,
I don't need the *light.*" The eye is utterly useless
without the light, so the spirit of man is utterly helpless
and powerless to discern the things of God apart from the
revelation of the Spirit of God (1 Cor. 2. 14). The true
Light *now* shineth. Oh, that the eyes of the *understanding*
might be opened (Luke 24. 31, 32).

III. **The Manner.** Christ is the Light of the World, but
there are two ways of looking at or dealing with this
Light. These are represented by the "single eye" and
the "evil eye," the pure and the impure, the honest
and the deceitful, the new heart and the old.

1. THE SINGLE EYE and its effects. The single eye is
one that has been anointed with the heavenly eyesalve
(Rev. 3. 18). The blood-washed spirit that looks
through this eye has been *reconciled* to God, and seeks
to know the truth as it is in Jesus. There is now no
mixed motives in the life, no mingling of self-interest
with the kingdom of God. The whole forces of the
soul are now concentrated in "this one thing I do,
forgetting the things that are behind, I press on toward
the mark." Such an eye fills the whole body with light,
because the Spirit of God takes the things which are

Christ's, and reveals them to those who have the pure eye for the glory of His Name. If our motives are single, one with Christ's, then we shall not walk in darkness, but shall have the light of His life within us. To be filled with the Holy Spirit of Truth is to be filled with light. The spirit of wisdom and revelation in the knowledge of Him: "The eyes of your understanding being enlightened" (Eph. 1. 17, 18).

2. THE EVIL EYE and its effects. The evil eye is the coloured lens of an unclean heart. The eye of prejudice can only see objects in a contorted fashion. The unrenewed heart of man can no more appreciate the light of revelation than the blinking owl of the night can enjoy the sunshine. The "evil eye" is like the eye of the hawk, always staring *downward* when flying upward. Remember Lot's wife. "If thine eye be evil, thy whole body is full of darkness." The darkness within is an evidence of an evil and doubting heart. We look to Christ with an evil eye if we look to Him only that *self* may be honoured and gratified; as Keble put it:

> "We see far in holy ground
> If duly *purged* our mental view."

IV. The Message. "Take heed therefore that the light which is in thee be not darkness" (v. 35). If the light that is in us is not a revelation from God it is but the flickering "spark of our own kindling," a light that is certain to deceive. The light that was in the Church of Laodicea was darkness, for although they said that they had need of nothing, yet was Christ, the Light, outside (Rev. 3. 17-20). There is no darkness so great as the darkness that is mistaken for light (Matt. 6. 23; Prov. 16. 25). Woe unto them that put darkness for light (Isa. 5. 20). "When the *pilot* is drowned, the *light* quenched, and the *captain* taken prisoner, what hope is left for the crew?" While ye have the light, *believe* in the Light (John 1. 9).

THE HYPOCRITE.
Luke 11. 37-44.

" A lie which is half a truth is ever the blackest of lies !
A lie which is all a lie may be met and fought outright,
But a lie which is part of a truth is a harder matter to fight !"
—TENNYSON.

THIS mongrel lie which is part of a truth finds its incarnation in the hypocrite. The one is as difficult to deal with as the other. The names *scribe* and *Pharisee* as used by our Lord here are synonymous of hypocrite. Their characteristics as detailed before us in these verses are the outstanding features of the hypocrite.

I. **He is more concerned about the traditions of men than the truth of God.** "The Pharisee marvelled that He had not first washed before dinner" (v. 38). The Pharisee of Christ's day not only held the traditions of the elders about hand-washing, but in their superstitious zeal bathed their bodies before meat (Mark 7. 4, R.V.). Jesus Christ in the heavenly truthful dignity of His character simply ignores it, so that the hypocritical marvel at His liberty. The sons of God are not to be in bondage to the opinions of men. Whom the Son of God makes *free* are free indeed. Although Christ Himself, the embodiment of truth and holiness, stood before this Pharisee, yet would he despise Him because He did not conform to his petty theory of hand-washing. The popular tradition about the way of salvation is, "Do as well as you can," to the denial of the truth of God's saving grace. There are other traditions concerning the Lord's coming and Church worship that are equally subvertive of the truth as it is in Jesus.

II. **He is more careful about outward than inward purity.** "They make clean the outside of the cup, but the inward is full of ravening and wickedness" (v. 39). The only good side of a hypocrite is the outside, for they do "*make clean* the outside." They live as in the eyes of their fellow-creatures, seeking not the honour that comes from God only. They are *men* pleasers. They will make their *hands* clean, although their hearts should be full of wickedness. They look upon the things which are *seen*. They *profess* to know God, but in works they deny Him (Titus 1. 16). They practically deny that "out of the *heart* proceed evil *thoughts*," etc., and that these are the things which defile a man (Matt. 15. 19, 20). He is utterly indifferent about the righteousness of God if he can only get his own established (Rom. 10. 3); and when he prays it is with himself (Luke 18. 11). He flatters men with his outward manners, while the inward manner of the heart is an abomination to God (James 4. 8).

III. He stickles for trifles, and neglects the things which are indispensable. "Ye tithe all manner of herbs, and pass over judgment and the *love of God*" (v. 42). God demanded that the *fruit* of the land should be tithed (Lev. 27. 30), but they would tithe even the fragrant plant, and *pass over* justice and the love of God as if these were unworthy of notice. Such would not rob a child of a pin, but they would unblushingly rob God of their whole life. "Behold, to obey is better than sacrifice" (1 Sam. 15. 22). By their fruits ye shall know them; they stand up stoutly for *orders* and *forms* of worship, while they pass over the promises of God and the power of the Holy Ghost. They will argue vehemently for the rules of the Church, and pass over the law of the spirit of life which is in Christ Jesus. He is very particular in adapting certain tunes to certain psalms, but it concerns him nothing as to whether he himself is reconciled to God and adapted to the kingdom of Heaven. He could not pass the plate at the Church door without putting something into it, but he can pass through a whole service without giving to God one grateful feeling for the gift of His Son. They *pass over* the LOVE OF GOD.

IV. He seeks self-glorification through his religious profession. "Woe unto you, Pharisees! for ye love the uppermost seats in the synagogues," etc. (v. 43). The hypocrite is religious, but only so far as it will help to honour himself and minister to his vanity. He has no thought of *adorning the doctrine* of God our Saviour, but he seeks to be adorned by the doctrine. If he holds office in the Church it is that it may add to *his* dignity. He would appropriate all the privileges purchased by the agony and death of the Son of God for the exaltation of his own deceitful self. He is seldom out of his place in the house of prayer, but his god is himself. It is not the synagogue or church that he loves so much as those *"uppermost seats"* that help to *lift him up*. He will be very zealous in religion if he can thereby gain the flattery of others. He is one who sits in the place of God, and who robs Him of His honour and glory. A hypocrite, it has been said, is "like a glow-worm, it seems to have both light and heat, but when you touch it it has neither."

V. His real character is loathsome, although it appears not in the sight of men. "Woe unto you, hypocrites! for ye are as graves which appear not, and the men that walk over them are *not aware* of them" (v. 44). Those who walked over or passed by those *whited* sepulchres little thought of the foulness and rottenness that were inside. "Within, full of dead men's bones and of all uncleanness" (Matt. 23. 27). A sow that is washed is only a washed *sow*. A hypocrite may manage by his white-washing to give no offence to his fellow-man, but God looketh upon the heart (1 Sam. 16. 7). Be not deceived, God is not mocked; the hidden man of the heart is naked and bare before the eyes of the Lord, and that is *the man* that must give his account unto God (Psa. 7. 9). The hypocrite lives for that which is "highly esteemed among men," but this is "an abomination in the sight of God" (Luke 16. 15). Your woe, O hypocrite, is coming, for hath not the Lord Jesus Christ said, "I am He which SEARCHETH THE HEARTS?" (Rev. 2. 23). What wilt thou do on that solemn day?

BIBLE READINGS.

BALAAM; OR, THE EXPERIENCES OF A CASTAWAY.

Joshua 13. 22; 1 Corinthians 9. 27.

"Not change of place, but change of heart
Winneth the sweet wounds of love's dart;
Coming or leaving, Thy power alone
Shattereth or melteth heart of stone.

Not change of place, but unchanged heart
Removes us, Lord, from where Thou art;
Darkened love! thrice saddest wonder!
Putteth God and us asunder."

"BALAAM, the son of Beor, did the children of Israel slay with the sword *among them* that were slain by them." This is a very brief statement, but it is a terrible *revelation*. He who once declared the Word and will of God is found slain among His enemies. A striking example of the "withered branch" referred to in John 15. 6. It may be true in our Christian experience what Felicia Hemans said in another connection:

"No outward thing is changed,
Only the joy of purity is fled."

A tree may have every appearance of health and stability even while in heart it is rotting away. It is possible to have the *form* of godliness while there is an utter absence of the power. The character of Balaam is somewhat enigmatical, but enough has been given us to make a beacon fire of warning to every servant of the Lord Jesus Christ. Let us look at—

I. His Character and Privileges.

1. HE WAS BROUGHT INTO CONTACT WITH GOD (Num. 22. 9-12; 23. 4). What an angelic privilege to have God

Q Vol. IV.

to speak to us, and to *know* that it is God who speaks!
One would think that such an evidence of His existence
and personal interest in us would be enough to bind our
souls for ever in faithfulness to Him. But, alas, how many
of us hear His Word, and believe it to be His Word, yet
fail in obedience to it?

2. HE HAD THE COURAGE TO ACKNOWLEDGE GOD BEFORE
OTHERS. "Balaam said, The Word that God putteth in
my mouth, that shall I speak" (Num. 22. 38). Nobly
spoken. In form this is the confession of the *faithful*
(1 Kings 22. 14). This is a hopeful start on the prophetic
career. Ye did run well. Who did hinder? Remember
Lot's wife.

3. HE HAD THE WORD OF THE LORD PUT IN HIS MOUTH
(Num. 23. 5). In this he was as highly favoured as the
true and tender-hearted Jeremiah (Jer. 1. 9). Nor was he
alone in this honour. "But what saith it? The Word is
nigh thee, even in thy mouth and in thy heart, that is, the
Word of faith which we preach" (Rom. 10. 8). To have
the Word of God put in our mouths when young is good,
but that is not enough to make faithful servants of Christ.

4. HE WAS CONVINCED OF THE SAFETY AND HAPPINESS
OF GOD'S PEOPLE (Num. 23. 21-24). Balaam's testimony
is: "He hath *not beheld iniquity* in Jacob; the Lord his God
is *with him*, and there is *no enchantment* against him."
Indicating a threefold privilege that belongs to all His
redeemed ones: 1, Forgiveness; 2, Fellowship; 3, Safety
(Rom. 4. 7, 8; Heb. 13. 5; Rom. 8. 33). It is never very
difficult to convince the ungodly that the Christian has
the best of it. When the magicians *failed* to imitate the
works of Moses they were ready to confess that "this
is the finger of God" (Exod. 8. 16-19).

5. HE HAD HIS EYES OPENED TO SEE THE VISION. "He
saw the vision of the Almighty falling into a trance, but
having his eyes open" (Num. 24. 3, 4). To have one's

eyes open to see the vision of the Almighty in His
wondrous grace and mercy in Christ Jesus is imperative
to a holy God-pleasing life. There are those who seek to
witness for God who have never seen the vision, whose
inner eyes have never yet been opened; and there are those
who, like Balaam, have seen the vision, and have turned
back. Zechariah had understanding in the "visions of
God," and as one has lately said, "Eternity itself will be
needed to measure the life of the man who has seen the
visions of God." It is an awful thing to see God in Christ
and die. The vision will haunt the impenitent through
eternity.

6. HE DECLARED HIS FAITHFULNESS TO GOD. "I cannot
go beyond the commandment of the Lord to do either
good or bad, but what the Lord saith, that will I speak"
(Num. 24. 13). These words have a very pleasant sound
in our ears, coming as they do after seeing the "vision
of the Almighty." They were spoken in a firm, decisive
tone. "If Balak," he says, "would give me his house
full of silver and gold, I cannot go beyond the Word of
God." Alas, alas, Peter has a fearful comment to make
on this loud-lip profession. "Balaam, who *loved* the
wages of unrighteousness" (2 Peter 2. 15; Jude 11). Not
every one that *saith* shall enter into the kingdom.

7. HE WAS AT TIMES MOVED BY THE SPIRIT OF GOD.
"The Spirit of God came upon him" (Num. 24. 2). Is
Balaam also among the prophets? Yes. For a time the
tongue of prophetic fire rests upon him, and he speaks the
wisdom of God. The coming of the Spirit upon him, as
upon others, was entirely of the GRACE of God, an
opportunity and a provision brought within the reach
of a soul that may enrich the life for ever, or that may
be *heartlessly* received, and end in failure, darkness,
disappointment, and disgrace. Take heed lest the *light*
that is in thee be turned into darkness.

8. HE HAD A GREAT DESIRE TO DIE THE DEATH OF THE
RIGHTEOUS. "Let me die the death of the righteous, and
let my *last end* be like his" (Num. 23. 10). There are two
ends to the life of the righteous, the first and the *last*. The
first may not always be blessed, but the last is. "Blessed
are the dead that die in the Lord" (Rev. 14. 13). In the
sight of the Lord their death is precious (Psa. 116. 15).
He desired the blessed end of the righteous without living
their *separated* life. A vain hope. Balaam was found
slain among the enemies of the Lord (Josh. 13. 22).
Take heed to thyself.

II. His Guilt and Failure.

1. HE SOUGHT TO ALTER THE WORD OF GOD. "The Lord
afterwards declared that "He would not hearken unto
Balaam" (Josh. 24. 9). It would appear from this that
he pleaded with the Lord to change His manner of dealing
with Israel, and so break His Word of promise. The
backsliding in heart would always fain do this.

2. HE LOVED THE WAGES OF UNRIGHTEOUSNESS (2 Peter
2. 15). Like Lot's wife, he would like the *rewards* of the
righteous, but his *heart* was set on the gain of godlessness.
The *love* of the heart decides the character of the life in the
sight of God. Be not deceived, God is not mocked. The
Lord looketh upon the heart. *Love* is either the fulfilling
or the breaking of the law of God.

3. HE TAUGHT THE PEOPLE OF GOD TO SIN (Rev. 2. 14;
Num. 31. 16). This is an awfully solemn charge to bring
against a man whose eyes had been opened to see the vision
of the Almighty, but it is the Almighty One Himself who
makes the charge. Ye cannot serve God and Mammon. If
we fail to walk in the light, and turn aside, like Balaam, to
the company and fellowship of the ungodly we cannot but
"cast a stumbling block" in the way of others, and bring
woe upon our own souls.

4. HE WENT BACK TO HIS OWN PLACE. "And Balaam

rose up, and went and returned to his own place"
(Num. 24. 25). Back like the sow that was washed
to its wallowing in the mire. "They went out from us
because they were not of us; if they had been of us they
would no doubt have continued with us." Back to *his
own place* of curse after God had in mercy given him a
place of blessing. If he had gone out *heartily* for God
and His people he would have had no cause or desire to
go back. To turn away from God is to go back to *your
own* place of death and dishonour (Heb. 6. 4-6).

5. HE CAME TO A WOEFUL END. "Balaam also did the
children of Israel slay with the sword among them that
were slain by them" (Josh. 13. 22). In going back to his
own place he dug his own grave and sealed his own doom.
Backslider, beware. Return unto the Lord, and He will
restore again the joy of thy salvation. The *love of the world*
is a sin that will eat like a canker the spiritual life out of
the soul. It was not without good reason Paul wrote: "I
keep my body under, lest by *any means*, when I have
preached to others, I myself should be a castaway" (1 Cor.
9. 27; Acts 1. 25). ———

POWER FOR SERVICE.

"WHEN the Comforter is come, whom I will send unto you
from the Father, even the Spirit of truth, *He shall testify*
of Me; and *ye also* shall bear witness" (John 15. 26, 27).

"Ye shall receive power, after that the Holy Ghost is
come upon you, and ye shall be witnesses unto Me"
(Acts 1. 8).

"God bearing them witness, both with signs and
wonders, and with divers miracles, and gifts of the
Holy Ghost" (Heb. 2. 4).

When the Holy Spirit was given through Jesus Christ
from the Father He came as the Comforter (Advocate),
and as the Spirit of truth to bear witness of the resurrection and ascension of Christ, and to endow His followers

with power to testify of Him. Every son of God should be
a servant. "Son, go work to-day in My vineyard." Every
delivered one should serve Him without fear in holiness all
the days of his life (Luke 1. 74, 75). For divine service
divine equipment is required.

I. Power is Needed.

"*Tarry ye* in the city of Jerusalem *until* ye be endued
with power from on high" (Luke 24. 49). The Lord Jesus
tarried for thirty years until the time of His showing
Himself when He was endued with power from on high
at the Jordan. But it is not their *tarrying* we wish
to emphasise so much as the fact that they were *not
to go* in His Name until they had received a special
spiritual endowment for this definite work of witnessing.
Jesus Christ knew the strength of the forces of evil to
be overcome, and that without the presence of the Holy
Spirit of power all their self-effort would be worthless.
"He wrestled not against *flesh and blood*, but against
principalities and powers, against the *rulers of darkness*"
(Eph. 6. 12). Therefore the whole ARMOUR OF GOD must
be put on ere they set out on this holy warfare. A man
may as soon hope to beat back the tide with a pitch-fork
as to overcome the works of darkness without the power
of the Holy Ghost. The enduement or baptism of the
Holy Spirit stamps the service of the man of God with
divine authority. Without this power our work for God
will only be a laughing stock to wicked spirits.

II. Power is Provided.

"Ye shall *receive power* when the Holy Ghost is *come upon
you*" (Acts 1. 8, R.V.). "This is that which was spoken.
. . . I will pour out My Spirit" (Acts 2. 16; 10. 45).
When the Holy Spirit came He came as a MIGHTY
RUSHING WIND, the symbol of power. As wind He is
within the reach of all, and all the pressing powers of
hell shall not be able to withstand His mighty *rushing*

(Isa. 59. 19). Fling thyself into this mighty rushing current and take full advantage of this all-sufficient spiritual influence waiting in the person of the Holy Ghost to be linked on to your weakness. We may well glory in our infirmities when the power of Christ rests upon us (2 Cor. 12. 9).

III. The Nature of this Power.

It is *spiritual*—the power of the Holy Spirit. It consists of a fitness to adapt with unerring and convincing rectitude the "things of God" to the helpless and destitute spirits of men. It is not so much a *gift* of the Spirit as it is the working of the Holy Ghost Himself in and through the heart that has been wholly yielded to Him as an habitation of God. It is something entirely different from the powers that dominate in this present evil world. 1. It is not *money power*. "Silver and gold have I none, but such as I have I give." 2. It is not *intellectual* power. "They were unlearned and ignorant men" (Acts 4. 13). It is the *foolish* and the *weak* things that God hath chosen as channels of His *wisdom* and *power*, that no flesh may glory in His presence (1 Cor. 1. 27). 3. It is not *social* power. Those mighty men who stood in front of the battle in the early days were neither princes nor peers, but poor peasants clothed with the armour of God. This power is not of man, nor of the will of the flesh, but of God

IV. How this Power may be Received.

"Ye shall *receive* power, *after* that the Holy Ghost is come upon you" (Acts 1. 8). Just as we receive *life* by receiving Christ, so shall we receive *power* by receiving the Holy Ghost. Salvation is in the personal Saviour; power is in the personal Spirit. Your heavenly Father will give the Holy Spirit to them that ask Him (Luke 11. 13). Ask, and ye shall receive; ask of Him, and He will give you the *living water* (John 4. 10) Some, like Simon, would like to buy this power, if not with money, at least with prayers and works (Acts 8. 18-20). It cannot be *purchased*, it is the *gift* of God. When the suffering disciples prayed that "with all *boldness* they might speak His Word" God answered their cry by filling them with the Holy Ghost (Acts 4. 29-31). The only way by which God can *give us* power for service is by filling us with His Holy Spirit. It is not *ye* that speak, but the Spirit of your Father which is in you. "Have ye received the Holy Ghost since ye believed?" (Acts 19. 2).

V. How this Power is to be Used.

If we are not using this power we are abusing it. We must use the gift of the Holy Spirit as the servants were to use the pound delivered to them—in *"occupying till He comes."* We can only in a true sense occupy *His place* when we are entirely possessed by His Spirit. In doing *His business* we are to trade with *His gift*. He has not sent us on this great warfare on our own charges. We are to use this power as Peter and John used it when they healed the lame man *in the Name* of the risen Christ. We are to use it as Elisha used the mantle that was given him by his risen and glorified Master (2 Kings 2. 14, 15). We are to use it as Gideon used the "sword of the Lord" (Judges 7. 20). We appropriate the power of the Holy Spirit when by faith we act, *depending on Him* to accomplish the work and will of God in us and by us. This is the victory, even our *faith*, "I will go *in the strength* of the Lord God, making mention of His righteousness, even of His only" (Psa. 70. 16).

THE CHRISTIAN'S CROWNS.

"AND round about the throne . . . I saw four and twenty elders sitting, clothed in white raiment, and they had on *their heads crowns* o gold" (Rev. 4. 4).

"And the four and twenty elders . . . *cast their crowns before the throne*, saying, Thou art worthy, O Lord, to receive *glory*, and *honour*, and *power*" (Rev. 4. 10, 11).

These "four and twenty elders" seem to represent the company of the redeemed in Heaven. They evidently bear all the characteristics of the glorified Church. 1. They are *clothed* with white raiment. 2. They worship the *Lamb* (Rev. 5. 8). 3. They have been *redeemed* by the blood. 4. They are *round about* the throne. 5. They are *crowned* with glory and honour. 6. They are *kings and priests* unto God. 7. They hope to *reign on the earth* (Rev. 5. 8-10).

I. What these Crowns Signify.

The elders cast their *crowns* at the Redeemer's feet, saying, "Thou art worthy to *receive glory*, and *honour*, and *power*." Then these crowns are symbolic of "glory, honour, and power," put upon them through the grace of God their Saviour as a reward for their faithfulness and the fulfilment of His promise, "Enter thou into the *joy of thy Lord*." But this "glory, and honour, and power," represented in the crowns, those redeemed ones seek to lay at Jesus' feet, saying, "Thou art worthy," etc.

II. What these Crowns are, and How they are Won.

1. Incorruptible Crown. "Now they do it (practise temperance) to obtain a corruptible crown, but we an incorruptible" (1 Cor. 9. 25). Much self-denial was practised by the Olympic runners to gain the *glory* and the *honour* of being crowned with a wreath of parsley, which faded and withered in a few hours. But we deny self and keep the body under, "bringing *it into subjection*" (v. 27), that we might obtain a glory, and an honour, and a power (crown) that is as incorruptible as the *Word* of Him who hath promised. We are to strive for the *mastery*, not in our own strength, but panoplied with the "whole armour of God" (Eph. 6. 12). This crown of glory and honour is within the reach of all the saints (Heb. 12. 1).

2. Crown of Life. "Blessed is the man that endureth temptation, for when he hath been approved he shall receive the crown of life, which the Lord hath promised

to them that love Him'' (James 1. 12, R.V.). We may have *life* through faith in Christ without ever having the *crown* of life. This crown, or the *"glory,* and *honour,* and *power,"* of life is only given to those who have been *tried* and *approved,* and who *love Him.* Faithfulness to God in times of testing, because of sincere and whole-hearted love for Himself, will win the crown of life (Rev. 2. 10). Are there not many Christians whose lives are not crowned with glory, honour, and power, but who are more like unto the withered branches, trodden under foot of man, and gathered and burned at their pleasure? (John 15. 6).

3. CROWN OF RIGHTEOUSNESS. "There is laid up for me *the crown* of righteousness, which the Lord, the righteous Judge, shall give to me at that day, and not only to me, but also to all them that *have loved His appearing"* (2 Tim. 4. 8, R.V.). We win the crown of righteousness, rightness in our daily life, by *"loving* His appearing." The coming of our Lord is a most practical doctrine. No truth has a mightier influence in *righting* our lives. "He that hath *this hope* in him purifieth himself as *He is pure."* The soul that loves the Lord will long for His appearing, and will daily seek to be like Him. Many do not *love* His appearing, because their own lives are not right. Such will not "at that day" receive the "glory, and honour, and power" (crown) that belongs to those whose lives here have been righted by the hope and love of His coming. This constraining love was no factor in their earthly spiritual history, so the fruit of it cannot be reaped by them.

4. CROWN OF REJOICING. "For what is our hope, or joy, or crown of rejoicing (glorying, R.V.). Are not *even ye* in the presence of our Lord Jesus Christ at His coming? For *ye are* our glory and joy" (1 Thess. 2. 19, 20). This crown of glorying is won through soul-winning (Phil. 4. 1). What a *glory* and *honour* it is to be used of the Holy Spirit to lead others into a saving knowledge of the Son of God. This is

the end of your faith, "even the salvation of souls" (1 Peter 1. 6). This crown is given when the soul-winner and the soul won meet together *"in the presence* of the Lord Jesus Christ at His coming." "Behold, I and the children whom the Lord hath given me" (Isa. 8. 18).

5. CROWN OF GLORY. "When the chief Shepherd shall appear ye shall receive the everlasting crown of His glory" (1 Peter 5. 4, Alford). To be blessed with the everlasting crown of *His glory* is to be made a partaker of that "glory, and honour, and power" which is eternally His. The glory which Thou gavest Me, I have given them" (John 17. 22). We shall be *like Him* when He, the chief Shepherd, shall appear, crowned with glory, and honour, and eternal life.

III. How these Crowns were Used.

"They fell down before Him, and *cast their crowns before the throne*, saying, Thou art worthy, O Lord, to *receive*," etc. (Rev. 4. 10, 11). They are thankful for the crowns, that they might have something wherewith to honour Him who redeemed them and who sits upon the throne. We don't labour and strive to win crowns for the grandisement of ourselves in the kingdom of Heaven, but that we might have something to lay at His feet, whereby His glory and *honour* may be exalted. "Crown Him Lord of all." "Worthy is the Lamb that was slain to receive *power*, and *riches*, and *wisdom*, and *strength*, and *honour*, and *glory*, and *blessing*" (Rev. 5. 12). This is He who once was crowned with thorns, but now "on His head are *many* crowns" (Rev. 19. 12). _____

THE SELF-ABNEGATION OF THE LORD JESUS
AS REVEALED IN THE GOSPEL BY JOHN.

IN the Gospel of John we are brought, as it were, into the "holiest of all." That disciple "whom Jesus loved," and who *leaned* upon His bosom, seems to have drunk most deeply of the Spirit of the Master. In the self-abnegation of our Lord we are taught one of the profoundest lessons on the Christian life. Our Lord and Saviour was so truly human that He had a self which He did not live to please. "He pleased not Himself." In this also He *suffered*, leaving us an example. The disciple is not greater than his Lord. If He through self-denial finished the work given Him to do, how shall we follow Him if we will not deny ourselves and take up the cross? Let us *hear* HIM. He says—

I. "My meat is **to do the will of Him that sent Me,** and to finish His work" (chap 4. 34).

"My *meat*." The very strength and satisfaction of His soul lay in the doing of His Father's will. His hungry heart could only be appeased with the knowledge that the purposes of Him that sent Him were being fulfilled. "Man shall not *live* by bread alone, but by *every word* that proceedeth out of the mouth of God." Do we find *food* for our souls in the doing of the will of God?

II. "Verily, I say unto you, **the Son can do nothing of Himself,** but what He seeth the Father do: for what things soever He doeth, these also doeth the Son likewise" (chap. 5. 19). "I can **of Mine own self do nothing**" (v. 30).

What a revelation this is of the self-emptying of the Son of God, and of His entire relinquishing of everything that was calculated to mar the accomplishing of the will of God through Him! As the SON He could do nothing of Himself apart from the Father. He *could not* do it because of the great love He had for His Father. May the love of Christ so constrain us. The plan of Christ's life was not His own making. He lived in such close fellowship with the invisible Father that He could say, "The Son can do nothing of Himself, but what He SEETH *the Father do*." Do we live in such close fellowship with Christ that His

doings are ever before *our eyes* as a pattern for us.
The Father had honoured the Son in doing nothing
without Him (John 1. 3). Now the Son, even in His
humiliation, will do nothing without the Father (John
10. 30). Into this holy and blessed relationship have
we been brought by being made the "sons of God"
(Heb. 2. 11). "WITHOUT ME *ye can do nothing.*"

III. "I came down from Heaven, **not to do Mine own
will**, but the will of Him that sent Me" (chap. 6. 38).

He came down from Heaven with the express purpose
not to do His own will, but *the will of the Father* who sent
Him. Every believer in Jesus is sent down into the world
with the same message and for the same purpose (John
17. 18). Not to do their own will, but the will of Him that
sent them. Why did our Lord make such frequent reference
to the fact that He did not come, and work, and speak to
please Himself? Was it not to manifest His *oneness* with
the Father, and to bring His hearers into personal contact
with Him? Although Jesus Christ had done *His own will*
we are not to suppose that *that will* would have been contrary to the will of His Father, but He emptied Himself
that He might be a pattern to those who should hereafter
believe and follow. "Not My will, but Thine be done."
Does this not help us to understand that oft-repeated
petition, "Thy will be done on earth as it is done in
Heaven?"

IV. "Jesus said, My doctrine is **not Mine**, but **His
that sent Me**" (chap. 7. 16). "I speak to the world those
things which I have heard of Him" (chap. 8. 26). "I do
nothing of Myself, but as My Father hath taught Me, I
speak these things" (chap. 8. 28).

These gracious words which fell from our Saviour's lips
assure us that His *teaching*, spoken *to the world*, was the
teaching of God the Father who had *taught Him*. Nor is
it otherwise now with every true servant of God. Did not

Jesus say, "I have called you friends, for all things that I have heard of My Father I have made known unto you?" (John 15. 15). He received the teaching from the Father; we receive it from Him that we might "speak it to the world," as we have heard of Him. In this sense each one of us may truly say, "I can do nothing of myself." This is the place we must take before Him if His Word and doctrine are to be taught with power. "Not I, but Christ." He who so yields himself to the will of God will be declared to be a son of God with power, according to the spirit of holiness (Rom. 1. 4).

V. "I do always those things that please Him" (chap. 8. 29). "I must work the works of Him that sent Me while it is day" (chap. 9. 4). "I have not spoken of Myself; He gave Me a commandment what I should say" (chap. 12. 49).

These texts we have grouped together might be taken separately, as they reveal three deeply significant truths in connection with our Lord's earthly ministry. 1. He spake by *commandment* of the Father. He was as a man under authority. 2. He was impelled by the *necessity* of the obedience of love. "I *must* work." 3. His life was an unqualified success in the sight of God His Father. "I do *always* those things that please Him." His choice was always for the will of God. Christian worker, how is it with your life in the light of these facts? Is the *command* of God in your testimony? Is the constraining love of Christ the impelling force in your daily service for God?

VI. "I speak not of Myself, but the Father that dwelleth in Me, He doeth the works" (chap. 14. 10) "The Word which ye hear is *not Mine*, but the Father's which sent Me" (chap. 14. 24).

So perfectly was the Son abandoned to the will of the Father that He *dwelt in Him*, and spoke *through Him*. He claims that His *will*, His *words*, and His *works* were not

His own, but the Father's. Is it so with us in this present evil world? Christ is giving us the secret of His own blessed life when He says "If ye abide *in Me*, and *My words* abide in you, ye shall ask what ye will, and it shall be done unto you. *As* the Father hath loved Me, *so* have I loved you" (John 15. 7-9). He is also putting us, as His servants, into the same relationship with the Father and the world that He Himself had when He says—

VII. "I have given them the words **which Thou gavest Me**" (chap. 17. 18). "As Thou hast **sent Me into the world**, even so have I sent them into the world" (chap. 17. 18).

Having received the same words and the same commission as the Son of God Himself received, what manner of persons ought we to be? Faithful is He that calleth you, who also will do it. ———

SUCCOUR FOR THE TEMPTED.

"As when a sudden storm of hail and rain
Beats to the ground the yet unbearded grain,
Think not the hopes of harvest are destroyed
On the flat field, and on the naked void:
The light, unloaded stem, from tempests freed,
Will raise the youthful honours of its head,
And soon restored by native vigour bear
The timely product of the bounteous year."—DRYDEN.

"WE have not an high priest which cannot be touched with the feeling of our infirmities, but was on *all points* tempted like as we are, yet without sin" (Heb. 4. 15). "For in that He Himself hath suffered being tempted, He is *able to succour* them that are tempted" (Heb. 2. 18).

The *nature* of *our* temptations will generally prove what we really are. The higher the moral and spiritual character is the higher and more subtle will the temptations be. Christ could never be tempted by the coarse and common forms of sin. The devil brought his tempting baits up to the dignity of the Son of God. Therefore, being tempted as a Son on all points like as we (sons) are, He is able to succour them that are tempted with the comfort wherewith He Himself was comforted of God. Shall we look at some of those "points" in which He, like us, was tempted, and by which we are made partakers of His sufferings?

I. **He was tempted to seek a lawful thing in an unlawful way** (Matt. 4. 3, 4). "Afterward He *hungered*, and the tempter said, If Thou be the Son of God, command that these stones be made *bread*." Is not this a common temptation, especially to those struggling with the difficulties of a *business* world? That coveted thing, longed for with a *hungry* heart, seems to be within reach just by the speaking of a word, but a word which is forbidden by the inner conscience. The very thought of it is the whispering of Satan. In this the Lord tasted what is now generally known as "the struggle for bread." But He fought this temptation with "Man shall not live by bread alone," etc. "He trusted in God" (Matt. 27. 43).

II. **He was tempted to make a display of His power for the honour of His own Name.** "If *Thou* be the Son of God, *cast Thyself down*, for it is written, He shall give His angels charge over Thee" (Matt. 4. 6). We will never be able to demonstrate our *divine sonship* to the world or the devil by "*casting ourselves down*." One thing is certain, that if the devil had been able to cast Him down he would not have asked Him to "cast *Thyself* down." Are we not also tempted to make a display of our gifts or powers—money, song, speech, or works—just for the sake of proving to others that *we* are the sons of God, instead of for the glory of God. He was tempted on all points like as we are, yet without sin

III. **He was tempted to accomplish the purposes of God by adopting a God-dishonouring method.** "The devil showeth Him all the kingdoms of the world,

and the glory of them, and said, All these will I give thee
if Thou wilt *fall down* and worship me" (Matt. 4. 8, 9).
It was the purpose of God to give Him all the kingdoms
of the world and the glory of them (Zech. 14. 9; 1 Chron.
29. 11; Rev. 11. 15). The temptation is to step out of
the Father's plan, to shun the agony of the Cross, and
to expect the promised blessing by using means that are
opposed to the Word and character of God. This was the
temptation by which Adam and Eve fell, and a temptation
that seems to be growing increasingly powerful in these
present times. The devil is always ready to meet the
devoted servant of Christ who is *hungering* after the
kingdom of God with his "If thou wilt *fall down.*"
Abram *fell down* when he took Hagar, that he might
hasten on the promise of God. The Gospel of Christ,
preached in the Holy Ghost, and received by faith, is
THE POWER OF GOD. To substitute anything else for this
as the means of bringing the world to Christ is to fall
down before the temptation of the devil.

IV. **He was tempted to speak unadvisedly with
His lips.** "The Pharisees began to urge Him vehemently,
and to *provoke Him* to speak of many things, that they
might catch something to accuse Him" (Luke 11. 53, 54).
Christians who have to mingle much with ungodly men are
often assailed in this manner. They argue hotly, that they
might provoke the follower of Christ to utter some word
thoughtlessly, that they might seize it as a sword to smite
the innocent. Tempted one, remember He was tempted
like as you are, and that He is able to succour them that
are tempted. There is no member of the body so ready to
play the Judas as the tongue   Set a watch.

V. **He was tempted to save Himself by forsaking
the Cross.** "*Save Thyself.*" "If Thou be the Son of God
come down from the Cross, and *we will believe*" (Matt.
27. 40-43). To deny the cross and *save ourselves* the

suffering and the shame connected with it is an oft-repeated temptation to the servant of Jesus Christ. There is
additional force in it when there seems to be the prospect
of others *believing* in us through so doing. The world, the
flesh, and the devil are ever crying in some way or other
"*save thyself*" to every son of God who would be crucified
with Christ (Gal. 2. 20). The enemy knows that if we save
ourselves our *lives* will be lost (see Matt. 16. 24, 25). To
take up His cross is to lose our self-life, as the corn of wheat
dies in the earth and lives again in a *new* and more fruitful
form. "If Thou be the Son of God, save Thyself." It
never becomes the *sons* of God to *save themselves*, although
they may be sometimes constrained to ask: If I am a *child*
of God, why should I suffer so? He was tempted in all
points like as we are, therefore He is able to succour them
that are tempted.

The temptation to shrink from suffering for the good of
others is ever before us; but as Jesus *suffered* without the
gate *that He might sanctify* the people with His own blood,
so are we called to go forth, therefore, unto Him without
the camp, *bearing His reproach* (Heb. 13. 12, 13). The
reproach of Christ is a glorious *burden* (1 Peter 4. 14;
Heb. 11. 26). ———

THE SERVANT OF CHRIST.

THE hearty servants of the world have their distinguishing
marks; the true servant of Christ has his. He is—

I. Obedient. What wilt thou have me to *believe*
rather than what wilt thou have me to do? seems to be the
inquiry of many. The willing servant has always an open
ear for the Master. "Speak, Lord, for Thy servant
heareth." "My sheep hear *My* voice, and they follow
Me." Among the babel of the world's voices *His* voice
will he obey (Josh. 24. 24). Christ pleased not Himself;
the servant is not greater than his Lord. Many would
rather mourn than follow. It is easier for the flesh to

offer the sacrifice of tears than to obey; but obedience is better than sacrifice. Jesus, who hath left us an example, said: "I do always those things which please *Him*" (John 8. 29). Are you ready to obey then, "Whatsoever He saith unto you, *do it*?" In 2 Samuel 15. 15 we see servants ready for anything.

II. **Diligent.** The hand of the diligent maketh rich; the hand of the slothful is in his bosom. He that observeth the wind shall not sow; he that regardeth the clouds shall not reap. "Sow beside all waters; be instant in season, out of season." The hand of a diligent servant searcheth for work. Whatsoever thy hand findeth to do, do it; and do it heartily as unto the Lord, for ye serve the Lord Christ. Do not trifle with the Lord's work, for it is written, "Cursed is he that doeth the work of the Lord negligently" (Jer. 48. 10, margin). Do not hide your Lord's money (gifts), remember the unprofitable servant was cast out (Matt. 25. 30). Serve the Lord with a pure conscience (2 Tim. 1. 3).

III. **Humble.** "In honour, preferring one another" is to be the rule among the servants; the servant of the Lord *must not* strive (2 Tim. 2. 24). *Envy*, like Miriam's leprosy, totally unfits for service. Do we praise God as heartily for service rendered by others as by ourselves? If not, are we not seeking in some measure our own and not the Master's glory? "Our highest place is lying low." Uzziah was marvellously helped till he was strong; but when he was strong pride and destruction followed (2 Chron. 26. 15). The mark of Jacob, the wrestling victor, was a halt. The humble servant gives himself no place, that the Master be not robbed. Joseph, the faultless servant, said, "It is not in me." Paul, the successful servant, said, "Yet not I." Let us follow his example, serving the Lord with all humility of mind (Acts 20. 19).

IV. **Persevering**. Jacob served fourteen years for the
object of his affection. "Ye shall reap if ye faint not."
If the Master give us a work to do it should be ours
faithfully to do it. Elijah sent his servant *seven* times
with the one message, and he went and murmured not.
It was not the servant's place to *make* the cloud, nor yet
to despair at the seeming fruitlessness of his journeys;
his duty was to *go* and *look*. How often the servant
goes discouraged because he does not see signs of coming
blessing. Does the Master send? Well, go again! Be
assured that He hears the sound of abundance of rain.
He shall not be discouraged (Isa. 42. 2). "Serve the Lord
with gladness" (Psa. 100. 2).

V. **Faithful**. It is required of a servant that he be
found faithful. I am thankful that it is not that he be
found successful, and yet every one that "serves with
a perfect heart and a willing mind" (1 Chron. 28. 9)
will be successful according to the Master's reckoning,
though others may brand it as a failure. The servant
is to be faithful with the few things, "the little that a
man hath." He that hath only one pound will not be
responsible for ten. Nothing is trifling that is done for
Him; the cup of cold water will not lose its reward.
Eternity gives dignity to the lowliest service. "Be thou
faithful unto death, and I will give you a crown of life."

VI. **Courageous**. Be of good courage, be strong and
very courageous. Moses as a servant was very courageous
when he demanded of Pharaoh the surrender of all Israel.
He was a bold ambassador. Well he knew that he was not
sent to warfare on his own charges. His authority was,
"I AM" hath sent me. Why are ye fearful? "Lo, I am
with you." Well may the servant tremble that goeth forth
in his own name, instead of having the "Thus saith the
Lord." Would that all God's servants had the courage to
make the same demand of the world that the Master makes:

entire surrender, entire separation, entire consecration. Add to your faith courage.

VII. Devoted. In Exodus 21. 1-6 we have the confession of the devoted servant. "I love my Master; I will not go free." That which is devoted to the Lord shall not be redeemed. Ye are *not* your own, for ye *are* bought with a price, therefore glorify God. The constraining power is the love of Christ, our Master. We love Him because He first loved us. The Levites were called to serve at the age of twenty-five and were discharged at fifty. They gave the best of their lives to God. God requires the best, He is worthy. Many live in the expectation of doing God a favour by presenting Him a worthless, wasted life when they are going to die. "Present your bodies a *living* sacrifice unto God, which is your *reasonable* service" (Rom. 12. 1).

VIII. Uncompromising. *First,* with the world. Pharaoh said, "Go, but ye shall not go very far. Go, but leave your little ones and your flocks." The servant's answer was as emphatic as a thunderbolt, "Not a hoof shall be left behind." Let us build with you, says the world; but the whole-hearted servant answered, "Ye have nothing to do with us to build," etc. (Ezra 4. 3). "Come down to the plain of Ono." The response of Nehemiah was, "I *cannot* come down." Jephthah said, "I have opened my mouth unto the Lord, and I cannot draw back." Let us not be among those that draw back. *Second,* with sin. The command given to Israel was, "Drive out," "Destroy," "Dispossess." Every spared enemy is a spared trouble, every unconquered sin is an enemy in the camp. The compromising Saul spared Agag, but the uncompromising Samuel hewed him in pieces. So let us do with every hidden sin. "Crucify the old man with his lusts." As servants let us stand on the dignity of God's Word, and "dwell with the King for His work."

Then others will be constrained to say, "Happy are these Thy servants." Remember that the eyes of the Master are on us. "I know thy service" (Rev. 2. 19).

"YE ARE THE TEMPLE OF THE LIVING GOD."

"THUS saith the high and lofty One that inhabiteth eternity, whose Name is Holy, I dwell in the high and holy place, *with him also* that is of a contrite and humble spirit" (Isa. 57. 15).

"Let them make Me a sanctuary, that I may dwell among them" (Exod. 25. 8). God's delights were always with the sons of men. He dwelt with Adam in the garden, with Israel in the wilderness, in the temple among His worshippers, and in the Person of His Son. Now He abides in His believing people. The temple is a type of the body of Jesus (John 2. 21), of the Church of Christ (Eph. 2. 21), and of the individual believer (1 Cor. 3. 16). In the tabernacle God *walked* with His people. In the temple His people *dwelt* with Him. Suggestive of the present and past dispensations. As a type of the believer we might look at—

I. The Building of the Temple.

1. THE THOUGHT ORIGINATED WITH GOD (Exod. 25. 8). God always takes the first step. "Chosen in Him before the foundation of the world."

2. THE FOUNDATION WAS LAID BY GOD (1 Cor. 3. 11). Both the place and the stone were His own choosing. Man was helpless, and has no standing apart from "Redemption."

3. THE MATERIAL WAS UNFIT TO BEGIN WITH (1 Chron. 22. 2, 3). At that time ye were (1 Cor. 6. 9, 11), but ye are washed.

4. SOME OF THE MATERIALS WERE WON IN BATTLE (1 Chron. 26. 27). Every thought is to be brought into captivity to the obedience of Christ.

5. THERE WAS A GREAT VARIETY OF MATERIALS. Gold,
silver, brass, iron, wood, stone. All sorts. Many members,
but one body; many gifts, but one Master.

6. THE STONES WERE PREPARED BEFOREHAND (1 Kings
6. 7). You hath He *quickened* who were dead, and now as
lively stones are built up (1 Peter 2. 5).

7. THEY WERE FITLY FRAMED TOGETHER (Eph. 2. 21).
So we are builded together for an habitation of God
(Eph. 2. 22). All one in Christ Jesus.

8. THE TEMPLE WAS BUILT ACCORDING TO A DIVINE
PATTERN (1 Chron. 28). Christ is the image of the
invisible God, and believers are created anew after the
image of Christ. "As He is, so are we."

II. The Purpose of the Temple. It was—

1. THE HABITATION OF GOD (Exod. 25. 8). Believers
have been saved, not merely to be saved, but to be a
spiritual house, indwelt by the Spirit of God.

2. THE PLACE IN WHICH GOD WALKED (2 Cor. 6. 16). As
God walked in the tabernacle of old, so in grace doth He
desire to walk in His people. "Ye are the temple of God."
"I will dwell in them, and walk in them."

3. THE PLACE OF HOLINESS (Psa. 93. 5). If holiness
becomes His house, surely holiness becomes His saints in
whom He dwells. "Be holy for I am holy."

4. THE PLACE OF PEACE. "In this place will I give peace"
(Haggai 2. 9). Those indwelt by the Spirit of God have
their hearts filled with the peace of God.

5. THE PLACE OF STRENGTH AND BEAUTY (Psa. 96. 6).
Strength of character and beauty of life characterise all who
are filled with the Holy Spirit; they are strengthened with
might by His Spirit in the inner man (Eph. 3. 16).

6. THE PLACE WHERE HIS GLORY WAS REVEALED. "I
will fill this house with glory (Haggai 2. 7), and will be

the glory in the midst of her'' (Zech. 2. 5). May Christ so dwell in our hearts by faith that we might be filled with all the fulness of God (see Eph. 3. 16, 20).

7. THE PLACE WHERE EVERYTHING SAID ''GLORY'' (Psa. 29. 9, R.V.). One would like to write more on this point, it is so full of meaning. Does everything in you and me say ''Glory?'' If everything has been given to Him it will.

III. **The Possessing of the Temple.** The temple was finished; man had done everything he could, but he could not fill it with glory. The glory of His presence—

1. WAS NEEDED IN IT (2 Chron. 7). It was still an empty house till He possessed it. Oh, may God fill us; we are empty indeed, with all our furniture, till He fills.

2. FILLED IT (2 Chron. 7. 1). As soon as it was finished it was filled. We are possessed as soon as we are wholly yielded.

3. TRANSFORMED IT. It became a *spiritual* house when possessed by God the Spirit (1 Peter 2. 5). Ye are not carnal but spiritual if God dwell in you.

4. CLAIMED IT (Psa. 132. 14). If your body is the temple of the Holy Ghost ye are not your own (1 Cor. 6. 19). ''Your body and your spirit, which are God's.''

5. SANCTIFIED IT (Psa. 93. 5). ''The Lord hath set apart him that is godly for Himself'' (Psa. 4. 3). ''Know ye not that ye are the temple of God?'' (1 Cor. 3. 16).

THE WORLD.

I. **The State of the World.** The world was made by Him (John 1. 10)—*Creation.* Sin entered into the world (Rom. 5. 12)—*Corruption.* The whole world lieth in wickedness (1 John 5. 19)—*Desolation.* The devil is the god of the world (2 Cor. 4. 4), and in Matthew 4. 8 we see him offering to sell it.

II. **The Hope of the World.** God loved the world (John 3. 16)—*Compassion*. "Behold the Lamb of God, which taketh away the sin of the world" (John 1. 29)—*Substitution*. That the world through Him might be saved (John 3. 17)—*Salvation*. He is the propitiation for the sins of the world (1 John 2. 2).

III. **The Need of the World.** He will convince the world of sin (John 16. 8)—*Conviction*. That all the world may become guilty (Rom. 3. 19)—*Contrition*. That the world may know Thou hast sent Me (John 17. 23)—*Confession*. The gift of tongues at Pentecost is a proof that God desires *all* to hear and live. The message was for "every creature under Heaven" (Col. 1. 23).

IV. **The Believer and the World.** He is *given* to Christ *out of the world* (John 17. 6)—*Divinely separated*. He is *sent* by Christ *into the* world (John 17. 18)—*Divinely commissioned*. He is *indwelt* by Christ *for the* blessing of the world (John 17. 23)—*Divinely equipped*.

SOME THINGS POURED OUT.

THE poured out—

I. **Blood** in ATONEMENT (Lev. 4. 7). How? All have sinned. Where? In the altar of the Cross. Who? His own blood.

II. **Blessings** in SALVATION (Mal. 3. 10). The Blood of Christ bought superabundant blessing. *Prove* Him by trusting and yielding.

III. **Spirit** in POWER (Acts 2. 16-18). Power for sanctification and service. Ability to see visions of God, and witness to His Son.

IV. **Heart** in PRAYER and ADORATION (Psa. 62. 8). Where? "Before Him." How? "Pour out." Why? "God is a refuge for us." He filleth the hungry soul with goodness (Psa. 107. 9).

V. **Wrath** in JUDGMENT (Rev. 14. 9, 10). Its objects: "Worshippers of the beast," marked in their *heads* and *hands*, thoughts and deeds. Its nature: "Without mixture;" no mercy, pure justice, the final fruit of unbelief (Jude 5). ———

THE BELIEVER'S PAST AND PRESENT,
AS SEEN IN EPHESIANS 2.

1.—The Past.	Verse	2.—The Present.	Verse
We were dead in sin, ..	1	We are quickened, ..	1
We did live according to the world, ...	2	We are saved, ...	5
		We are raised, ..	6
We were the servants of the flesh, ...	3	We are seated, ..	6
		We are created in Christ,	10
We were the children of wrath, ...	3	We are made nigh, ..	13
		We are made one, ..	14
We were without Christ,	12	We are made new, ..	15
We were aliens, ..	12	We are reconciled, ..	16
We were strangers, ..	12	We have access, ..	18
We were foreigners, ..	19	We are fellow-citizens,	19
We were without hope,	12	We are built, ...	20
We were without God,	12	We are fitly framed, ..	21
We were afar off, ..	13	We are an habitation of	
We were at enmity, ..	16	God, ...	22

———

PLEASING GOD.

"YE ought to please God" (1 Thess. 4. 1).

I. Those who are not pleasing God.

1. They that live ONLY FOR THEMSELVES are not pleasing God. "We ought not to please ourselves, for even Christ pleased not Himself" (Rom. 15. 1-3). *Self* is all the god that many worship.

2. They that only seek to PLEASE MEN are not pleasing God. "Do I seek to please men? If I yet pleased men, I should not be the servant of Christ" (Gal. 1. 10).

3. They that are IN THE FLESH cannot please God. "But ye are not in the flesh, but in the Spirit" (Rom. 8. 8, 9).

4. They that have NO FAITH cannot please God. "Without faith it is impossible to please Him" (Heb. 11. 6). A man might have faith in the minister, in the Church, and Bible, and yet have no faith in God.

II. Those who are pleasing God.

1. Those who ASK RIGHT THINGS from God. "David asked for an understanding heart to discern between good and bad, and the speech pleased the Lord" (1 Kings 3.9,10).

2. Those who are SEPARATED FOR GOD. "No man that warreth entangleth himself, that he may please Him who hath chosen him" (2 Tim. 2. 4). How numerous are the entanglements!

3. Those who are WHOLLY YIELDED TO GOD. Now God "working in you that which is well-pleasing in His sight" (Heb. 13. 20, 21).

4. Those who WALK WITH GOD. "Enoch walked with God" (Gen. 5. 24), "and he pleased God" (Heb. 11. 5).

5. Those who PRAISE GOD. "I will praise the Name of God. This also shall please the Lord" (Psa. 69. 30, 31). All singing is not praising. God judgeth the heart.

III. Promises to those who please God.

1. "Their ENEMIES shall be at peace with them" (Prov. 16. 7). This is a different thing from being at peace with our enemies. *They* surrender.

2. Their PRAYERS shall be answered (1 John 3. 22). If we are always doing what pleases Him we may always expect what we ask.

3. Their NAME shall be everlasting (Isa. 56. 4, 5). "Choose the things that please Me, and I will give an everlasting name." "They shall be called by His Name, and His Name endureth for ever."

CUPS OF THE BIBLE.

1. The cup of suffering, ... John 18. 11
2. The cup of salvation, ... Psa. 116. 13
3. The overflowing cup, ... Psa. 23. 5
4. The cup of communion, ... 1 Cor. 11. 25
5. The cup of devils, ... 1 Cor. 10. 21
6. The cup of wrath, .. Psa. 75. 8; Rev. 16. 19

THE CHOICE OF MOSES.
Hebrews 11. 25.

IT is a blessed privilege to have an early godly training, but a personal choice must be made.

I. What this choice was. "To suffer with the people of God." This implies—

1. That God has a people (Exod. 6. 4; 1 Peter 2. 10).

2. That they are a suffering people. "In the world ye shall have tribulation" (Matt. 5. 11; Phil. 3. 10).

II. What constrained Moses to make this choice? "Faith."

1. By faith he saw the nature of godless pleasure. "Pleasures of sin" (Dan. 5; Rev. 3. 17-20).

2. By faith he saw the riches of Christ. "Esteeming reproach for Christ greater riches," etc. (1 Peter 4. 14).

3. By faith he saw the rewards of eternity. "He had respect unto the recompense of the reward" (v. 26). "In the world to come eternal life" (Mark 5. 30).

III. What this choice implied.

1. A refusing (v. 24; Phil. 3. 7).

2. A forsaking (v. 27; 2 Cor. 6. 17).

IV. How he was sustained in his choice. "He endured, as seeing Him who is invisible" (v. 27).

Seeing Him who is invisible gives—
1. Patience in trial, ... verse 27
2. Strength for the battle, ...Josh. 5. 14
3. Comfort in affliction, ... Psa. 23. 4
4. Support in death, ... Acts 7

PEACE, PERFECT PEACE.
Colossians 3. 15.

I. **A Great Possession.** "The peace of God." 1, Peace through faith; 2, Peace that passeth understanding; 3, Peace the world cannot give.

II. **A Gracious Calling.** "To the which ye are called." Called of God. O hear Him.

III. **A Blessed Rule.** "Let the peace of God rule in your hearts." His yoke is easy. His burden is light. Submit to the reign of grace.

IV. **A Simple Condition.** "Let." The sun has arisen, open the window, let the light come in. Let the sceptre of His peace rule the heart and life.

V. **A Grateful Result.** "Be ye thankful." Be thankful that He is able, that His grace is sufficient, that He never fails.

THE LORD IS AT HAND.
Philippians 4. 5.

Therefore—
1. Be diligent, ... 2 Peter 3. 14
2. Be prayerful, ... Mark 13. 33; Luke 21. 36
3. Be patient, ... James 5. 8
4. Be pure, ... 1 John 3. 3
5. Be watchful, ... Mark 13. 36, 37
6. Be hopeful, ... Luke 21. 28; Rom. 8. 19-23
7. Be ready, ... Matt. 24. 44
8. Be comforted, ... 1 Thess. 4. 18

GRACE.
1. The Source of Grace, .. 1 Peter 5. 10; John 3. 16
2. The Channel of Grace, ... 1 Cor. 1. 4
3. The Administration of Grace, .. Heb. 10. 29
4. The Gospel of Grace, ...Acts 20. 24
5. The Application of Grace, ...Rom. 3. 24
6. The Reign of Grace, ...Heb. 4. 16

GOSPEL OUTLINES.

DRINK FROM THE GREAT DEPTHS.

"HE clave the rocks in the wilderness, and gave them drink as out of the great depths" (Psa. 78. 15).

This Psalm is to be regarded as an historical parable (v. 2), and as such it is full of deep spiritual significance that we might "set our hope in God, and not forget His works" (v. 7).

I. **The Place of Need.** "In the wilderness." The wilderness, like this present world, is the place of trial and testimony. Many fail here, saying, "Can God *furnish a table* in the wilderness?" (v. 19). In the *wilderness* the Israelites were dependent on God for everything, so while in this world we must live by *faith* upon the Son of God.

II. **The Blessing Mentioned.** "Drink." Water is here typical of the blessings of the Gospel (Isa. 55; John 7. 37; Rev. 22. 17). It is something *real* to meet a real need—*thirst*. It is something that must be appropriated, "drink," and a something that *cannot fail* to accomplish this great end of refreshing and satisfying the receiver. Such is the Gospel of Christ to all who believe.

III. **The Means Used.** "He *clave* the rock." Moses *smote* the rock, but it was the Lord who *clave* it, so that the streams gushed out (v. 19). This precious soul-saving treasure was hidden in the bosom of the rock until it was smitten and *opened* by the grace of God. "He was wounded for our transgressions." It pleased the Lord to *bruise* Him; "with His stripes we are healed" (Isa. 53. 5).

IV. **The Freeness of the Blessing.** "He *gave* them drink." It was both free and full, for "the waters *gushed* *out*, and the streams *overflowed*" (v. 20). This was the gift of God to every thirsty soul. "Ho, every one that thirsteth, come ye." "By grace are ye saved" (Eph. 2. 8).

V. The Source of the Blessing. "Out of the great depth." Truly, the well is deep. This is not *surface* water; it was entirely beyond the reach of man till He clave the rock. The water of life that has come to us through the cleft Rock of Ages has come out of the great depths.

1. Out of the great depths of the MYSTERIOUS GODHEAD. The Three—one God—is the God of our salvation (2 Cor. 13. 14).

2. Out of the great depths of a PAST ETERNITY. Salvation was no after-thought with God, for Christ was "the *Lamb slain* from the foundation of the world" (Rev. 13. 8).

3. Out of the great depths of INEXHAUSTIBLE RICHES. There is no merit in man, but there is unsearchable riches in Christ. The grace that brings salvation has its source in the infinite heart of God.

4. Out of the great depths of UNFATHOMABLE LOVE. God so *loved* the world that He gave His Son. This stream gushing out from the heart of God is as broad as the world, and as deep as human need for time and eternity. "If thou knewest the gift of God, ask of Him, and He will give thee LIVING WATER" (John 4. 10).

THE BROKEN SNARE.

"OUR soul is escaped as a bird out of the snare of the fowlers; the snare is broken, and we are escaped" (Psa. 124. 7).

This was very literally fulfilled in the experience of the children of Israel when they escaped out of Egypt, out of the snares of Pharaoh. The snare was broken when the hosts of Pharaoh were overwhelmed in the Red Sea, and also when they escaped from their captivity in Babylon.

The antitype of this is found in those who have escaped like birds from the snare of that old fowler the devil, and from the bondage of a soul-ensnaring love.

I. The Fowlers. "Out of the snare of the fowlers." The devil has many snares, and he takes good care to keep them as far as possible out of sight. The fowler has no intention of *feeding* the bird when he fixes the tempting bait in the snare. His aim is to catch. The devil and all his angels, both human and diabolical, are ever busy plying their cunning and enslaving traffic, seeking to catch souls. These fowlers are wise enough to consider the *habits* and *desires* of all those they wish to entrap.

II. The Snare. What may be the snare that catches and holds one may not be the snare that holds another; but every unsaved sinner is *snared* by the *power of sin* in one form or another. *Love* of the world is a snare into which many fall. The "*fear* of man" also hinders multitudes from enjoying the liberty of the free. The "*lust* of the flesh" and the "*pride* of life" are snares that grip as firmly as fetters of iron.

III. The Captive. "Our soul." Not only our *life*, but our very *spirit* has been caught in the snare-coils of iniquity. The snared bird has lost the power of flight, so with the soul snared with sin, it cannot rise up into the pure atmosphere of Heaven's love and fellowship. A *soul*, made in the image of God, to company with Him and rejoice in all the privileges of Sonship, "free to roam the Heavens o'er," SNARED, caught, and led captive by the devil at his will. Alas! a willing captive.

IV. The Breaking of the Snare. "The snare is broken." Yes, thank God, *every* snare may be broken. Christ came to *destroy* the works of the devil, and to give deliverance to the captives. One believing look at the crucified One will instantly break the soul-binding spell of sin. When sin has lost its attractive power the *snare is broken*, and the soul may escape. "Behold, I have set before you an open door." Escape for your life.

V. The Escape. "Our soul *is escaped* as a bird." How instantly the liberated bird turns its back on the fowlers and their snares when a way of escape is offered. It would sing as it soars a new song (Exod. 15. 1). A man said, who had lost a lark, "The next time I get it I will clip its wings," but he did not get it. Every *back-comer* is sure to get his wings clipped. Our soul has escaped the condemnation of the devil through the snare-breaking power of the blood of the Lamb. Hallelujah!

THE SURE AND STEADFAST ANCHOR.

"Which hope we have as an *Anchor* of the soul, both sure and steadfast, and which entered into that within the veil, even Jesus" (Heb. 6. 19, 20).

Life apart from Jesus Christ is full of uncertainties, because it is outside the plan and purpose of God. Only the Christian can say "*We have a hope both sure and steadfast.*"

I. What this Anchor is. It is Jesus Himself, who is entered within the veil as our Hope. It may not be easy to define Love, Peace, or Hope, but we *knew Him*.

II. How this Anchor was formed. There are two elements in it, the *divine* and the *human*. Our Anchor is both God and Man. "Christ our Hope" as an Anchor. He was severely tested, being tried by God, man, and devils, and is abundantly able to bear any strain that may be put upon Him.

III. How this Anchor is to be had. All who have *fled for refuge*, by laying hold of Jesus as their hope, are made partakers of its saving power. *A felt need in*

view of the coming storm is all the *fitness* needed.
It is too late to seek the anchor when the ship has
split on the rocks.

IV. **How this Anchor is to be used.** We are not to
leave it behind to be called for when the danger appears
(Acts 27. 29); it must be *with us continually*. "Lo, I am
with you alway." What a privilege to be in constant
touch with Him who is almighty to keep! Every look of
faith is a casting of the anchor within the veil (Col. 3. 1).

V. **How this Anchor holds.** "It is sure and steadfast," taking hold of the unseen and eternal　Jesus in
the presence of God *for* us has made our standing sure,
having entered by *His own* blood. As our representative
He is rooted in God by an eternal covenant. His anchor
holds in the *day of adversity* when all around gives way.
It holds in the *day of death*, when the "cold dark billows
roll." It holds in the *day of judgment*, "when the elements
shall melt with fervent heat." Which hope *we have* as a
present enjoyment. He that is without Christ is without
hope. "Will your anchor hold?"

SEVEN MARVELS OF MERCY.

"COME now, and let us reason together, saith the Lord:
Though your sins be as scarlet, they shall be as white as
snow," etc. (Isa. 1. 18).

This invitation of grace shines out in this chapter like a
morning star from between the rifted clouds of universal
gloom. There are, it is said, seven wonders in the world,
but the wonders of the grace of God are seventy times seven,
and more to follow. What a marvel—

I. That God should **forgive** at all. He might have dealt
with us only according to law and justice. Man sinned at
first without a cause; why should he expect a God so
gratuitously insulted to forgive?

II. That God should be willing to forgive **all**. All who accept this invitation are offered forgiveness. He is not willing that any should perish, but that all should come to Him and live.

III. That God should condescend **to reason with** sinners. The fact that God offers to reason with us shows how *unreasonable* we have become in turning out of His way and will. What a revelation this is of man's reluctance to deal with God, and of God's yearning love for man. This is the opening of that fountain of the great deep that's able to cover the mountain sins of multitudes.

IV. That God should offer to reason with us **after all that He hath done for us**. Think of what He had done for Israel in the past in bringing them out of Egypt into the promised land. Think of what He has done for us in the gift of His Son and in the agony of the Cross. ''Come *now*,'' though you have killed the Prince of Life. ''Behold, *now* is the accepted time.'' ''Where sin abounded, grace did much more abound'' (Rom. 5. 20).

V. That God should not only forgive, but **transform the sinner**. ''Though your sins be as scarlet they shall be as *white as snow*.'' The cleansing blood of Jesus Christ does not wash scarlet *sins* white as snow, but scarlet *sinners* (1 John 1. 7). Paul the saint was once Saul the sinner.

VI. That God should forgive and transform on **such easy terms**. The simple terms are, ''Come now, and let us reason together.'' Those who ''plead together'' with Him will have their sins blotted out for *His own Name's sake* (Isa. 43. 25, 26). ''Knock, and it shall be opened unto you.''

VII. That God should still **bear patiently with refusals**. The greatest marvel of all is the *longsuffering*

mercy of God. "How often would I have gathered you,
but you would not." "Will ye also weary ME?" saith the
Lord. As grace and truth have come by Jesus Christ, so
will judgment (Acts 17. 31).

THE CHOICE OF THE IMPOVERISHED.

"HE that is so impoverished that he hath no oblation
chooseth a tree that will not rot" (Isa. 40. 20).

Even the heathen idolater, who is so poor that he cannot
make for himself a graven image of gold or silver, will, in
seeking a god, make it of *incorruptible* wood; even in their
ignorance and blindness they desire as an object of trust
that which will *abide*. This *tree* that will not rot may fitly
represent the Cross of Christ, and all that is thereby
signified.

I. **The Cross of Christ is called a Tree (1 Peter
2. 24).** As a tree—

1. It speaks of CURSE. "Cursed is every one that hangeth
on a tree" (Gal. 3. 13). "He that is hanged is accursed of
God" (Deut. 21. 23).

2. It speaks of SUBSTITUTION. "He bore our sins in His
own body on the tree" (1 Peter 2. 24). "Made sin for us"
(2 Cor. 5. 21).

II. **The Cross of Christ is a Tree that will not rot.**
"God forbid that I should glory, save in the Cross of our
Lord Jesus Christ."

1. The CHRIST WHO DIED will not rot. "He is *alive* for
evermore. He could not see corruption. He is the Living
Bread."

2. The BLOOD THAT WAS SHED will not rot. "He hath
obtained *eternal* redemption for us. Ye are not redeemed
with *corruptible things*, but with the *precious* blood of
Christ."

3. The BLESSINGS PURCHASED will not rot. *Eternal* life. A *peace* that passeth knowledge, a *joy* unspeakable, and an inheritance *incorruptible* and undefiled.

III. The Cross of Christ is a Tree worthy of being Chosen. "He *chooseth* a tree that will not rot." Moses made this choice, so did Ruth. Reasons why this choice should be made—

1. Because THE PLEASURES OF SIN will rot. "They are only for a season" (Heb. 11. 25).

2. Because THE HONOURS OF THE WORLD will rot. Those who would build for themselves *a name* will be put to shame and confusion (Gen. 11. 4-8).

3. Because EVERY OTHER FOUNDATION will rot. Other foundation can no man lay than that is laid. None other name given among men whereby we can be saved.

IV. The Cross of Christ is a Tree chosen by the Impoverished. The self-righteous, who seek to establish their own graven images of gold and silver, despise this tree (Rom. 10. 1-3). The *poor* publican made this choice (Luke 18. 14). "He came not to call the righteous, but sinners to repentance." "Blessed are the poor in spirit, for theirs is the kingdom of Heaven."

A SAD FUNERAL.

"I SAW the wicked buried, who had come and gone from the place of the holy" (Eccles. 8. 9).

Death is a busy worker, and funerals are no uncommon sight. But some funerals are infinitely more sorrowful than others because of the character of the life that has been lived. "Blessed are the dead that die in the Lord," but cursed are the dead that die out of Him.

I. A Solemn Sight. "A burial." There is always something mournful about a burial, whether the body be that of a prince or a pauper, and surely the inhabitants of both Heaven and hell are interested in the departure of every soul.

II. **A Solemn Reflection.** "I saw the *wicked* buried." There are some who never seem to see the *wicked* buried, they always seem to be turned into saints, either immediately before or after death. "Where are all the bad people buried?" said a little girl to her mother as they walked through the cemetery. We see the funeral of one such in the sixteenth chapter of Luke.

III. **A Solemn Warning.** "I saw the wicked buried who had *come and gone* from the *place of the holy.*" He had seen them coming and going from the Temple, the house of prayer, just as the faithful and the holy did They came and they went, and they went as they came, and were buried as wicked persons. I saw the wicked buried who had come and gone from the communion table. Alas, this is no uncommon sight! Many "come and go," and go as they come, from the house of God, thinking that their *coming* and *going* is all that is needed. But it may be that our churches are largely blameworthy for many that are buried as *wicked*, because they have "come and gone," and have failed to hear the saving Gospel of God. Many come and go through force of habit, having been trained from infancy. Others, because it helps their respectability in the eyes of men. Others to make a display of themselves. Others because they love and fear God. Unless our *coming* brings us to Christ, and our *going* takes us out to His service, what shall it profit?

EBENEZER.

"THEN Samuel took a stone, and called the name of it Ebenezer, saying, Hitherto hath the Lord helped us" (1 Sam. 7. 12).

Every mile-stone along our life's journey ought to be to

us an Ebenezer, and will be if we have been walking in
His ways. There were no Ebenezer stones raised in the
far country by the prodigal. This stone set up by Samuel
has many tongues. It speaks of—

I. Redemption. "Hitherto." The meaning of this
word stretches away back to Egypt, and embraces the
great deliverance there wrought. Our Ebenezer goes
back to the Cross of Christ.

II. Preservation. "Hitherto *hath.*" There were many
dangers and temptations by the way from Egypt to Canaan,
but the Lord *helped* all the way. This He has promised
to do. What encouragement for the young convert, the
weak, and the tried.

III. Answered Prayer. This stone was raised after
Samuel had *"cried unto the Lord* and the Lord had
thundered from Heaven"* (vv. 9, 10). Our Ebenezer must
also bear this inscription: "I cried unto the Lord, and
He heard me, and delivered me."

IV. Victory. The victory mentioned here was after
Samuel had "offered a *young lamb"* (v. 9). It was
victory through the Lamb. We may always triumph
through the power of God's uplifted Lamb. He who was
lifted on the altar of the Cross is now lifted into the
glory of the Father's throne to give gifts unto men.
They overcame by the blood of the Lamb.

V. Divine Faithfulness. "Hitherto hath the *Lord
helped us.*" In looking back we can easily trace the presence and working of the hand of God in our behalf. He
hath proved Himself faithful wherein He hath promised.

VI. Present Testimony. The Lord who *hath helped* is
now helping. "I will never leave thee nor forsake thee; so
that we may boldly say, The Lord is my helper, I will not
fear" (Heb. 13. 5, 6).

VII. **Encouragement for the Future.** This "hither-to" is the guarantee of *henceforth*. The God of our help in ages past will be our hope for years to come. The unsaved have no Ebenezer in their lives, but they may have if they will but trust that other Stone, which is tried and precious and sure (Isa. 28. 16).

NOTICE TO FLIT.

"ARISE ye, and depart, for this is not your rest; because it is polluted it shall destroy you, even with a sore destruction" (Micah 2. 10).

The good land given them by the Lord had ceased to be a place of rest for them because of their sin. There is no peace saith my God to the wicked.

I. **The Nature of the Call.** It is twofold. It is a call—

1. To ARISE. "Arise ye." 1. Arise from the dead (Eph. 5. 14). From among the dead in trespasses and sin. 2. Arise and go to your *father* (Luke 15. 18). Be reconciled to God. 3. Arise and *worship* (Jer. 31. 6). 4. Arise and *shine* (Isa 60. 1).

2. To DEPART. To depart from all iniquity. "Come out from among them, and be ye separate" (Isa. 52. 11). "Ye cannot serve God and mammon."

II. **The Reasons given.**

1. Because this is NOT YOUR REST. There is a great danger of seeking rest in a condition of heart that is not pleasing to God. Refuge of lies. It would have been the prodigal's doom if he had found *rest* in the far country. That an unsaved state is not a state of rest is attested by many proofs. The hunger of the heart has never been satisfied.

2. Because IT IS POLLUTED. Sin has poisoned the spring of every worldly pleasure. The whole land and kingdom of the godless is blighted with the polluting breath of sin.

The outward life, like the city of Jericho, may be pleasant, but the waters of the inner life are naught.

3. Because IT IS DESTRUCTIVE. "It shall destroy you." To abide out of Christ is to abide in the Sodom of destruction. Flee for your life, tarry not in all the plain. Like Bunyan's Pilgrim, stop your ears to the evil entreaties of men and devils, and make for the narrow gate. Arise ye, and depart, or this condition of life will destroy you. "I flee to Thee to hide me." "Come unto Me, and ye shall find rest" (Matt. 11. 28).

THE KINDNESS OF GOD.

"THAT in the ages to come He might show the exceeding riches of His grace in His kindness toward us through Jesus Christ" (Eph. 2. 7).

Here the *fountain* of the great deep of the goodness of our God is opened up. "Come ye to the waters." Here is a river that maketh glad the city of God.

I. **The Character of God's Grace.** "The exceeding riches of His grace." He is gracious, and His grace contains *exceeding riches*. He is rich in power and in wisdom, but He is *exceeding* rich in grace, so that he can *abundantly* pardon. All the needs of this great perishing world could not exhaust the riches of His grace. "Where sin abounded, grace did *much more* abound."

II. **The Merciful Purpose of God.** "That *He might show*," etc. So exceeding rich was this grace that filled the infinite heart of God that it could not remain unseen or unfelt, but had to burst forth in overflowing floods of blessing. The exceeding riches of this grace is shown first of all in creation, then in the making of man in His own image, in the salvation of Noah, in the call of Abraham, of Moses, and of the prophets, and most of all in the gift of His Son (John 1. 17; Eph. 2. 8; 2 Tim. 1. 9).

III. The Special Manner in which this Grace was shown. "That He might show the exceeding riches of His grace *in His kindness towards us*." Let us bless His Name that He should be pleased to make an exhibition of the *riches of His grace* in showing kindness *to us* who "were by nature the children of wrath" (v. 3). He has not been pleased to *show* such kindness to the angels who kept not *their first* estate. This kindness toward us is seen in the laying of our sins on His own Son (Isa. 53), in the forgiving of all who believe (Acts 13. 38, 39), in making us sons and daughters, in giving us the Holy Spirit to serve Him now, and in preparing a place for us in the Father's house.

IV. The Channel through which this Kindness flows. "Through Jesus Christ." So that now "the kindness and love of God our Saviour towards man hath appeared" (Titus 3. 4). There is but one Mediator between God and men, the Man Christ Jesus. That Man whom God hath filled with all His own fulness (unsearchable riches), that through Him His kindness might be shown to needy, miserable men.

V. The Time and Duration of this Kindness. "In the ages to come." These ages or dispensations embrace the present, and stretch on through all the countless epochs that are yet to follow. The exceeding riches of that grace that has come to us in *His kindness* through Jesus Christ will be continued to us as an ever-abiding revelation through all the ever coming eternity.

THE GOSPEL OF CHRIST.

"I AM not ashamed of the Gospel of Christ, for it is the power of God unto salvation to every one that believeth" (Rom. 1. 16).

I. What this Gospel is. The Gospel of Christ is the good news of peace with God, through the blood of His

Cross. Not only is the *message* good, but the *Messenger* Himself is full of grace and truth. The law was given with many symbols of terror, but grace came with an agonising heart. The Gospel embraces the life, death, and resurrection of Christ as the Saviour of the world.

II. Paul's Estimate of the Gospel. "I am not ashamed." He doubtless remembered the words of the Lord Jesus in Mark 8. 38.

1. He was not ashamed to BELIEVE IT. Never since the day he met the Lord and surrendered himself to Him, saying, "What wilt Thou have me to do?" (Acts 9. 6).

2. He was not ashamed to CONFESS IT. He was determined to know nothing else among men (1 Cor. 2. 2). Ready also to preach it at Rome (v. 15).

3. He was not ashamed to SUFFER for it. Suffering for the Name of Christ was part of his heritage in Him (Acts 9. 16). A list of his sufferings are detailed in 2 Corinthians 11. 23-28. If any man would live godly he must suffer.

III. Why he was not ashamed of it. "For it is the power of God."

1. It is the POWER OF GOD. It is the going forth of the mighty Word of Him who created the heavens and the earth by the same Word. It is the medium through which the *omnipotence* of God works in *mercy* and in *love*.

2. It is the power of God UNTO SALVATION. The same power that *created* of old is now directed through the Gospel to the *salvation* of the lost. Salvation has been a more costly work to God than creation. Surely there is power enough here to meet the need of all. "Is not My Word a fire and a hammer?" (Jer. 23. 29).

3. It is the power of God unto salvation TO EVERY ONE THAT BELIEVETH. *Every one* that *believeth* comes within the scope of this uplifting, saving power. Many are so

bewitched by the pleasures of sin that they heed not
the saving news from Heaven (Gal. 3. 1). The *freeness*
and *graciousness* of this Gospel is the glory of it, yet for
this very cause many are ashamed of it, because it rebukes
their pride and ignores self-righteousness.

RESCUED FROM THE FIRE.

''Is not this a brand plucked out of the fire?'' (Zech. 3. 2).
Joshua here may represent a fallen and degraded priest-
hood. The vision is a transformation scene. The one who
has taken his stand before the messenger of the Lord in his
filthy garments is seen to be cleansed, pardoned, clothed,
and crowned, and declared to be a ''brand plucked out of
the fire.''

I. The Fire an Emblem of Sin.

1. Fire like sin, is very SUBTLE. It is not easily dealt
with. You cannot *touch* it without smarting for it. Who
can weigh it or measure it?

2. Fire, like sin, is very DESTRUCTIVE. Its tendency is
to change and destroy all that abide within its influence.
It may have fascinations, as the flame has for the moth,
but its end is death.

II. The Brand an Emblem of the Sinner.

1. A brand is quite FIT FOR THE FIRE. The nature of the
one is exactly suited to the nature of the other. Sinners love
sin, and roll it under the tongue as a sweet morsel. The
brand and the fire never quarrel, but water is its sworn
enemy, and so is *blood*.

2. A brand in the fire is IN A PERISHING STATE. The
process may be slow, but the end is certain destruction.
To be living *in* sin is to be living in a *perishing* condition
(John 3. 18). The brand is utterly unable to help itself;
it is entirely at the disposal of the consuming flame. ''Not
by works of righteousness which *we have done*.''

III. The Plucking Out Emblematic of Salvation.

"Is not this a brand *plucked out?*" There are two ways of saving a brand from the fire. By plucking it out or by quenching the fire. Christ our great Deliverer has done both; He has put away our sins, and plucked us out of the kingdom of Satan.

1. It was SUDDEN. "Plucked." Snatched up out of the devouring element in a moment. One moment in the place of death, the next *saved*. The Son of Man saves suddenly. "This *day* is salvation come to this house" (Luke 19. 9). There is life for a *look*.

2. It was COMPLETE. "Plucked *out*." It was not taken half out. Some seem satisfied with merely getting turned in the fire instead of getting turned out of it. If sin is not to have dominion over us we must get *separated* from it.

A CALL TO DECISION.

"THEN Moses stood at the gate of the camp, and said, Who is on the Lord's side? let him come unto me" (Exod. 32. 26).

In the absence of Moses sin and iniquity, like an armed host, came into the camp of Israel. The whole nation is in danger of being swept away from the faith by a popular flood of idolatry. As it was then, so is it now. There is a great need for the *stepping out* of men in the Name of God. "*Who* is on the Lord's side?" Amidst the present confusion it is sometimes difficult to know.

I. There are but Two Sides.

The Lord's side, and the *other* side. The other side may be divided into many ranks and companies, but they are godless. "He that is not *for* Me is *against* Me." Those who are not for the Prince of Peace are fighting in the ranks of the prince of darkness. There is no neutrality in this warfare. Mr. Face-both-ways is a traitor to God.

II. What is Implied in being on the Lord's Side?
There is implied—

1. A KNOWLEDGE of Him. God hath manifested Himself to us in His Son, who hath said, "He that hath seen Me hath seen the Father."

2. A FAITH in Him. If we know Him as the "Lord God merciful," etc., surely this will lead us to *believe* in Him (John 5. 24).

3. A DECISION for Him. Because Ruth believed Naomi she *decided* to live and die with her. True faith always leads to entire surrender.

4. An ABIDING with Him. Clinging to His presence, and entering heartily into all His plans and purposes. A perfect acceptance of His will.

5. A RESTING on Him. The battle is the Lord's. Those "out and out" for God rest on His strength for victory. "Greater is He that is for us," etc.

III. What is Demanded of those on the Lord's Side?
That they declare themselves—

1. By SEPARATION. "Let him come unto Me." Let us go forth unto Him without the camp, bearing His reproach (Heb. 13. 12, 13).

2. By CONSECRATION. "Consecrate yourselves" (v. 29; *fill your hands*, margin). All true consecration is a *filling* and fitting for the service of God.

3. By WARFARE (v. 27). We wrestle not with flesh and blood (Eph. 6. 12). Take heed lest the curse of Meroz come upon you (Judges 5. 23).

THE DOOM OF THE DISOBEDIENT.
"WHAT shall the end be of them that obey not the Gospel of God?" (1 Peter 4. 17).

This is a solemn question   Who can answer it fully?

It is a question that deeply concerns every one who *hears* the Gospel. God hath *commanded* all men everywhere to repent and believe the Gospel.

I. What is the Gospel? Gospel is simply "good news," or the God-spell; spellbound by the goodness of God.

1. As to its *Source*, it is the GOSPEL OF GOD (Rom. 1. 1). The good news of God's love for a perishing world (John 3. 16).

2. As to its *Channel*, it is the GOSPEL OF CHRIST (Rom. 1. 16). The good news of a holy life lived, and an all-sufficient atonement made for the sinner.

3. As to its *Purpose*, it is the GOSPEL OF SALVATION (Eph. 1. 13). The good news of a perfect deliverance from sin and from the wrath to come.

4. As to its *Nature*, it is the GOSPEL OF GRACE (Acts 20. 24). The good news of a full salvation, without money or price, to whosoever will.

5. As to its *Endurance*, it is the ETERNAL GOSPEL (Rev. 14. 6, R.V.). The good news that shall never lose its freshness through all the coming ages.

II. What is required of those who hear the Gospel? "Obey." This obedience is shown—

1. By BELIEVING it. "Faith cometh by hearing, and hearing by the Word of God. He that believeth not God hath made Him a liar."

2. By LIVING it. "It is the *power of God* to every one that believeth" (Rom. 1. 16). This glad news when received, and the heart and life yielded up to its influence, will transform the whole character.

3. By DECLARING it. "Freely ye have received, *freely give*."

III. **What shall the end be of those who obey not
the Gospel?** Not to repent and believe the Gospel is to
disobey the *command* of God (Acts 17. 30).

1. It will be the LOSS OF EVERY PRIVILEGE. The broad
way leads to the *destruction* of every hope. To disobey
the Gospel is to refuse God's only means whereby man
can recover his lost estate by being reconciled to God
(Heb. 2. 3; 10. 29).

2. It will be the BLACKNESS OF DARKNESS. The blackness and darkness of a lost eternity (2 Thess. 1. 7-9;
Matt. 25. 46; 13. 40-42).

3. It will be the SECOND DEATH. The doom of those
who are cursed because they would not be blessed
(Luke 16. 23-26; Rev. 20. 15; Luke 12. 5).

THE MISSION OF CHRIST.

"FOR the Son of Man is come to seek and to save that
which was lost" (Luke 19. 10).

Zaccheus *sought* to see Jesus, and Jesus *sought* to save
Zaccheus. "This is a faithful saying, that Jesus Christ
came into the world to save sinners" (1 Tim. 1. 15).

I. **The Seeker.** "The Son of Man." As the *Son of
God* He was the offspring of all that God the Father is
in Himself. As the *Son of Man* He is the offspring of
humanity. Divinity and humanity are both represented
in Jesus, who is called the Christ. He is not the Son of
angels, but He is the Son of Man, our *kinsman* Redeemer.

II. **The Objects.** "That which was *lost*." Not only
what man *had lost*, but *man himself* as a lost one. Man
as a spirit is lost to Heaven and to God as long as he is
enslaved by the power of sin, although he may be as rich
and honoured as this publican. He may be *insensibly* lost,
like the piece of silver, or *miserably* lost, like the poor
sheep, or *wilfully* lost, like the prodigal (Luke 15); but

to be out of the Shepherd's count, or out of the Father's fellowship, is to be *lost*. "She that *liveth in pleasure* is dead while she liveth."

III. The Purpose. "The Son of Man is come to *save*." "He came not to call the righteous, but sinners" (Luke 5. 32). "He came not to condemn the world, but that the world through Him might be saved" (John 3. 17). This saving search began in Eden. "Adam, where art thou?" The *Maker* has come to readjust man as a spiritual mechanism with Himself. Man can only be saved by regeneration. When the Son of Man came to save the lost He came prepared to sacrifice all that He had in order to secure this end. He made Himself of no reputation, and became obedient even unto the death of the Cross. "He shall see of the travail of *His soul*, and shall be satisfied."

IV. The Manner. "The Son of Man *is come to seek*." He has come—come into our very nature, into our room and stead, into the curse that was due to us, and into the death penalty of our sins. He has come *seeking* to save. He came not to be ministered unto, but to give His life a ransom for many. Seeking to save. He still continues His ministry of *seeking*.

REFRESHING NEWS.

"As cold waters to a thirsty soul, so is good news from a far country" (Prov. 25. 25).

I. The Comparison Made. "Good news, like cold water." What is more terrible than the *pangs of thirst*? And what more fearful than the ragings of a sin-convicted conscience? *Cold* water is divinely adapted for a thirsty soul, so is the good news of the Gospel of Christ. Water is the gift of God brought within the reach of man in the up-flowing spring. The *good news* has been published, and brings refreshing to every believing heart (Luke 2. 10, 11).

II. The Source of the News. "From a far country."
From the kingdom of Heaven, into which our Kinsman-
Redeemer has gone (Luke 19. 12). To have good news
from a far country implies that we have a deep interest in
that country because of loved ones there. "We love Him,
because He first loved us." The Gospel of God is no good
news to those who love the world, and whose affections are
set on the things of earth, like the man with the muck rake.

III. The Nature of the News. "It is good."

1. Because it tells of a GOD WHO IS LOVE. "God is
Love," and "Love is of God." This love is manifested in
the gift of His Son (1 John 4. 9), even while we were yet
sinners (Rom. 5. 8). A love that many waters could
not quench.

2. Because it tells of a FINISHED REDEMPTION. "It is
finished." He came to give His life a ransom for many,
and He could say, "I have finished the work which Thou
gavest Me to do" (John 17. 4; Col. 2. 14, 15).

3. Because it tells of a HOME PREPARED (John 14. 2).
"A better, that is, an heavenly" (Heb. 11. 16). The
house of the Lord for ever (Psa. 23. 6). "Within the veil"
with Jesus (Heb. 6. 19, 20).

4. Because it tells of a COMING KING, who shall give to
this waring earth peace (Zech. 14; Rev. 11. 15). "All
the ends of the earth shall see the salvation of our God"
(Isa. 52. 10). Have you heard the good news, and has it
been as cold water to your thirsty soul?

THE LEANING PILGRIM.

"WHO is this that cometh up from the wilderness leaning
upon her Beloved?" (S. of S. 8. 5).

"Come hither, and I will show thee the bride, the Lamb's
wife" (Rev. 21. 9). The Church of the living God is still
coming up from the wilderness of this present world leaning

upon her Beloved, while the men of the world still keep asking, "Who is this?"

1. The Unknown One. *"Who is this?"* Those who know not the Beloved know not them that are His. The world that knew not Christ cannot know those who are Christ's. The fact is that Christians have been so transformed by the Spirit of God that the world knows them not.·

II. The Company She Keeps. *"Her Beloved."* Despised and rejected by others, but the Beloved of her soul. To her He is the chiefest among the thousands, and the altogether lovely. This is the language of endearment, and speaks of the closest relationship. To the Beloved she is both a sister and spouse (chap. 5. 1). Related both by *birth* and *marriage*.

III. The Place of Her Fellowship. *"The wilderness."* There was nothing in her *surroundings* to satisfy her heart, but the presence of her Beloved filled her soul with gladness. Into the wilderness places He may still allure us that He may speak comfortably to us (Hosea 2. 14). Here we have no continuing city; we are pilgrims and strangers with Him who has said, "Lo, I am with you alway."

IV. The Position She Occupies. *"Leaning upon her Beloved."* This attitude is very suggestive, and speaks to us most plainly of—

1. CONSCIOUS WEAKNESS. It is when we are weak that we are made strong by leaning on the Strong One. They that be whole need not a physician.

2. FELT NEED OF GUIDANCE. In the pathless *wilderness* she needs one to lead her in the right way, as Israel was led by the cloudy pillar (Psa. 107. 4-7). "He leadeth me beside the still waters" (Psa. 23. 2).

3. GREAT PERSONAL CONFIDENCE. She has no doubt at all of His wisdom and love, so she leans her whole soul and

life *upon Him*. She proves her faith by leaning hard. A
negro servant said to her mistress as she sat leaning upon
her for rest, "If you love me, missis, lean hard."

4. BLESSED FAMILIARITY. "Leaning upon her Beloved."
John leaned upon the bosom of Jesus, and became "the
disciple whom Jesus loved." The more we lean by faith
upon Him who is our Beloved, the more beloved shall we
be to Him.

V. Where She is Going. "Coming up from the wilderness." Her path is an *upward* path that leads to the city
whose Builder and Maker is God. From the wilderness to
the many mansions prepared in the Father's house. It is
a journey like Rebekah's, away to a prepared home, and to
a blessed and eternal union with the Beloved (Gen. 24).

FLEEING FROM THE REDEEMER.

"WOE unto them! for they have fled from Me: though I
have redeemed them" (Hosea 7. 13).

Ephraim is here said to be like a silly dove (v. 11).
Could anything be more silly than to flee from Him
who hath *redeemed us*. To flee from Him is to flee to
destruction (v. 13). Alas, that such silliness should be
so very common.

I. See what the Lord has done for them. "I have
redeemed them." Think of their wretched condition in
Egypt, and how He redeemed them out of the house of
slavery (Micah 6. 4). Think of His condescension in
coming down to dwell in a bush, that He might manifest
His purpose of grace to Moses (Exod. 3. 8). Think of what
He hath done for us in coming down to dwell in the
Man Christ Jesus, that He might show forth the riches of
His grace in redeeming us by His own blood. What a
sacrifice of the wealth of divine love is here. "He is the
propitiation for our sins."

II. **See what they did with the Lord**. "They fled from Him." It is impossible to flee from that presence which is everywhere, or from the all-searching of His eyes; but we may flee from Him in the *love* and *confidence* of our hearts and in the choosing of our own will and way. It is a sure sign that there is something wrong within when we turn away from those who love us. The guilty child is ashamed to look its father in the face; its eyes flee from him. Some flee from the Lord, like Jonah, by refusing to obey His Word; but there be many who flee from Him, like Adam, because they *know* that they have sinned against Him. It was not so with David. "I flee *to Thee* to hide me." It is utter madness for a thirsty soul to flee from the fountain of living water to broken and empty cisterns.

III. **See what they said about Him**. "They have spoken lies against Me" (v. 13). Those who flee from the mercy of God are likely to think and speak lies about Him. They would drag the Holy One down to their own level. They speak lies against Him when they say: 1. That God does not love them. 2. That they need to make themselves better before coming back to Him. 3. That the death of Christ was not for them. 4. That simple faith in Him will not justify. 5. That their sins are too many to be forgiven. 6. That He does not answer prayer. 7. That He is not able to keep from falling. Those who speak such lies against Him show that they have come under the power of the devil, who is such a liar from the beginning.

IV. **See where they go who flee from the Redeemer**. "Woe unto them" (v. 13). They rush into grief and misery and into the destruction of all peace and fellowship with God. To turn away from our *Redeemer* is to turn back to the bondage and slavery of our own restless self-will. "He that is without Christ is without hope" (Eph. 2. 12).

A LIVING REFUGE.

"A *man* shall be as an hiding place from the wind, and a covert from the tempest; as rivers of water in a dry place, as the shadow of a great rock in a weary land" (Isa. 32. 2).

"Behold the Man." Human, yet divine; sinless, yet accursed; the Beloved of God, yet exposed to the *wind* and *tempest* of the wrath of men and of devils.

I. This Man Saves. He is "as an hiding place." He is well able to save, for He is God's *fellow* (Zech. 13. 7). "He thought it not robbery to be *equal* with God." The refuge of our souls is a Man, a living Man, with a loving, glowing heart throbbing with the grace of God. Not a doctrine or a creed, nor a duty. Salvation means *fellowship* with the Son of God. He *hides* from the wind of temptation and the tempest of wrath due through the guilt of sin. Your life is *hid* with Christ in God.

II. This Man Satisfies. He is "as rivers of water in a dry place." The world will always be a *dry place* to those whose hearts are set on heavenly things. Those who know not this *hiding place* with *rivers of water* take to digging wells in the earth. Wells whose waters are polluted. The "water of life" cannot be found in those man-made wells of earth. These "rivers of water" speak of the abounding fulness that is in Christ for all who hide in Him. Unsearchable riches. "All my springs are in Thee" (Psa. 87. 7).

> "When all created streams are dried,
> His fulness is the same;
> I will with this be satisfied,
> And glory in His Name."

III. This Man Shelters. "He is the shadow of a great rock in a weary land." This shadow is not like that of Jonah's gourd. It is a shadow that follows the pilgrim right through the *weary land*. "That rock which followed them" (1 Cor. 10. 4). The way at times may be weary.

1. Because it is *rough*. Trials may come thick and fast; the heat of oppression may be great, but He is a shadow. 2. Because it is *long*. Old age or great suffering may make the way seem long, but abide in the Shadow. 3. Because it is *lonely*. Loved ones have gone, tender and holy ties have been broken, and the heart longs for *somebody*. Behold the *Man*, who is the shadow of protection in this weary land, and rest in fellowship beneath His wings (Ruth 2. 12).

LIVING EPISTLES.

"YE are manifestly declared to be the epistle of Christ ministered by us, written not with ink, but with the Spirit of the living God" (2 Cor. 3. 3).

An epistle is just a letter or something one has written for the good of another. It may contain the *revelation* of one man's thoughts and feelings to another. The visible creation is a great letter spread out before the eyes of men, in which we may read the wisdom and power of God. Providence is another letter written by the finger of God, but not every one can read it aright; it is very frequently read "through a glass darkly." The Church is *the epistle of Christ* written by the Spirit of God, and sent to the world as an expression of His love and grace and power and of the *"manifold* wisdom of God." Every Christian is a paragraph of this great letter, written not in tables of stone, but in fleshy tables of the heart. "Ye are His workmanship."

I. A letter is written on prepared material. Not on the table of the *stony* heart, but on the fleshy table of the *new* heart (Ezek. 36. 26, 27). Not on the rotten rags of our own righteousness, but on the *white linen* of His own righteousness, which is unto all that believe (Jer. 31. 33).

II. A letter bears the expression of the writer. Every true believer is an *expression* of the character and mind of Christ. "The Epistle of Christ." "The words which Thou hast given Me, I have given them." "Thou shalt speak My words faithfully." "We have the *mind* of Christ."

III. A letter bears the signature of the writer. His Name is put upon His people. His Name is to be signed at all we do and added to all we ask. "If ye ask anything in My Name I will do it." "Yet not I, but Christ."

IV. A letter should be legible. What is the use of a letter if it cannot be understood. Some professing Christians are about as difficult to make out as the autograph of some writers, the letters are so badly formed that it is next to impossible to get the right message out of them. Peter and John, as epistles, were large and legible (Acts 4. 13). Let your light so shine.

V. A letter should be free of blots. If there is a big blot on the letter you send, the blot will likely be the *first* thing noticed. Faults are easily seen. If as epistles of Christ we are blotted, it is certain the blots are not the writer's doing. His work is perfect. If there are blots, thank God there is a blot-eraser provided (1 John 1. 7).

VI. A letter is known by its handwriting. There was no mistaking the "writing on the wall" (Dan. 5. 5, 6). Does not the world look on the character of every Christian and still keep asking, "Whose image and superscription is this?" If we have been made partakers of the divine nature, the Lord, whose writing we are, knoweth them that are His, although the world should know us not. There is another handwriting that He will not own (Matt. 7. 23; 13. 40-42). ———

JOHN THREE SIXTEEN.

"God so loved the world, that He gave His only begotten Son," etc. (John 3. 16).

The most familiar, and most comprehensive, yet most simple text in all the Bible.

I. **The Origin of Redemption.** "God so *loved*." The fountain-head of salvation is the *love* of God; not holiness, justice, power, or truth, but LOVE. The outgoing of the *heart* of God in tenderest and abounding compassion (John 4. 10).

II. **The Object of Redemption.** "The *world*." The ungodly world in all its wreck and ruin and unlovableness. A world nursed in the lap of the wicked one. A world so blind that it did not know its Maker when He came (1 John 1. 10).

III. **The Plan of Redemption.** "*Gave His Son*." This was love's sacrifice to win back an alien world from the love of sin and power of the enemy. God, in planning redemption, planned that He Himself should provide the price. Such is grace. This great sacrifice could not be bought. It is the gift of God. "Behold the Lamb of God." God's appointed Lamb alone could suffice to meet the world's dire need.

IV. **The Purpose of Redemption.** "Should *not perish*." Salvation. That the world through Him might be saved (v. 17). He came not to destroy men's *lives*, but to save them (Luke 9. 56). Jesus Christ does not only save souls, He saves *lives*. "To me to *live* is Christ."

V. **The Extent of Redemption.** "*Whosoever*." In this provision made by the sovereign grace of God there is ample satisfaction for all. This is no mock fountain with its imitation jugs and painted streams. Whosoever will may take the water of life *freely* (Rev. 22. 17).

VI. **The Application of Redemption.** "Whosoever *believeth on Him*." Faith is not the water, but it is the cup that hangs at the well by which you drink. There are many who believe after a fashion who are utterly destitute of salvation. It is not He that believeth only, but he that believeth *in Him* that hath everlasting life. The faith must be *in the Son* (v. 36).

VII. The Result of Redemption. "Not perish, but *have everlasting life*."

Not perish like the old world, but have life, like Noah.

Not perish like the Sodomites, but have life, like Lot.

Not perish like the foolish builder, but have life, like the wise man.

Not perish like the rich man, but have life, like Lazarus.

Not perish like the devil, but have everlasting life, like Christ.

THE WATER OF LIFE.

"And let him that is athirst come, and whosoever will let him take the water of life freely" (Rev. 22. 17).

The Spirit and the Bride unite in saying "Come," to the bright and morning star, referred to in verse 16, and him that heareth the promise of His coming, are invited also to say "Come." Then the invitation goes out to the thirsty ones of earth, that they might come and drink of this water of life. It is surely very fitting that the last invitations recorded in the book of inspiration should be to an absent Saviour, "Come, Lord Jesus" (v. 20); and to the absent sinner, "Let him that is athirst come."

I. The Blessing Mentioned. "The *Water* of Life."

1. Its source. "It proceeds out of the throne of God *and of the Lamb*" (v. 1). Coming from the throne it comes with all the authority and dignity of the glory of God. Coming through the Lamb it comes in mercy and at great sacrifice, for He was slain for us.

2. Its nature. "The Water *of Life*" in fulness like a "*pure river*" (v. 1). *Water* here may be emblematic of that pure stream of "grace and *truth*" that has come to us by Jesus Christ (John 1. 17). The words, He said, that I speak unto you, they are spirit and *life*. Life is the one thing needed by those who are dead in trespasses and sin (John 4. 10). This good news is as cold water to a thirsty soul.

II. **The Parties Invited.** Two classes are suggested here.

1. HIM THAT IS ATHIRST. He that *feeleth* his need and whose soul eagerly longs for satisfaction. Not the righteous or the learned, but the *thirsty*. The invitation is one of mercy, therefore it is to the needy.

2. WHOSOEVER WILL. Those *thirsty* in soul, and those *willing* in mind. "If any man willeth to do His will he shall know" (John 7. 17).

III. **The Conditions Stated.**

1. They are SIMPLE. "Let him *take*." It is not, Let him *make*. As the waters flowed from the smitten rock in the wilderness, so flows this river of life for all. "As many as receive," etc. (John 1. 12).

2. They are LIBERAL. "Let him take *freely*." Take without money and without price as much as ye need (Isa. 55. 1, 2).

————

GREAT ENCOURAGEMENT TO STABILITY AND SERVICE.

1 Corinthians 15. 57, 58.

I. **The Exhortation.**
    1. In faith be *steadfast* (Col. 1. 23).
    2. In trial be *unmovable*.
    3. In work be *always abounding*.

II. **The Encouragement.**
    1. Your work is *in the Lord*.
    2. Your labour is *not in vain*.
    3. Your *triumph is sure*. "He giveth us the victory."

SEED THOUGHTS.

CONVERSION.

"If he turned not " (Psa. 7. 13).

I. Why you should turn.

1. Because you are going the wrong way, ..   Isa. 53. 6
2. Because God calls you to turn, ... Ezek. 33. 11
3. Because you will suffer if you don't,   ..   Psa. 7. 13

II. How you should turn.

1. Personally, ... Ezek. 18. 30
2. Immediately, ... Matt. 3. 10
3. Completely, ... 1 Thess. 1. 10

JUSTIFICATION.

"How can a man be justified with God?" (Job 25. 4).

There are many opinions as to how this is to be done. Here are a few—

1. I believe that some need to be justified more than others,   Rom. 3. 10-19, 22, 23
2. I believe that if a man keep the law
   he shall be justified, ...   Rom. 3. 20
3. I believe that God justifies the good,   Rom. 4. 5; 5. 6
4. I believe that every man must justify
   himself, ...   Rom. 8. 33
5. I believe that if a man trusts in Christ
   and does as well as he can he shall
   be justified, ...   Acts 13. 39
6. I believe that there is something more
   to do than merely believe,   ..   Rom. 3. 28
7. I believe in Jesus Christ, and *know
   that I am justified*, ...   Rom. 5. 1

NO DIFFERENCE.
Romans 3. 22.

I. Some points in which there is a difference.

    1. In the circumstances of birth.
    2. In mental ability.
    3. In manner of upbringing.
    4. In degree of sinfulness.

II. Some points in which there is no difference.

1. All are mortal,	Heb. 9. 27
2. All have sinned,	Rom. 3. 23
3. All under condemnation,	John 3. 18
4. All loved by God,	John 3. 16
5. All provided for in Christ,	1 John 2. 2
6. All invited through the Gospel,	Rev. 22. 17
7. All saved who believe,	John 3. 36

SELF-DECEPTION.
"He deceiveth himself" (Gal. 6. 3).

1. When he thinketh he is *good enough*.

2. When he thinketh he can *save himself*.

3. When he thinketh that no one can *know* whether he is saved or not.

4. When he thinketh that he must *wait* till he is better before he can be saved.

5. When he thinketh that he is *doing the best he can* while doubting God.

6. When he thinketh that if lost he is *not to blame*.

7. When he thinketh that the work is not *already finished*.

8. When he thinketh that there is something more to do than *believe* (Acts 13. 38, 39).

9. When he thinketh that he shall *escape* if he neglects salvation (Heb. 2. 3).

GRACE.

1. Saved by Grace, ...   Eph. 2. 8
2. Falling from Grace, ...   Gal. 5. 4-9
3. Continuing in Grace, ...   Acts 13. 43
4. Growing in Grace, ...   2 Peter 3. 18

A SEVENFOLD COMPLAINT.
Hosea 7. 13-15.

IT is worthy of notice that the ME's here are all emphatic in the Hebrew. They—

1. Have *fled from Me* (v. 13).
2. Have *transgressed against Me.*
3. Have *spoken lies* against Me.
4. *Have not cried* unto Me.
5. *Rebelled* against Me.
6. *Imagine mischief* against Me.
7. *Return, but not to Me.*

A SOLEMN QUESTION.
"What will ye do in the solemn day?" (Hosea 9. 5).

I. **The Time.** "The solemn day."

1. In the solemn day of *affliction.*
2. In the solemn day of *death.*
3. In the solemn day of *judgment.*

II. **The Question.** "What will ye do?"

1. Will you *deny?*
2. Will you *flee?*
3. Will you *resist?*

"SEEING THAT ALL THESE THINGS SHALL BE DISSOLVED, WHAT MANNER OF PERSONS OUGHT YE TO BE IN ALL HOLY CONVERSATION AND GODLINESS?" (2 Peter 3. 11)